A POPULAR DICTIONARY OF

Cornish Place-Names

O.J. PADEL

ALISON HODGE

First published in 1988 by Alison Hodge
Bosulval, Newmill, Penzance, Cornwall TR20 8XA

British Library Cataloguing in Publication Data

Padel, O.J. (Oliver James),   1948-
A popular dictionary of Cornish place-names.
    1. Cornwall. Place names. Etymology
    I. Title
    914.23'7'0014

ISBN 0-906720-15-X

Designed and originated in-house.
Printed and bound by A. Wheaton & Co. Ltd., Exeter.

Contents

Preface   v

Introduction   1
The study of place-names   3
Languages   7
Derivative names   10
Types of place-name formation   10
Recent English names   13
Personal names and place-names   14
Saints and place-names   19
Technical terms   25
   1. Periods of the Cornish language   25
   2. Sound-changes   27
   3. Mutation   35
   4. Compounds   38
   5. Epenthesis   40
   6. Hyper-correction   42
   7. Re-interpretation   44
Explanation of the entries   45

Dictionary of Cornish Place-Names   49

Index of Elements   183
1. Cornish   183
2. English   196
3. Old Norse   202
4. French   202

Index of Personal Names   203
1. Cornish   204
2. Old English (and Old Norse)   211
3. Middle English and surnames   211

Further reading   213

For

Martin Picken

Preface

I have written this book as part of the Survey of Cornish Place-Names at the Institute of Cornish Studies. The Institute is funded jointly by Cornwall County Council and the University of Exeter, and without the support of those two bodies the Survey would not exist and the work would not have been possible. Readers who enjoy any of it will be glad to know to whom their thanks are due.

The Survey of Cornish Place-Names has a place among other, similar, surveys of the counties of England, published by the English Place-Name Society. This is recognised as one of the world's foremost bodies in the study of place-names. It receives generous support from the British Academy for furthering its work, and this support has been of great benefit to the Survey of Cornish Place-Names (and, hence, to this book) — primarily in the form of the services of Dr Mark Bateson, the Society's research assistant, and his predecessor, Catherine Cubitt (née Coutts). It is doubtful whether either of them will actually remember any of the individual spellings of Cornish place-names which they have so diligently culled from early documents, but they are there.

Martin Picken has for many years now been a great friend and teacher to me in all matters to do with Cornish history and topography, and it is a pleasure once again to record the debt which I owe him. The number of errors from which he has patiently saved me, and the amount of information which he has so generously provided, are too great to be recalled. The documentation of many names in this book would be immeasurably poorer without his constant help.

Any place-names worker is dependent upon archivists and librarians for supplying his raw material, and I count myself very fortunate in those whom I encounter — especially Christine North and the staff of Cornwall Record Office, Angela Broome of the Royal Institution of Cornwall, and Dr Graham Haslam of the Duchy of Cornwall Office, all of whom have been both helpful and infinitely patient in supplying steady streams of documents, and sometimes much more than that — useful references, opinions in cases of doubt, and spellings which they have themselves found. All this has been of great benefit to the book. Similarly with the staff of the Devon Record Office, the Public Record Office, and the British Library. At Cambridge University Library, both Arthur Owen and the staff of the Map Room made useful suggestions.

The Tamar Valley Project gave me useful references concerning the names and history of Calstock parish; and Cornwall Archaeological Unit, now part of Cornwall County Council, gave information and helpful discussion on the archaeological aspects of place-names. I have also drawn extensively upon the work of two earlier collectors of Cornish place-name forms, Charles Henderson and J. E. B. Gover, both of whose work is deposited at the Royal Institution of Cornwall, in Truro. Other users of their work may care to note that I have never used a form cited by Gover without checking it in its original source, for I have found it thoroughly unsafe to do so. With Henderson's work, by contrast, I have occasionally taken his forms on trust.

Tomos Roberts and Bernard Tanguy have given useful advice concerning Welsh and Breton place-names respectively. Peter Pool and J. G. Thomas have generously supplied information from their own researches. I found it extremely beneficial to be able to use Peter Hull's edition of the Launceston Cartulary in advance of its publication. Julia Crick gave me the benefit of her expertise on the text of Geoffrey of Monmouth's *History of the Kings of Britain*; Dr David Dumville, likewise, on the *Historia Brittonum*; and Chris Sanders advised me on *Orkneyinga Saga*.

Other people have kindly commented upon parts or all of the typescript. In particular, Dr Margaret Gelling examined my attempts to deal with some of the more problematical English names, to their great benefit; Dr

Ken George, Caroline Humphreys and Michael Polkinhorn all read large amounts of typescript and made very useful comments; Father Job an Irien and John Skilbeck read parts in draft; and Professor Charles Thomas commented helpfully upon my efforts with the Scillonian place-names. Caroline Humphreys also generously gave her time and expertise helping me in the Public Record Office, and Stephen Smith likewise in the Royal Institution of Cornwall. Margaret Bunt typed the script, and also checked it and commented upon it, with her usual careful attention.

To all these, and to many others, my warmest thanks. I should make it clear that I alone am responsible for the mistakes which undoubtedly must remain. I shall be very grateful for corrections, amplifications and additional early spellings; they can be sent to me at the Institute of Cornish Studies.

Redruth, 1988   O. J. P.

Introduction

In one sense, the idea of a 'popular dictionary' of place-names is self-evident: everyone is interested in place-names, especially in Cornwall and Scilly where the names are so distinctive. Apart from their intrinsic interest, place-names can give important information about the country: archaeologists, local historians, family historians, those interested in the history of the landscape, and students of the Cornish language, all have questions that they would like to ask of the place-names.

In another sense, however, a 'popular dictionary' of place-names is almost a contradiction in terms. Place-names are a complex field of study. Trying to explain them requires an acquaintance with many different areas of learning, some of them very technical. In this book I have tried to give, for the general reader, comprehensible accounts of just over 1,000 place-names of Cornwall and Scilly, and in the attempt I have realised just how technical a process it is. It has often been necessary to omit or compress parts of the argument. Many of the names in the book could have a page or more devoted to them, usually without arriving at a definite answer. The inconclusive, and the unanswerable, question is a familiar phenomenon to the student of place-names. I have worked on the principle that it is better, when necessary, to say that the answer is not known, than to sound conclusive about questions which cannot be answered definitely.

The selection of names was simple. I have included all those place-names which appear on the Ordnance Survey Quarter-Inch Map of the county (1:250,000), plus any alternative names by which those places have been known, and any other names which I found it necessary to discuss in the course of treating the initial selection. The basic names total about 660; and the additional names bring the total to over 1,000. I have used the 1982 edition of the map, the one on sale when I started work on this book in 1985, and have not taken account of any changes made in more recent editions.

Allowing the map-makers to make the initial choice has produced an unexpected selection of names — not at all the selection that I might have picked for its interest to me as a philologist. Many villages in twentieth-century Cornwall are ones which have grown up quite recently, say in the eighteenth or nineteenth centuries, as a result of economic changes — perhaps the requirements of Cornwall's industries (tin, copper, slate, and china-clay), or the change in farming practices, whereby rough grazing-land, 'downs', was enclosed and taken into cultivation. Place-names such as CHARLESTOWN and DOWNGATE reflect the comparatively recent origin of their villages. The inclusion of such names has proved very instructive. For one thing, it is notable how many of the places in such a selection come into this category. For another, it is striking to discover that, even when a place-name has such a comparatively recent origin, it may not be at all easy to give the exact meaning. The derivation of the English names MERRYMEET, SUMMERCOURT and *Pennycome-quick* (FALMOUTH) is not in any doubt, but it is much harder to say what they may actually signify. This makes one realise that in asking, 'What does it mean?' the inquirer is posing the hardest question of all. If names so close to us in time and culture can be opaque, those given 1,000 years ago, in a language which is inadequately recorded and a culture far remote from our own, may never be fully understood.

It will thus be clear that, very often, one can only suggest the apparent derivation of a name, without explaining the actual meaning. Sometimes, when a derivation is here rejected because it 'makes no sense', it may nevertheless be the correct one, but for reasons which we can never know. But all too often, it is not possible even to suggest a derivation. Hence the many guesses and alternatives which appear throughout the book.

2

The study of place-names

There are two main principles to the study of place-names, in Cornwall or anywhere else. First, as most people are aware, is the requirement not to trust the modern forms of names, but to find, for each name, its earliest spellings, and to trace the development of the name from those earliest appearances into the modern form. Very often the early spellings will show that the modern form is misleading. See, for instance, BOLVENTOR, BROWN WILLY, CLUBWORTHY, GEORGIA, HALLWORTHY, HERODS-FOOT, MENHENIOT, MOUNTJOY, POLMASSICK, RED DOWN, SEATON, and TRENARREN. All of these, and many more, have been subjected over the years to re-interpretation or corruption — sometimes as a result of the change in language from Cornish to English, but not only because of that.

In other cases, such as MOUSEHOLE, REDRUTH and SALTASH, the meaning is quite clear from the modern name, but it has become a popular belief that the name is actually more complicated. It requires the early spellings to demonstrate that, just occasionally, things are indeed what they seem to be.

The collecting and processing of the early forms is an immensely long task. Just one or two early spellings are not sufficient. Very often the earliest spelling of all may be corrupt, especially if it comes from a source, such as Domesday Book, compiled or copied by people who were not local. Moreover, in the entries which follow I have normally given only two or three early forms, as few as are needed to show the derivation. That is itself misleading. Usually the forms cited are typical ones, selected from a number of others. The process is partly a statistical one: a single spelling divulges its meaning only when considered in the context of all the other spellings, of similar and other dates. Occasionally, explanations have to be offered on the basis of a single form, for lack of others; but any such explanation is tentative. For a few names, no early form is yet available, even though the name has the appearance of being an old one: see TREGURRIAN, for instance. That is especially true with names of coastal

3

features, which often have no available evidence before the nineteenth century, even though they may be very much older. (The reason is that early documents are mostly concerned with land ownership or tenancy, and so they mostly deal only with habitations, not with natural features of the landscape.)

The task of collecting forms is never ended. To complete it in a lifetime would require skimping the work. Even when it was all done, one still could not know what spellings in lost documents might radically have changed the interpretation of a name. Under the names MARK-WELL, STRATTON and TREVISCOE, it will be seen that those three places are exceptionally fortunate in having very early spellings, from the Anglo-Saxon period. By the time of their next recorded forms (respectively in 1199, 1086 and 1333), each name had changed drastically. In each case, the true derivation could not even have been guessed if the exceptionally early spelling had not survived. How many other names may have behaved similarly, but, by chance, have no forms early enough to show their true derivations?

That does not invalidate the scientific process. It simply means that the student must do the best he can, with whatever is available. But at the back of the mind there will always be the awareness that if only earlier and fuller references were available, all might seem different.

It goes without saying that, once collected, the forms must be understood. They cannot be read as if they were modern English words. Letters have had different values at different times. The letters *ch*, for instance, can mean at least three different things, depending upon the date of writing and the native language of the writer. Then one needs some knowledge of the historical development of the appropriate language or languages, to know what words are indicated by the sounds represented. By and large, names were written as they sounded: there was no fixed spelling at an earlier period. But this does not mean that it was a haphazard process. There was an accepted sound-value for each letter or combination of letters. It is surprising, at first, to notice how often the medieval spelling of a place-name in the Cornish language is exactly that which would have been used for writing the equivalent words in the literary Cornish texts at the same period. But that is not coincidence: both were being written according to accepted spelling conventions.

However, the situation is more complicated, for names were not always spelt just as they sounded. There has also been an opposite tendency at work, that of conservatism. Such is the power of the written word, and the respect in which it is held, that place-name spellings are often copied from older documents, sometimes from ones very much older. Occasionally this means that the spelling used today may be several centuries out of date; and very often, in looking through older records, one finds that a spelling at one date is an exact repetition of a much older form, even though one may know, from other sources, that the name had changed meanwhile.

Sometimes this can produce results confusing for the beginner. Having found, perhaps after weeks of searching, an early form such as *Kennery* 1699 for what is now called CANWORTHY, he may think that it is nearer to the original spelling, and a clue to the derivation. The opposite is true. Comparison with other forms, older still, shows that this name was originally *Carn-worthy*, that the spelling *Kennery* in 1699 was an up-to-date one indicating the contemporary pronunciation, and that our modern spelling Canworthy is in fact more archaic than the 'old' one of 1699. Spellings from the sixteenth and seventeenth centuries are particularly liable to mislead in this way, because names were often spelt in their colloquial pronunciations at that period, and have since reverted to more archaic spellings. Thus the spelling *Larrake* c.1605 is in fact more 'modern' than the current LANDRAKE, which is closer to the original form. Similarly, *Sanckras* 1580 and *Poffill* c.1605 are more 'modern' than the current SANCREED and POUGHILL used today. Such spellings of the sixteenth and seventeenth centuries are of great value for showing the contemporary pronunciation, but for the derivation one looks for something much older.

It is unclear why such names reverted from their up-to-date spellings at that period to the more archaic ones

5

used today; the answer may have to do with the spread of literacy. Perhaps as literacy became more widespread at that period, people tended to write names simply as they heard them; and then the conservative spelling traditions re-asserted themselves as the wider literacy took firmer root. But that can only be speculation.

The knowledge of these tendencies has in turn caused people, at times, to try to give what they mistakenly thought was the old spelling of a name. This has occasionally given rise to pseudo-archaic spellings, which are discussed further under the explanation of the technical term *hyper-correction*.

The study of older spellings is the first essential method of the place-names student. The other one, equally essential but often given less emphasis, is comparison. The importance of this method will best be shown by examples. The name of KILMAR TOR, considered on its own, appears to be 'nook of a horse', Cornish *kil + margh*. Its few earlier spellings agree with the modern form in suggesting that. But the hill has the form of a long ridge, and comparison with other names in Cornwall, and with similar names in Wales and Brittany, shows that the phrase *keyn margh*, literally 'back of a horse, horse's back', was often used fancifully to describe hill-ridges. In this instance there is another parallel further afield, for English uses the phrase 'hog's back' in the same fanciful way. Kilmar Tor has no early spellings which might show the older word *keyn* instead of *Kil*. But another place in Cornwall is found as *Kinmerch* in 1207, and had already changed to *Kil-* by 1346; so Kilmar Tor could easily have changed from an older *Keyn-* before the date of its first appearance as late as *c*.1605. It is impossible to be sure; but in this case the comparative method agrees well with the nature of the place. Together they override the inadequate evidence of the early spellings, and the great probability is that Kilmar Tor was originally *Keyn-margh*, 'horse's back', a fanciful description of the ridge.

The point here is that one cannot study the names of one district, or even of one county, in isolation. References to place-names in other counties, and in Wales and Brittany, will frequently be found in the pages which fol-

6

low, for the valuable light which they can throw upon the place-names of Cornwall. The English names MOU-SEHOLE and *Crowenest* (see CROW SOUND) are not readily explained on their own; in speculating as to their meanings, it is worth remembering that there is another Mousehole in Devon, and other Crow's Nests in many places. Any explanation for the places in Cornwall ought to be compatible with the occurrences elsewhere too.

Languages

Most place-names in this book are in the Cornish language. In the derivations it can be assumed that the language is Cornish unless something else is specified. Cornish is a Celtic language, one of the family of languages which were formerly spoken all over the British Isles and much of western Europe. During the Roman period one Celtic language, British, was spoken through the whole of England, Wales, and south Scotland. Over much of England there is now almost no trace of it remaining — its replacement by English was extremely thorough. But the British language survived in the western parts. As it developed it became differentiated into two distinct languages, Welsh and Cornish; and a third one, Breton, was used by overseas migrants who took the language with them. The closest similarities are between Cornish and Breton. Many place-names in the Cornish language have their exact counterparts in Wales and Brittany. The other group of Celtic languages, Irish and its relatives Scottish Gaelic and Manx, is much less closely related. Their similarities with Cornish are of great interest to the philologist, but the differences of naming-habits mean that many fewer place-names or words from that group will be cited in this book.

Even a casual glance at the place-names reveals striking differences between Cornwall and Devon. The reason is that in Devon there was a thorough replacement of the Celtic language by English, whereas in Cornwall the replacement was later and much more partial. The Anglo-Saxons must have settled over much of Devon, and reached the borders of Cornwall, during the seventh century; but there are very few historical sources from the period to give any precise idea of how this momentous change occurred. The place-names in two areas of east Cornwall show that they, too, were heavily settled by the Anglo-Saxons (probably in the eighth and ninth centuries), with the replacement of Cornish names by English ones. Those areas are the far north of the county, around Bude, and the area around Callington. In both of them the place-names have far more in common with those in Devon, just across the county boundary, than with the rest of Cornwall.

From this beginning, the English language spread gradually westwards through the county. The chronology of this westward spread is not fully established; but by the year 1200 there must have been English speakers in many parts of east Cornwall, as far as Bodmin. By 1600 Cornish had given way to English in most parts east of Truro, and thereafter the decline was rapid. In 1700 the language was probably kept alive mainly in fishing villages, where the contacts with Breton speakers must have helped to ensure its continued use, and by 1800 it had altogether died, except for words in dialect use which still survive today in the far west.

There are two important results of this change of language during the historic period. One is that the language of a place-name can give a suggestion as to when it was formed, according to the part of the county. In the eastern parts, a place-name in the Cornish language must be old, since it is unlikely to have been formed after about 1200 over most of eastern Cornwall. In the two areas of intensive English settlement, the few Cornish names are likely to be even older, going back over 1,000 years. Thus the Cornish name LAUNCELLS, in the heart of the English territory around Bude, is probably at least 1,000 years old. In the west of the county, on the other hand, places with English names, such as TWELVE-HEADS and BLACKWATER, are not usually recorded before the seventeenth century, and probably are not very much older than that. There are exceptions, such as MOUSEHOLE, which is an English name in the far west of the county, but which is at least 750 years old; and a few English names in west Cornwall are translations of Cornish ones, such as BLACK HEAD and NEW MILLS; but by and large the English names are those of the more recent villages. Sometimes they denote very recent ones, such as ASHTON and FOUR LANES, both only a century old.

There is also a third language, French, found in some place-names in Cornwall, as elsewhere in England. Most of the French names must have been given during the Norman period, when French was one of the official languages of the kingdom: DOUBLEBOIS, GRAMPOUND, MALPAS and ROCHE are of this kind. But the several Cornish examples of *Beau repair*, 'beautiful retreat', are curious. Although the name is found in other counties, Cornwall has an exceptional number of instances (at least six, all in the west of the county), and some extra explanation seems called for, though none is forthcoming. The name of The BRISONS, too, seems of a different kind. Here it may be that the name was never generally current locally — the rocks at Cape Cornwall may well have had some other name, of Cornish derivation; the name Brisons could have been a sailors' name, given general currency by being placed on charts in the sixteenth century.

In order to suggest a derivation, the first requirement is obviously to decide in what language the place-name was coined. Usually there is no problem about that: many place-names contain one of the common words used for forming place-names — *tre, poll* or *penn* in Cornish, or *tún, ford* or *héafod* in English. Under most circumstances the language of that element determines the language of the whole name, for truly bilingual names are so rare that the possibility of finding one can be ignored.

Sometimes it is less easy to decide the language of a name. For CAMBEAK, for instance, there is a possible explanation in either English or Cornish. Then only general plausibility (the type of name, the area where it is found, parallel names elsewhere, or parallel uses of the suggested elements) can say which is the more likely derivation. Or else there may be no ready explanation in either English or Cornish; then one can only fall back upon the comparative method, or the general look of the names, to decide the language. For the two adjacent headlands of GUNVER HEAD and Stepper Point (W9178, by Padstow), no ready derivation is available in either Cornish or English; all one can say is that the general appearance of *Gunver* is Cornish rather than English, while *Stepper* looks English rather than Cornish.

Derivative names

There is one apparent exception to the principle, mentioned above, that truly bilingual names are virtually non-existent. In names such as CARNON DOWNS and ROSEMULLION HEAD the first part is unquestionably of Cornish derivation, while the second part is equally clearly English. However, these are by no means to be considered as 'bilingual' or 'hybrid' names. They are, rather, examples of a very widespread phenomenon in name-giving, whereby a name which already exists is used as part of a new, longer name. Examples are extremely common in any language. At the most obvious level, Oxford Street means 'street leading towards Oxford', not 'street with a ford for oxen'. The original place-name is used without regard for its original meaning or derivation, simply to indicate a place. In the same way, names in Cornwall such as Carnon Downs and Rosemullion Head must be considered as purely English place-names in formation, and their meanings are 'downs belonging to Carnon' and 'headland near Rosemullion'. The Cornish meanings of the original Carnon and Rosemullion were irrelevant when these derivative place-names were coined by English speakers. To the modern inquirer, the more interesting question is what those original Cornish names meant; but that must not obscure the actual significance of place-names belonging to this type, nor should it be imagined that these names are in any way bilingual or 'hybrid' formations in the true sense.

Types of place-name formation

The great majority of place-names are formed from either one or two elements, and no more. Examples of names formed from a single word include BISSOE 'birch-trees', DRIFT 'village', KELYNACK 'holly-grove', and *Arwothal* 'beside-the-marsh' (from which PERRANARWORTHAL is named). (For these purposes prepositions, such as *ar*, and suffixes such as the plural (*-ow*), adjectival (*-ek*) and diminutive (*-ynn*) ones do not count as separate words.) Examples of names composed of two elements include any of the names starting with *Tre-*, and the great majority of all the other names as well. Perhaps the only true three-element Cornish name in this book is PENDOGGETT 'head of two woods', though PENJERRICK might count as another. THREEMILESTONE and SHORTLANESEND are examples of three-element names in English. Others which appear to consist of more than two elements are mostly derivative names.

There is one fundamental difference between the ways in which place-names are formed in Cornish and English. In both languages, each of the two words in a name has a different function, here termed the 'generic' and the 'qualifier'. The generic is usually drawn from a fairly small stock of words used frequently in place-names to denote, in broad terms, what sort of a place is being named: in Cornish, words such as *tre* 'farmstead', *nans* 'valley', *poll* 'pool', *penn* 'head, top' and *lann* 'church-site'; in English, words such as *ford* 'ford', *dún* 'hill', *tún* 'farmstead', *héafod* 'head' and *stów* 'church-site'. The Index of Elements shows that in this book there are several or many place-names containing each of these words.

The qualifier is so termed because it is used to qualify, to state more precisely what kind of *tre*, *ford*, *lann* or *stów* is being named. It may be purely descriptive — perhaps an adjective such as *meur* 'great' in PORTHMEOR and CRUGMEER, or *du* 'black' in POLDHU and BALDHU, or a noun such as *scaw* 'elder-trees' in TRESCO and TRESCOWE, or *lefant* 'toad' in POLYPHANT. In English, examples of adjectives used as qualifiers are *blæc* 'black' in BLACK HEAD and BLACKWATER, and *lang* 'long' in LONGDOWNS and LONGSHIPS; and nouns used as qualifiers include *myln* 'mill' in MILLBROOK and *rynel* 'water-channel' in RUNNEL STONE. In both languages one of the commonest types of qualifier is a personal name, saying simply whose farm, valley, church-site or

11

other feature is being named. The lists of personal names show how common this type of qualifier is.

The qualifiers are drawn from a far wider range of vocabulary than the generic words. Apart from the large number of possible personal names, any ordinary word in the language might be used as qualifier, and many words are so used once, and only once, among the names in this book.

Some nouns may occur either as generics or as qualifiers in place-names. The word *nans*, 'valley', is used as generic in names such as NANCLEDRA 'valley of Clodri', NANCEGOLLAN, 'valley of a whetstone', and NANPEAN, 'little valley', but in TRENANCE ('farm in a valley; valley farm') it serves as qualifier; *eglos* 'church' is the generic in EGLOSKERRY, 'church of Keri' and EGLOSHAYLE, 'church on an estuary', but it is the qualifier in TRENEGLOS, 'farm by the church'. In English, *wudu* 'wood' occurs as generic in HENWOOD, 'hens' wood', but as qualifier in WOODFORD, 'wood-ford, ford in a wood'. But it will be clear that adjectives and personal names cannot serve as generics in place-names, only as qualifiers.

The fundamental difference between the two languages lies in the way in which the two elements, generic and qualifier, are put together. In English the normal way is for the qualifier to precede the generic (just as, in the language, adjectives precede their nouns): BLACK HEAD, LONGDOWNS. A few generic elements in English are regularly used in the reverse order: *mount* in English place-names normally comes before its qualifier, as in MOUNT EDGCUMBE, MOUNT HAWKE, and Mount Pleasant, instead of the more prosaic Pleasant Mount, Hawke's Mount, and so on. (But note ST MICHAEL'S MOUNT, where *mount* as the generic comes in the normal English position, at the end.) Another English generic which normally precedes its qualifier, but which does not occur in Cornwall, is *fort*: Fort William, Fort Augustus, and Fort Knox, rather than William's Fort, etc. In Cornwall, *wheal*, 'a mine', is used similarly (Wheal Busy, Wheal Fortune, and so on), the usage as well as the word itself having been borrowed from the Cornish language.

For in Cornish, by contrast, the normal formation is for the generic to come first, followed by the qualifier, just as adjectives in Cornish normally follow their nouns: BAL-DHU 'black mine' (literally 'mine black'), PORTHMEOR, 'great cove' (literally 'cove great'), and so on. The difference is nicely shown by two examples of names which have been translated from Cornish into English: the translators have, quite naturally, reversed the order of the elements, in keeping with the normal usages of the two languages. Thus *Melynewyth* 1364, the Cornish name of NEW MILLS, is literally 'mill new', Cornish *melin* + *nowydh*. In translation the order of words is reversed to give the normal English one, *New Myll* 1596. Similarly with BLACK HEAD (St Keverne): the Cornish name, *Peden due*, is literally 'head black', *penn* + *du*; in the translated name the same words occur, but in reversed order. There is also one other example of a 'translated' name, MAWGAN PORTH. Although both parts of this name are of Cornish derivation, they are used in a completely English way, with the qualifier, *Mawgan*, preceding the generic, *porth*, and as it stands Mawgan Porth must be considered an English place-name; *porth* here is used as a dialect word within English. But one earlier form of the name is *Porthmawgan* 1755, and that is the same name, but in the normal Cornish order: 'cove of St Mawgan parish'. The name has been 'translated' from Cornish into English simply by reversing the order of words.

A few names in Cornish do have the elements in the typically English order: MORVAH is 'sea-grave', from *mor* 'sea' + *bedh* 'grave'; and CAMBORNE is 'crooked-hill', from *camm* 'crooked' + *bronn* 'hill'. This unusual type in Cornish is discussed further below, under the technical term *compound*.

Recent English names

Many of the English names which appear fairly late in the historical record (say, in the seventeenth century or later) seem to belong to particular categories which are less well represented at earlier periods. These would include jocular names, such as *Pennycomequick* (FALMOUTH),

MERRYMEET, and BOLVENTOR; one suspects that the two places called by the unexplained name of DOWNDERRY may come into this category in some way. At an earlier date, the places called MOUSEHOLE and *Crowenest* (see CROW SOUND) may also be jocular, but there are fewer such names known from the medieval period.

Another category is that of villages named from an inn, around which the village grew up. Names coming into this category include INDIAN QUEENS, London Apprentice, CRIPPLESEASE, BUGLE, VICTORIA, and the three places called TAPHOUSE; there is one such hamlet dating from the medieval period, WAINHOUSE CORNER. There are also villages named from blacksmiths' work-shops: SHOP, BRAY SHOP and probably MAWNAN SMITH; and several named from their locations upon streams: BLACKWATER, BUDOCK WATER, CANWORTHY WATER, and CHACEWATER.

Finally there are those names where the individual or family commemorated in the place-name is historically known: these include many of the places ending in *town*, discussed in the next section.

Personal names and place-names

As mentioned above, personal names are very often found as the qualifiers in place-names. In the case of Cornish, this creates severe problems, because of the lack of sufficient information about Old Cornish personal names. A glance at the Index of Personal Names will show that Cornish personal names were distinctive and very varied. If we had extensive lists of the Christian names used in Dark-Age Cornwall, many of the place-names which are now obscure could doubtless be explained as containing Old Cornish personal names. But, with one notable exception, no such lists exist. Such personal names had largely dropped out of use before the Norman Conquest, for even in the tenth and eleventh centuries Cornish speakers were beginning to take names of Anglo-Saxon derivation as well as Cornish ones. Cornishmen are known who were called by Christian names such as *Ælfeah*, *Wulfnoth* and *Wulfsige*, all good Anglo-Saxon names. No doubt some place-names where *tre* is followed by an Anglo-Saxon personal name are the farms of such Cornishmen: TRELILL, 'farm of Lulla', is the only such example appearing in this book, but there is a handful of other such place-names, all in the east of the county.

After the Norman Conquest, people all over England started to use Christian names favoured by the Normans. The Cornish were no exception to this tendency, with the result that by the thirteenth and fourteenth centuries, when records become fuller, the great majority of Cornishmen had names drawn from the rather limited range of Christian names popular over the rest of the country — Robert, Peter, John, Walter, and so on. Thus it is only pre-Conquest records which can give us ancient Cornish Christian names; and such sources are so scarce that many such names must have vanished without record. Fortunately there is one document which does give extensive lists of Cornish names: the records of manumissions (the setting-free of slaves) which were entered into the gospel-book kept at St Petrock's monastery in Padstow and Bodmin. This manuscript, now in the British Library in London, has marginal entries such as: '*Custentin* for the sake of his soul set free *Proscen* upon the altar of St Petrock, in the presence of these witnesses: *Mermen* the priest, *Riol* and *Cantgueithen* the deacons, *Tithert* the clerk, and many others.' These entries started to be made in the mid-tenth century, and continued through the eleventh. Approximately 140 Cornish names of men and women occur in them (and also a number of Anglo-Saxon ones), and they constitute the only extensive source for Cornish personal names.

For the large numbers of such personal names which are not recorded, and which might occur in place-names, one is dependent upon the comparative method — extrapolation from Welsh and Breton sources. These languages have much fuller lists of early personal names, partly because their records are more extensive in the early period, and partly because people in those two countries continued to use Celtic names until a later date. The community of language between the three countries was such that many personal names were common to all three languages (with, of course, appropriate changes of sound

15

corresponding to the differences between the languages). Very often a Cornish place-name shows that a particular personal name must have been in use in Cornwall, even though there is no other record of it in use, and it is deduced only from a corresponding Welsh or Breton name occurring in an early source.

Many of these Welsh, Cornish and Breton personal names were made up of two elements, much in the way that place-names were similarly composed. Some of the elements occur in a wide range of combinations, for instance Old Cornish *Wur-* (meaning 'over-, super-, very') in names such as *Wur-gustel* (literally 'super-pledge'), *Wur-ci* ('super-hound'), *Wur-lowen* ('very-happy'). The second parts of each of these three names, *gustel*, *ci* and *lowen*, recur in other personal names such as *Cat-gustel* ('battle-pledge') and *Tanc-wuestel* ('peace-pledge'); *Bren-ci* (possibly 'stink-hound'); and *Lowen-an* ('happy one'). These different combinations of recurrent elements are so common that we are entitled, when necessary, to invent other combinations of the same elements, even though they are not actually found. Thus, if a place-name required it, we could assume Old Cornish personal names *Cat-lowen* ('battle-happy') and *Cat-ci* ('battle-hound'), even though they are not actually recorded. (It so happens that the first of these is recorded in early Breton, and the second is not.) By this means many Cornish place-names which would otherwise be obscure can plausibly be explained as containing early Cornish personal names. But even this method cannot cover the full range of personal names which must have been in use in Dark-Age Cornwall, and there must be many unidentified ones lurking among those place-names of which the second part has had to be left unexplained, in this book, as an 'unknown word or name'.

It goes without saying that nothing at all is known of the people who have left their marks upon the modern map in this way. Occasionally one may wonder whether a person mentioned in the Bodmin Manumissions might be the same man as one commemorated in a place-name not far away; but there is no way of telling, for lack of historical sources.

16

Many Cornish Christian names were identical in form with ordinary words in the language, and it is then impossible to tell whether a place-name contains the ordinary word or the personal name. This is a problem shared with other languages, and there is no solution to it. We shall never know for certain whether TREMAR and TRETHURGY are the farms respectively of a horse and an otter, or of men called *Margh* and *Devergi*. But in some instances it is possible to make a guess: the frequency of names composed of *tre* + personal name makes the people much the more likely alternative in each of these cases.

It should also be emphasised that the meanings of the personal names are irrelevant in terms of the meanings of the place-names. Some of the personal names must have been still understood — those just mentioned, for example, which were also current words as names of animals. Others may have been half-understood to their users, as many are to the modern philologist; and others again, which have no apparent meaning in the Cornish language (or in Welsh or Breton) must have been as opaque then as they are now. But the situation is the same here as in the case of the derivative names as discussed above. As with those names, so here too, the meanings of the personal names are an interesting study in their own right; but they are not the immediate concern of the student of place-names.

All the personal names discussed so far were Christian names, for in the pre-Norman period people in Cornwall did not have surnames. Surnames came into use in Cornwall over an extended period, starting with a few Norman families in the twelfth century. Most people would have had fixed surnames by the fifteenth or sixteenth centuries, though at later dates there are still records of people who seem to have had variable surnames, or two alternative ones. Like Christian names in the earlier period, surnames have left their mark upon the place-names of the county. Generally it is obvious when that has happened: they appear in names like COAD'S GREEN and BRAY SHOP, which are first recorded at late dates (eighteenth or nineteenth centuries), and which belong to recognisable types. But occasionally it is less obvious; in

17

the case of DODMAN POINT and DOBWALLS, only a chance mention in records provides the local surname which proves the derivation. In the case of Dodman Point, the individual who is recorded may be the actual one who gave his name to the headland, or it may simply have been his family. As time goes on, and records become fuller, there are occasional instances where the individual is identifiable, for example at CHARLESTOWN, HALSETOWN and MOUNT EDGCUMBE; also at CANONSTOWN, though that does not contain a personal name.

As with the older Cornish personal names, there is occasional uncertainty whether a place-name contains a descriptive word or a surname of the same form. In SHORTLANESEND and WHITE ISLAND the descriptive word is the more immediately attractive; but early spellings with the genitive -s make one suspect a surname instead, and in the case of Shortlanesend a suitable family can be found in the area at the right period. Even then, certainty is impossible: as so often, the best one can do is make an informed guess.

There are also cases where uncertainty arises for the opposite reason: no plausible derivation is available for a name, either as place-name or as surname. Two examples occurring in this book are DARITE and FREATHY. In each case, the place-name is clearly connected with the similar surname which occurs in the area at an appropriate date; but it is uncertain which came first. Did the family take their surname from the place where they lived, or was the place named from the family? If there were a plausible derivation for the names, in either function, the question could be solved; but in these cases that does not apply. Similarly, if the surnames occurred elsewhere, in Cornwall or outside it, then it could be confidently asserted that the surname was the primary name; but, again, that does not apply. Both of these names will remain as problems until further comparative evidence becomes available. In the case of Freathy, the existence elsewhere of the surname *Friday* may provide a clue, suggesting that the surname was the primary name in that case.

Saints and place-names

In Cornwall, saints form a special and important category of the occurrences of personal names in place-names. Many people wonder why so many curious saints occur as place-names in the county. This is really two questions: why are so many Cornish place-names composed of a saint's name and nothing else? And, second, why are the saints such curious ones? The answer to both questions probably lies, as has long been recognised, in the nature of early Christianity in Cornwall and the other Celtic lands. More than elsewhere, the early church in the Celtic countries seems to have had a tendency to found a large number of local sites of worship and burial. These sites were not necessarily related to the centres of population, so there may have been no pre-existing name which they could borrow. By contrast, churches which were founded in existing communities, to serve the needs of the populace (as generally happened in England, it is assumed), would not so often have given rise to their own distinctive place-names. Many of the church-sites from which Cornish parishes are named have never been centres of population for those parishes. Often today the visitor to a Cornish church will find that there is just one farm beside the church, and no sign of any larger community; in many cases that single farm may be all the settlement that has ever existed there. The local term 'churchtown', used in this book, indicates the church and such habitation as there may be in its immediate surroundings — be it a single farm (a 'town'), a hamlet, or a full village.

When considering places such as OLD KEA, ST WINNOW and MEVAGISSEY, therefore, we are entitled to imagine them, in origin, as places inhabited by small groups of priests, perhaps two or three, living a religious life on sites founded for that purpose. The usual word for such sites was *lann*, here translated 'church-site', but to be envisaged rather as a curved enclosure, containing a chapel and a burial-ground; perhaps also a shrine at the tomb of the founding priest, who was later to be called a 'saint' although very few of them have ever been recognised by the Roman Catholic church. The monastic tendency of the

19

early church in Celtic countries has been exaggerated in the past. These sites would also have had a pastoral function, serving the religious needs of the surrounding district; but the place-names do require us to envisage such small, semi-isolated sites, their early inhabitants commemorated still in the place-names which we use today.

Some of the 'saints' occur at more than one site, perhaps in more than one country, for many of the Cornish saints have dedications also in Wales and Brittany. This makes it necessary to ask whether the saint in question must be thought to have visited all the sites bearing his name, or whether sites could be dedicated in honour of saints who had never been there. The latter must be the correct answer. A distinction can be drawn: on the one hand, there are saints such as Petrock and Piran, honoured at land-owning monasteries; these religious houses may later have brought about the dedication of other sites elsewhere to their patron saints. On the other hand, saints such as St EWE and St LADOCK are associated with no known places apart from the ones in Cornwall which bear their names. In the latter case, economy of hypothesis suggests that there actually were people called Ewa and Ladock, associated with the places bearing their names; but in the former case, an immediate association of the saint with all places bearing the names of Petrock and Piran is not necessary. But all is speculation here, and there are intermediate cases where one cannot know whether or not the saint ever visited the site which bears the name.

People wanted to know about the saints to whom their churches were dedicated, so accounts of their lives were compiled. These were based on a wide variety of sources. A few of the early *Lives* may have had access to reliable oral traditions of the saints whom they celebrated: the *Life* of St Samson (see GOLANT) was probably written in the seventh century, and claims to have used direct spoken traditions about the saint. The *Lives* of St PAUL and St Winwaloe (see GUNWALLOE) were written in the late ninth century, about 400 years after their subjects' lives. These earlier *Lives* may have used local legends of

20

some reliability, though it is a problem to know how much of their content is of that nature. Sometimes the authors drew on other tales as well. In a few cases one can identify an episode, or even a whole *Life* of a saint, as being a shameless crib from some completely different story, with only the names being changed to suit the new setting. Most of these *Lives* are too late to be of use in telling us anything about the saints themselves; all we can say from them is that the saint was believed, at a later date, to have taken part in the events related. Thus very little indeed is known about the Cornish saints except for their existence (and even that is in doubt in some cases), and perhaps something of their way of life, if the general impression gained from the *Lives* is correct.

Two sources are of particular importance in telling us about Cornish saints. The first is a legend that a considerable number of the saints in north-east Cornwall were sons and daughters of a Welsh king, called Broccan. This legend is found in the *Life* of St Nectan, to whom were dedicated chapels in the parishes of St Winnow and Newlyn East, and an important abbey in Devon at Hartland, just outside Cornwall. The legend was probably composed at (or for) Hartland Abbey, and the surviving copy is of the early fourteenth century. It says that King Broccan, from whom the Welsh region of Breconshire (Brycheiniog) took its name, left his queen Gladwys and went to Ireland to lead a holy life. After staying there 24 years, he returned to visit his wife, and subsequently had 24 sons and daughters by her. These are named in the legend, and we are told that they all later became saints in Devon, Wales or Cornwall. In addition to St Nectan, the following places in this book commemorate saints who appear in that legend: St Endellion, St Minver, Landulph (St Dilic), St Teath, St Mabyn, St Wenn, St Issey, Morwenstow, Gwennap, St Clether, and Egloskerry. It will be seen that the majority of these are located in north-east Cornwall. The list of saints is to some extent arranged in geographical order, with the patron saints of adjacent Cornish parishes appearing next to one another in the list.

There are also Welsh versions of the legend. They differ considerably in the names of the king's 24 sons and daughters, supplying many more Welsh saints, and fewer Cornish ones. However, the Welsh versions are of importance from the Cornish point of view, since they mention two saints honoured in Cornwall who do not appear in the Cornish version: St Berwin (honoured at Fowey), and St Kein, honoured at ST KEYNE and, latterly, at KENWYN.

There may be a grain of historical truth in one aspect of the legend, for it is notable that the area where most of these saints have dedications is also the chief area settled by Irish speakers in the fifth and sixth centuries, as shown by inscriptions of that period which contain Irish names, and are found at places such as St Kew and Lewannick. The significance of this is that Breconshire was one of the chief areas in Wales where Irishmen also settled at the same period, as shown by similar inscriptions there. The possibility, then, is that the Irish settlers in north-east Cornwall did not come direct from Ireland, but from Breconshire; and that the later legend of the sons and daughters of King Broccan preserves a dim memory of that.

The other important source for Cornish saints' names is not a legend, but a list of unknown purpose, copied into a Breton manuscript now in the Vatican Library, in Rome. It is simply a bare list of 48 names, with nothing to explain what the names denote, or why they are inserted there; but over half of them turn out to be the names of Cornish saints, of whom several are unknown in Wales or Brittany. This list was written in the early tenth century, before English influence became widespread in the county, and its early date gives it a considerable importance, even though its purpose is unknown and it can tell us nothing about the lives of the saints.

Its significance lies particularly in two factors. One is that it is arranged partly in geographical order, indicating that the cults of the saints already existed at certain sites where they are still honoured today. This carries with it the further possibility that the areas of influence of those sites (the later parishes) may also have been in existence already at that early date. The other importance is that it is written in Cornish, by someone who knew the language, and not in Latin by English officials, as were most other medieval records of Cornish saints. This means that its forms of the saints' names are much more authentic than most other medieval spellings, and in several cases it supplies crucial evidence concerning the original Cornish form of a saint's name. 'The List', as the document will be termed, includes saints who have given their names to the following places in this book: St Levan, St Just in Roseland, St Anthony in Meneage, Gerrans, Philleigh, Ruan Lanihorne, Mawgan in Meneage, St Keverne, St Buryan, Phillack, Gwithian, St Neot, Probus, Ladock, St Austell, St Mewan, Creed, Gorran, St Ewe, and Mevagissey.

It will be noticed that many places taking their names from saints have dropped the prefix 'Saint'. In the selection just cited, the place-names Gerrans, Philleigh, Probus, and others have become standardised in those forms, and the villages are never now called 'St Gerrans', 'St Probus', etc. The prefix was formerly dropped even more widely, and places such as St Endellion and St Enoder used normally to be named without the prefix; but the names of those villages have now been standardised with it. In the case of St Buryan, both forms are still used.

In other cases, the prefix 'Saint' has been added falsely to a name, inventing a saint where none previously existed. One example of that is the island of St AGNES in Scilly. The early forms show that the place-name did not originally refer to a saint, but was later thought to do so. Similarly, under LUDGVAN, MERTHER, MORVAH and TALLAND will be found instances where 'Sanctus Ludewanus', 'St Murther', 'Sancta Morvetha', and 'Sanctus Tallanus' have been claimed, though again the early forms generally lack the prefix. Two more cases where it is very likely that the saint was invented from a descriptive place-name are St DENNIS and KENWYN.

The fact mentioned above, that most early records of Cornish saints are in Latin documents, often written by non-Cornish officials, has caused confusion in terms of the forms of saints' names. In some respects, this confusion is still current today. A good example of the confusion is seen in the name of PHILLACK. The List shows that the saint here was originally called *Felec*. Subsequent medie-

23

val records of the church and parish almost always give the Latin form *Sancta Felicitas*, wrongly equating the Cornish saint with one of the several universal saints called Felicity or *Felicitas*. But Cornish *Felec* cannot originally have been a version of Latin *Felicitas*. Vernacular spellings of parish names start to become common in the sixteenth century, and when they are found for Phillack parish, it becomes clear that local usage had retained the Cornish form *Felek*, ignoring the officials' attempts to turn the saint into someone more familiar. However, it is only the mention of the saint in the tenth-century List which proves the point. We cannot know how many other Cornish saints' names may have been corrupted in the same way, and lack the early native evidence to show it.

There is another way in which the Latin forms used in the Middle Ages have confused the forms of saints' names. For the purposes of working the names grammatically into the syntax, Latin declensional endings had to be added to the names. Thus the saints who were locally known as St Breage, St Columb, St Senar (Zennor), St Ladock and St Newlyn had grammatical endings added for Latin purposes, becoming *Sancta Breaca, Sancta Columba, Sancta Senara, Sancta Ladoca* and *Sancta Newlina*. In modern times it has become a habit to use these Latin forms of the saints' names even when writing or speaking English. This incorrect usage is partly due to the fact that most of our knowledge of the saints comes from Latin sources; and it may be partly also intended to impart a spurious air of authenticity to the names. Forms such as *Breaca, Columba* and *Newlina* should be used only when writing or speaking in Latin. As the records show, Cornish people, when speaking English or Cornish, would always have referred to the saints as 'St Breage', 'St Columb', 'St Newlyn', and so on, correctly omitting the Latin endings.

However, there is a further complicating factor in the matter of Latin and vernacular forms of saints' names. The List shows that some Cornish saints' names originally ended in an open vowel or diphthong, with no consonant closing the syllable. Thus the forms shown by the List for Saints Creed, Ewe and Meva (of Mevagissey) are *Crite*, *Euai* and *Memai*. (*Crite* and *Memai* indicate the pronunciations 'Cride' and 'Mevai'.) These final syllables, by regular sound-changes, would anyway have become simple *-a* in the vernacular forms of the names. But the process was hastened by the Latin forms, for when these saints are next found in Latin sources, instead of having the Latin endings added to the whole names, their final syllables had themselves become the Latin endings, thus *Sancta Crida*, *Sancta Ewa*, and *Sancta Meva*. In these cases, the vernacular and Latin forms of the names are identical. The correct vernacular pronunciation of St Ewe's name is still seen in the name of the churchtown farm, Lanuah, which shows the pronunciation 'Ewa', the direct descendant of the tenth-century *Euai*. Other evidence shows that this is also true of the patron saints of St WENN and St KEW: it is clear that the vernacular forms of these saints' names were *Wenna* and *Kewa*.

It will be noticed that in all these cases, the Latin ending added was a feminine one, *-a*. There is a simple reason for this, in that it was the Latin ending most similar to the open syllables of the Cornish names. But it raises the doubt as to whether there was any further justification for the choice of gender. It may well be that the reason why we think of those saints as female is entirely spurious, based on the mere fact that their Cornish names ended in open syllables. This means that even the one fact which was all that was considered to be known about many Cornish saints, their gender, is itself in doubt. Under several other names, it will be noted that a local saint has the same name as one who is known in another Celtic country, but who is of the opposite sex. (See, for instance, MADRON, ST MERRYN and SENNEN.) It seems that the genders of Cornish saints in medieval records are very unreliable.

Technical terms

1. Periods of the Cornish language

For convenience, the history of the Cornish language is divided into three periods, called Old Cornish, Middle Cornish and Late (or Modern) Cornish. This division is of course arbitrary, and forms of words might be found which displayed intermediate characteristics between the periods. The dates correspond to some extent with those used for the sister languages of Welsh and Breton. Old Cornish means the language from the ninth to the twelfth centuries. The remains from this period include the Bodmin Manumissions and the Saints' List, names in Anglo-Saxon charters (such as *Hryd worwig* 960: see REJERRAH), and, towards the end of the period, an important Vocabulary in which some 960 Latin words are listed, with their Cornish equivalents.

Middle Cornish is the language of the twelfth to the sixteenth centuries. This is the classical period of Cornish writing. The surviving texts include a cycle of three plays, the *Ordinalia*, telling the story of the Bible from the creation of the world until Christ's resurrection; a long poem, related to the second play and concerned with Christ's passion; a fourth play, telling the life story of St Meriasek, the patron saint of Camborne; and some further scraps, including a group of sermons translated from English.

Late Cornish means the language in the seventeenth and eighteenth centuries, until its death in about 1800. Its remains include a play, *The Creacion of the World*, based upon the first of the *Ordinalia*, re-written and with some material added; various short poems, letters, one folk-tale, and some other scraps including the mottoes of some ancient Cornish families. From this period, too, comes the work of the great Welsh scholar, Edward Lhuyd, who took an interest in all the Celtic languages and wrote a grammar of Cornish, published in 1707.

To some extent the various periods of the language can be characterised by some of the sound-changes given below. Changes nos. (1) and (2) happened at the end of the Old Cornish period and the beginning of the Middle one respectively; so that words which do not show those changes are generally classed as Old Cornish, and words which do so as Middle Cornish. Similarly, changes nos. (4) to (7) occurred towards the end of the Middle period, or at the beginning of the Late period. Some place-names actually show some of the changes long before that date; but in the written language the changes were not usually shown until after about 1600, so that words showing

26

those changes are characteristic of Late Cornish in literary texts.

2. Sound-changes

All languages change over time. Grammar changes, the
meanings of words change, and the sounds of words
change. The reason for a particular change cannot usually
be given, but the fact of its occurrence can be chronicled.
Such changes are not haphazard, but tend to occur regularly throughout a language, or under certain definable
conditions, so that the study of sound-changes can be par-
tially a scientific one: rules can be deduced from the
available evidence, and predictions can be made, such as
'If a Cornish word corresponding to this Welsh word were
to be found, it ought to have the form X in the fourteenth
century and Y in the sixteenth.' Alas, such predictions
can only rarely be tested, when new evidence becomes
available; but the rules are essential for studying early
forms of the language, including place-names. A grasp of
some of the sound-changes which occurred in the Cornish
language is necessary to understand why certain early
spellings can imply one derivation but not another.

Seven particular sound-changes occur frequently in
Cornish place-names, and they will be considered in, very
roughly, chronological order. Two general principles must
be discussed first. As stated earlier, spellings of place-
names are liable to be highly conservative. This means
that they may well fail to show a sound-change which
happened long before the date of the spelling, and which
all speakers incorporate without thinking when pro-
nouncing the name. English speakers are familiar with
the pronunciation 'Gloster' for the name which is spelt
Gloucester. The spelling *Gloster* is recorded in 1666, so
that our spelling *Gloucester* is at least 300 years out of
date — probably much more than that, for the pronunciation had doubtless existed for a considerable period
before being recorded in writing. The more important a
place, the more likely are its spellings to be archaic. Within Cornwall, this can be seen in the principle that names
of parishes are more likely to be archaic than names of
farms; but any name may happen to become standardised

in an archaic form. There are examples of farm-names in Cornwall currently spelt in forms at least four centuries behind the pronunciation.

The other general principle is peculiar to the conditions of Celtic speech in Cornwall. As the language died out from east to west across the county, place-names in areas where Cornish was no longer spoken failed to show sound-changes which occurred after the death of the language in their area. Thus Cornish *penn* became *pedn* in the later sixteenth century (change no. (6) below); but that change is seen only in areas where Cornish was still being spoken at that date. In other areas, the older form *penn* appears. For this reason, place-names in the east of the county consistently tend to show earlier forms of the language than names in the west.

However, because of the conservatism of place-name spellings, a name may fail to show a sound-change even though it did occur in speech within that area, and even in that particular name. Thus BELOWDA became 'Belowsa' in speech (change no. (2) below) in the thirteenth century, and the *s*-sound is recorded in 1302. But the spelling used today fails to record the change, and might at first glance make one think that Cornish was no longer spoken in the area when that change occurred. The form of 1302 and other, later, ones show that it did indeed occur, and that the modern form is, misleadingly, seven centuries out of date.

In addition to this hazard, several of the changes listed below have, as yet, been insufficiently studied to make it possible to say precisely when they occurred, or even precisely what form they took, though considerable advances in these questions have been made in recent years. But the general principle, that place-names tend to show earlier forms in the east of the county, and later forms in the west, is broadly correct.

(1) Final *nt* became *ns*. This change probably occurred in the twelfth century. Forms in *-nt* are rare except in pre-Norman documents and in Domesday Book. In the present selection of names, there are only two elements which show this change, *nans* 'valley' (older *nant*) and *pons* 'bridge' (older *pont*) and its compound *carr-bons* 'causeway'; also the personal name *Sant*. Note that LE-ZANT, in the far east of the county, shows the final *nt* still surviving, as also do GOLANT and *Nancent* (ST BREOCK), though Golant did change in pronunciation (*Golenance* c.1462). But of the other names containing these words, none of the forms is early enough to show the older *nt*, except for *Eglossant* (SANCREED) in the twelfth century; however, for names not in this book, pre-Norman spellings and those of Domesday Book, 1086, regularly show the older form.

The change also happened, though not always, in the middle of words. In TREVANSON the personal name *Ansun*, from older *Antun*, is an instance. Under these circumstances, the *s* sometimes went on to become 'dj'. That applied, not only within a word, but also within a single place-name composed of more than one word. There is only one instance in the present book, PENJERRICK, where the *ns* of *penn nans* has become *nj*. Other names such as Nanjewick, 'hind's valley' (*nans + ewig*) and Nanjizal, 'low valley' (*nans + isel*) show it most clearly. In Penjerrick, the *s* of *penn nans* survives as *j*, but it is uncertain whether the spelling *Penhegerik* 1327 is already intended for 'Penedjerrick': more likely, the *g* is merely an attempt to write the distinctive *s*-sound arising in *nans* (compare the spellings *lagek* and *Reyg* in no. (2), below).

(2) Final and medial *d* became *z*. This change occurred slightly later than no. (1), around 1200. To use 'z' is an approximation. The *d* must first have become the sound of the *dy* in English 'would you' when spoken quickly. In final position it then became a full *z*-sound, but internally it may have remained as the 'dzy'-sound (spelt sometimes with *g*: see below).

In areas where English was already strong by 1200, the original final *-d* often survived, and was not changed. In names where that is so, the original *d* is usually spelt with *t* in place-names (for instance, TREGADILLETT and MENHENIOT). The *z*-sound is normally spelt with *s*.

The commonest instances of this change in place-names are in the words for 'ford' and 'dwelling', which were *rid* and *bod* in Old Cornish, but appear as *Res-* and *Bos-* in medieval spellings. Note spellings such as *Hryd* in 960 (see REJERRAH) and *Bot-* in 1086 (BOCONNOC, BOS-SINEY). There is one instance of *Ris-* in 1086, which is anomalously early for the *s* to appear (see RILLA MILL). In place-name spellings, the change tends to appear at a later date in the middle of words than it does in final position. Thus BISSOE is found with *d* in the thirteenth century, and *s* is not found until the fifteenth; whereas *Bos* is found in 1282 *Boskennec* (BOCONNOC) and in 1291 *Boscini* (BOSSINEY). Note also the form *Ponsmadek* 1301 (now POLMASSICK), where change no. (1) has already occurred (*Pons*), but change no. (2) is not seen (*madek*). This agrees with other evidence in suggesting that change no. (1) was a little earlier than no. (2).

It is common for place-names in east Cornwall to show this change in medieval spellings, but to revert to the more archaic *d/t* in more recent ones. Thus we find *Liskyrres* in 1298, and occasionally at later dates, but the modern name has reverted to *d*, LISKEARD. Similarly, the anomalous form *Risleston* in 1086 is supplanted by the more archaic *Ridlehtuna*, with *d*, in the twelfth century (see RILLA MILL); and PENDOGGETT shows both forms simultaneously, *Pendewegoys* and *Pendouket*, in a document of 1302, but has now settled on the more archaic one with *t*. So also further west: by and large, it is the later *s*-forms which have prevailed in that part of the county, but some names have preserved the older *d*, including BE-LOWDA. Note that *s*-forms of that name continue to appear as late as 1699 *Belowsey*, but that nevertheless it is the archaic *d* which has prevailed.

It has been suggested that these sets of parallel forms for a single name indicate the language of the informant, Cornish speech using the later forms with *s*, and English speech the more archaic ones with *d/t*; but it is doubtful whether the evidence is strong enough to support this interesting suggestion. Parallel forms of a name are perfectly capable of co-existing within one language, and moreover an *s*-form is just as capable as a more archaic one of being copied from an older document, so that it cannot prove anything about the language being used at the

30

date of the document. But, of course, an *s*-form does prove that Cornish was being spoken in the area of the place-name at the time of the sound-change.

The change of *d* to *z* regularly fails to occur when the following word begins with *r*: thus we find, even in west Cornwall, BEDRUTHAN, REDRUTH, and other examples of *d-r*, and no counter-examples of names where *sr* appears. Note the unusual change seen in the personal name *Otcer*, which must have become *Osker* in TREVISCOE: it is the only example in this book of a *t* before another consonant becoming *s*, for normally the *d/t* which became *s* was either at the end of a word, or between vowels.

Internally the *z*-sound (or, more accurately, 'dzy' sound) went on eventually to become a full 'dj' (as in English 'adjoin'). This further development has been dated *c*.1625, though earlier examples are known. There are occasional medieval spellings with *g*, but they probably do not indicate the full 'dj' sound yet. Note, for instance, *lagek* 1354, for what was later to be spelt *Lazacke* and has now reverted to the archaic LADOCK; and the *g* in *Reyglubith* 1249, later *Res-* (now RELUBBUS); and compare the spelling *Penhegerik* 1327, above, under no. (1). In such medieval spellings the *g* probably indicates the stage here indicated by 'dzy'. But in the early-modern forms *Bojewyan* and *Cadgwith* 1699, *Ringie* 1660 (now reverted to RINSEY), and *Velingey* 1566 (BOLINGEY), the spellings *j*, *dg* and *g* probably do indicate the full 'dj' sound.

(3) Between vowels, *d* sometimes became *th*. This change is largely restricted to east Cornwall, where *d* had not undergone change no. (2) to *z*, as it normally did further west. It seems to have been one which happened in English, after the Cornish names had been borrowed. In this book, the names which show it are BRADDOCK, ST CLETHER, LITTLE PETHERICK, NORTH and SOUTH PETHERWIN, and QUETHIOCK. All of these contained original *d* which later became *th*. The earliest forms to show the change are *Brothac* 1201, *Pitherwyne* 1275 and *Seyntclether* 1405, but most names do not usually show it until the sixteenth century. Since they are all parish-names, conservatism of spellings may mean that the change was

31

not written until some time after it had occurred; Braddock has reverted to an archaic form with *d*.

(4) Final *-o, -ou* and *-ow* became the neutral vowel, spelt *a*. In Cornish, *-ow* is the usual plural ending, and occurs in other words too, so that it is quite common in place-names. It became reduced to the neutral vowel, spelt with *a* as in English 'arena'. The remains of the language show that this change had occurred by the mid-sixteenth century, but in place-names it sometimes appears rather earlier. A good example is *Nansmornou* (LAMORNA), which had become *Nansmorna* by 1387. TREGONETHA shows the reduction of *o* (itself from original *-oe*) to *a* by 1341 *Tregenhetha*. Other names in this book which show it in their modern forms are BOHORTHA, CRIBBA HEAD, DELABOLE, REJERRAH and TREVERVA; and the pronounced, but not the written, forms of TRABOE, PORTHALLOW and PORTSCATHO also show it. In one case, *Lanreythou* 1266 had become *Lanretha* by 1591, and the reduced ending was then dropped altogether, giving modern LANREATH; but that is exceptional.

Some other endings were also reduced to *-a*. BELOWDA, GRUMBLA, MORVAH and Mulfra (see NEWMILL) show *-a* from older *-e*. NANCLEDRA shows it from original *-i* probably, but that is exceptional, and is not acknowledged in the pronounced forms ('Cledry', etc.): it might be a written development.

It is uncertain whether change no. (4) is due to English influence: probably so. Certainly it coincides with a similar change in English: compare Cockney 'barrer' and 'sparrer' for 'barrow' and 'sparrow', and 'fella' for 'fellow' is almost standard now. And people seem to have remained very conscious of it, so that it is one of the principal types of hyper-correction: see below.

(5) The sounds *dh, gh* and *th* were often lost. Again, the dates of these changes are very variable. There are some very early examples of the loss of *gh*, such as LOOE, *Lo* 1237, and DULOE, *Dulo* 1283: the word in these names must earlier have been *logh*, but no spelling of any place-name shows the final sound in that word. Even earlier, if BODMIN contains *meneghi*, as is likely, then *Bodmine* in

32

the tenth century already shows the loss of *gh* and confla-
tion of the two final syllables; and note its loss also in
Lesmanaoc 967 (11th) (Lesneage, see MENEAGE). Other
names retained the sound for longer; note *Lannergh* 1327
(LANNER), *Penleigh* 1337 (PENLEE POINT), *Gromlogh*
1503 (GRUMBLA), and *Kilmarhe c.*1605 (KILMAR TOR).
Sometimes *gh* was preserved by becoming 'f' (GODOLPHIN
and perhaps LANDULPH), 'k' (LANDRAKE and MUCHLAR-
NICK) or, most often, 'th' (CARNYORTH, ST ERTH and
POLZEATH, and note *Brethiek* 1336, ST MARTIN'S, Scilly).

In the names in this book, the loss of *dh* occurs mainly
in the element *penn-ardh*, 'headland', found in NARE
HEAD, NARE POINT and PENARE. The element *fordh* 'way'
often loses *dh*, and if GUNVER HEAD contains it, the loss
has occurred. CARHARRACK and MORVAH are further
examples of its loss. But in some names *dh* has been
preserved, surviving as *th*: CADGWITH, LESNEWTH and
REDRUTH are examples, and BEDRUTHAN if that contained *dh* originally, as is likely. In two names, LIZARD
and TREWELLARD, original *dh* seems to have been
preserved by becoming *-d*.

By contrast, *th* is usually retained, as in TREGONETHA
and the second part of PORTSCATHO. Its loss occurs widely, but not consistently, in the element *porth*. Forms
without it can occur as early as the thirteenth century, as
in *Porquin* 1201 (PORTQUIN), *Porruwan* early thirteenth
(POLRUAN) and *Porkehuuson c.*1242 (PORTHCOTHAN).
But there are plenty of cases where the *th* survived very
much longer, often to the present day. Sometimes, particularly when a vowel follows, there is a reduction of
written *Porth-* to spoken 'Per-' or 'Pr-': PORTHALLOW,
PORTHOUSTOCK and PORTSCATHO (the latter name can
even lose it altogether, 'Scatha'). If PAR is a variant of
nearby Porth, as is likely, the same name survives in contrasting forms for the older farm and the more recent
village. In other cases *Porth* is replaced by its relative,
English 'Port'. 'Bohurra', the pronounced form of BOHOR-
THA, also shows loss of *th*, again after *r*.

There is an English parallel to the loss of *dh* in one
word, for the Old English element *worthig* was often reduced to *-ery* in pronunciation (see CANWORTHY). But on

the whole it is unlikely that the changes in Cornish were due to direct English influence.

(6) Cornish *nn* became *dn*. This change occurred in the second half of the sixteenth century. Its main occurrence in place-names is in the common element *penn* 'head'. The only names in this book which show it are BOSKEDNAN, TOWEDNACK and *Peden due* 1699 (BLACK HEAD); it is common in minor names on the coast, mainly west of Truro but occasionally to the east. There was also a comparable change in words containing *-mm*, which became *-bm* and then *-bben*; the only example in this book is Gilly Gabben (from *Kelli gamm* 'crooked grove'), but it is also suggested that CRIM ROCKS may have been a hyper--correction for an original *Cribynn* (though that is not found).

(7) Cornish *u* became *i* (often spelt as English *ee*). In the Middle Ages, the sound of Cornish *u* was similar to that of French *u* (as in *tu* 'thou'). It became *i* (as in English 'machine') about 1600 in monosyllables, though once again place-names occasionally show earlier instances. The main words showing this change are *crug* 'barrow', *rudh* 'red', and *yuv* 'lord'; but in most instances in this book, the place-names in question have retained their archaic spellings with *u*, even though older (but more 'modern') spellings show that they did actually change. Thus CRUGMEER (which was *Crucmur* 1336) shows the form *Crigmeare* in 1702, but has now reverted to *u*; and REDRUTH has a few forms which may suggest the pronunciation 'Red*reeth*'. But in BODIEVE (*Bodyuf* 1323) and its equivalent names Bogee and Bojea, the *u* has changed to 'ee' in each case. The *ee* is seen in other names which do not appear in this book, all in west Cornwall, such as Creegbrawse 'great barrow', *crug* + *bras* (in Kenwyn, W7443), and Gonreeve 'red downs', *goen* + *rudh* (in St Gluvias, W775370).

In open syllables, Cornish *u* did not become 'ee', and it either remained written as *u* (BALDHU, POLDHU) or was rendered with English *ew* (CARTHEW), both spellings indicating the same pronunciation, like English 'dew'.

3. Mutation

In all the Celtic languages, certain regular changes, 'mutations', take place in the sounds at the beginnings of words under certain grammatical conditions. Thus in Cornish *tre*, 'farm', the *t* becomes *d* after *an*, 'the': *an dre*, 'the farm'. But after *ow*, 'my', it becomes *th*: *ow thre*, 'my farm'. There are several separate regular patterns of these changes, but the only type which occurs in Cornish place-names is the one called 'lenition'. In this type, the following changes happen to initial sounds under certain grammatical conditions:

b, m	→	v
d	→	dh (*th* as in 'then')
g	→	w or zero
gw	→	w
p	→	b
t	→	d
c, k	→	g

The sound *g* is lenited to *w* when it is followed by *o* (*goen* 'downs', *an woen* 'the downs'); when followed by most other sounds it is lenited to zero, but there are no examples in this book. All other initial sounds (*f, h, l, n, r, s* and the vowels) remain unchanged in those grammatical conditions which produce lenition.

It follows that, in Cornish, a word appearing with initial *d* may be either one which originally began with *d*, or one which originally began with *t* but has been mutated to *d*. Therefore it is essential to know the grammatical conditions under which the mutations occur, in order to know which word is present. Thus Cornish *a*, 'from', causes lenition in the following word; *davas* is 'sheep', so 'from a sheep' is *a dhavas*. By contrast, *a davas*, with *d*, cannot mean 'from a sheep', for the *d* must be a mutation of *t*, so the word is *tavas* 'tongue' instead: 'from a tongue'.

Among the place-names found in this book, lenition occurs in words occurring in the following grammatical situations:

(1) Feminine singular nouns after the definite article *an*, 'the'. Examples: Praze-an-Beeble, Ponsanooth, *Pen an ulays* (Land's End), *Trengyer* (Tregeare). Often *an* never

appears in the spellings, but is merely implied by the presence of the mutation: Drift, Greeb, Gribbin, Grumbla, Penwithick, *Penvounder* (Shortlanesend), and probably Praa.

(2) Adjectives after feminine singular nouns. Examples: Carthew, Goonbell, Kenwyn.

(3) Qualifying nouns or personal names after feminine nouns. Examples: most names containing *bod*, *lann* and *tre*, which are all feminine in gender; Brown Willy, Hallworthy, *Halldrunkard* (see Hallworthy), *Plu vuthek* (Budock), Rejerrah, Roseworthy, Seworgan, Ventonglidder (see St Clether).

(4) The second word in a compound (see below), irrespective of gender. Examples: Carbis, Morvah, Mulfra (see Newmill), Rinsey, Cambeak (if it is Cornish); see also the compound elements *troen-goes*, *crow-ji*, *melin-ji* and *meyn-ji*.

(5) Words after the prepositions *ar* 'facing' and *war* 'upon'. Examples: Perranarworthal, Trethevey (see River Allen), Trevena (Tintagel), Tywardreath.

(6) Words after the prefixes *go-* 'little', *gor-* 'over', *to-* 'thy', and *try-* 'triple' or 'very'. Examples: Godrevy, Godolphin, Georgia, Landegea (Old Kea), Towednack, Truro.

(7) Words after the numeral *dew* 'two': Pendoggett.

(8) Under some other conditions. In North and South Petherwin, the adjective *gwynn* is lenited after a male saint's name; this happens also in Welsh with titles or epithets of people. In Delabole the reason for the mutation of *pol* to *bol* (assuming the name to contain that word) is not clear. In Vellan Head, the derivation is uncertain, but if the name is Cornish then *V* must be a mutation of *b* or *m*. Adjectives which were regularly used to denote contrasting subdivisions of an older single farm, such as *meur* and *byghan* ('great' and 'little'), *gwartha* and *goles* ('upper' and 'lower'), acquired a fossilised mutation, so that they regularly appear in the forms *vear* and *vean* (Penhalvean), *wartha* and *wollas* (Predannack Wollas).

There are some names where lenition should grammatically have occurred, but it fails to do so. There are several possible reasons for this. Names in east Cornwall often fail to show mutation: KELLY BRAY, LINKINHORNE and TREMAIL are examples. Here the early date at which the names were borrowed by the English may perhaps have a bearing upon the matter, even though the sound-changes which gave rise to the mutation had already occurred some centuries before the English arrived in Cornwall. In other instances of non-mutation, the form of the place-name may have been influenced by the un-mutated form of a personal name which it contains: thus the *m* preserved in LAMORRAN may be due to the local currency of the saint's name *Moren*. Indeed, many instances of non-mutation come into no. (3) of the grammatical situations given above: it seems to be the one most liable to produce instances of non-mutation (e.g. ROSEMULLION, in addition to Lamorran, and indeed Linkinhorne and Tremail). The lenition may have been felt less grammatically essential in these phrases.

Names starting with *eglos* 'church' usually fail to show the mutation expected after that feminine noun. The reason may be partly as with Lamorran, local currency preserving the saint's name in un-mutated form; and, more important, there may have been a phonological reason. The voiceless *s* of *eglos* evidently prevented *p*, *t* and *c/k* from becoming *b*, *d* and *g*. Thus we find *Eglos Cutbert* 'church of St CUBERT', which grammatically ought to be *Eglos gutbert*; and *Egloscuri*, 'church of St CURY', not the expected *Eglosguri*. The phonological reason cannot be the only one, for it does not apply in the case of *Egglosbrec* (BREAGE) and *Eglos Maderne* (MADRON); but it was probably one factor.

In CAMBORNE, too, there may be a phonological reason for the failure to mutate: *Camvron* would have been expected, but the adjacent *m* may have helped to preserve the *b* from lenition. In Rosemullion, variation in gender could be the reason for the non-mutation: there are other suggestions that *ros* was occasionally masculine instead of feminine. Early written forms of place-names often failed to show mutation, and in some names this may have influenced the pronunciation: BODMIN, CARDINHAM and LAMORRAN could be such instances. If Tregaverne (see PORTGAVERNE) contains a stream-name or personal name *Gavran*, the failure of mutation may be either due

37

to the influence of Portgaverne, nearby, or due to the fact that Tregaverne might be a late name, formed by analogy and not a true *tre*.

4. Compounds

As mentioned earlier, the normal word-order in Celtic place-names was *generic + qualifier*, the opposite of the normal English order. This standard type of name in the Celtic languages is best termed a 'name-phrase'. A few names in this book show the opposite order, as in English names, *qualifier + generic*. In deciding the derivation of a name, it is essential to decide the structure of the name, since that affects the meaning. Thus the name Lanteglos (originally *Nant eglos*) has sometimes been cited as meaning 'church in a valley'. In fact, it is a name-phrase, and means 'valley with a church'. ('Church in a valley' would be *Eglosnant*, like EGLOSHAYLE, 'church on an estuary'.) Thus Lanteglos is originally the name of the valley, not of the church.

There are several reasons why a name in a Celtic language may be composed in this manner. One is that it may be extremely old. The evidence seems to show that in the pre-Roman period, the Celts had formed their place-names mainly in the order *qualifier + generic*, just as in English. Place-names such as *Branodunum* 'Bran's fort' (Brancaster, Norfolk) and *Moridunum* 'sea-fort' (Carmarthen) show this well. The change in the regular order of the elements came about at a period of other major changes in the Celtic languages, in about the fifth century; so this change in the grammatical structure of place-names took its place among many others, both grammatical and phonological. One reason, then, for a place-name to be a compound may be that it is extremely ancient, going back to the Roman period or earlier.

Another reason is that some adjectives in Cornish either must or prefer to come before their nouns, thus creating compounds. These compounds can be created at any time, so that names showing such formations do not need to be very early. The adjective *hen* 'ancient' is one which must do so: *hen-lys*, 'ancient court', never *lys hen*. One adjective which prefers to come before its noun, but does not always do so, is *camm* 'curved', 'crooked'. Thus we find the compounds *cromm-legh*, 'curved slab', and CAMBORNE, 'curved hill'; but also the name-phrase Gilly Gabben, 'crooked grove', where the adjective follows its noun in the more usual manner (*kelli gamm*, with mutation of *c* to *g* after *kelli*, feminine noun). Similarly, *rudh* 'red' is used to form a compound in RUTHVOES, 'red-bank', but to form a name-phrase in REDRUTH, 'red ford' (literally 'ford red'). It may have been partly a matter of personal preference which type was used in forming place-names with such adjectives; there is a possibility that the compound type was felt to be more formal, more poetic, or more 'name-like', and it may have been preferred in some farm-names for that reason.

Some compounds became established as ordinary words in the language, for instance *hen-lann* 'ancient church-site' (*hen* + *lann*), *carr-bons* 'cart-bridge, causeway' (*carr* + *pons*) and *gwavos* 'winter-dwelling' (*gwav* + *bod*). These could then be used at any date to form place-names in their own right: HELLAND, CARBIS. Such compound words would count (and feel) as single words within the language; so that place-names such as TREWAVAS, ('farm of a winter-dwelling', *tre* + *gwavos*) and KEHELLAND ('grove of an ancient church-site', *kelli* + *hen-lann*) do not violate the principle that place-names normally consist of only two elements: although *gwavos* and *hen-lann* are compounds in derivation, they each count as single elements. The full names Trewavas and Kehelland are thus ordinary name-phrases, of which the second element happens to be a compound word.

One distinctive feature of compound names is that the initial letter of the second element is lenited: *mor* 'sea' + *bedh* 'grave' becomes, as a compound, *Mor-vedh* 'sea-grave' (MORVAH). A normal name-phrase giving the same meaning would be *Beth mor*, 'grave of the sea', with the stress on the second syllable, and with no mutation. Another distinctive feature in compound names is the stress. In all place-names, this comes on the qualifying element, the one which makes the place distinctive. In an ordinary name-phrase, this will be the second element: 'Red*ruth*', 'Gilly *Gabben*'. But in a compound, it means that the stress is on the first element: '*Ruth*voes', '*Mor*vah'.

The following elements in this book are compounds: *carr-bons*, *cow-nans*, *cromm-legh*, *crow-ji*, *goel-va*, *hen-lys*, *hen-lann*, *hir-yarth*, *legh-rys* (?), *melin-ji*, *meyn-ji*, and *troen-goes*. The following place-names are compounds: Burras, Camborne, Cambeak (if it is Cornish), Gwynver (see Gunver Head), Morvah, Mulfra (see Newmill), Newlyn, and Rinsey. In addition, Crowlas and Gwenter are of uncertain derivation, but their appearance is of being compounds, since they are stressed on the first syllable; so any suggested derivation would need to take that into account. Similarly, if Gunver (Head) and Morval are Cornish at all, their appearance is of being compounds.

5. Epenthesis

A vowel inserted between two consonants, for ease of pronunciation, is called 'epenthetic'. A good example is seen in sound-change no. (6) above: the form *Peden* 1699 (see BLACK HEAD) shows an epenthetic vowel inserted into the late Cornish form *pedn*. Epenthetic vowels seem to appear in the early forms of the names BURLAWN and GOLANT: spellings such as *Bodolowen* and *Golananta* (as compared with *Bodlouen* and *Gulnant*) show vowels inserted, between *d* and *l* in the first name, and between *l* and *n* in the second. Note also the modern form TREBE-THERICK, contrasted with the form *Trebethrick* 1657: again a vowel has been inserted, between *th* and *r*.

Epenthetic vowels did not count for purposes of stress in Cornish. The stress in Cornish words is regularly on the last syllable but one. So *Trebethrick* was naturally stressed on *beth*. In the modern form, Trebetherick, it has remained on that syllable; so that the stress now appears to be on the last syllable but two instead. The reason is that the *er*, with epenthetic vowel, does not count as a full syllable.

Epenthesis sometimes occurred very early in Cornish. Some words and names already contained epenthetic vowels in the tenth century, earlier than most dated place-name forms. There is a good early example of it in the form *Tretdeno* 1086, for what is now TREKNOW, having lost the epenthetic vowel again. The second word in this name is *tnow*, 'valley' (here mutated to *dnow* after *tre*). The spelling of 1086 shows an epenthetic vowel, *e*, between *d* and *n*. The Welsh equivalent of *tnow* is *tyno*, with a similar epenthetic vowel between the first two consonants.

Epenthesis is not usually a datable sound-change, in either Cornish or English pronunciations. It has already been seen that some names have acquired intrusive vowels and then lost them again during their history. So it can appear at very variable dates. In LUDGVAN the form *Ludewon* 1291 shows it, but others of similar date do not. In SEWORGAN it seems to have arisen after part of the first element *rys* was lost: *Rys-wothgan* became *'Swothgan*, and a vowel was intruded between *s* and *w*, giving *Sewothgan* 1614.

Sometimes it is necessary to assume that a vowel in an early form is epenthetic, in order to explain the position of the stress in the modern form of a name. The importance of realising that a vowel is intrusive in this way is that of determining the original form of the name, in case corresponding Welsh or Breton words are being considered. In the names TREVIGRO and TREWIDLAND, the modern stress indicates that the early forms *Trevigora* and *Trewythelan* probably contain epenthetic vowels (respectively *o* and *e*) which have since dropped out again, so that the original forms which must be envisaged are *Trevigra* and *Trewythlan*.

Similarly, the modern stress of the name TREGONY, on the first syllable, is unexpected. It is best explained by assuming that in the earliest forms *Trefhrigoni* and (emended) *Trerigani*, the *o/a* is epenthetic. (Such an intrusive vowel was usually the neutral vowel, so that there was uncertainty how to spell it, and variation is to be expected.) If it were *not* epenthetic, it would have borne the stress, and the resulting 'Tre-rygony' should have given modern 'Tregony', not the actual 'Tregony'. But if it were epenthetic, it would not have counted for stress purposes, and the name would have been stressed 'Tre-rygony' (from older 'Tre-rygny'); this, with conflation of the two first syllables, would then satisfactorily explain the unexpected stress in the modern name. Forms such as *Tregny* *c.*1540, showing that the first-syllable stress already existed, would thus show the epenthetic vowel having been lost again, as elsewhere.

6. Hyper-correction

Often there is an awareness that a sound-change has occurred, and that the colloquial pronunciation of a name is different from its 'correct' or its older pronunciation, or from its written form. Occasionally people may have two pronunciations of a name, one used in quick, colloquial speech and another used when speaking formally, slowly or emphatically. As a result, there can be a general awareness that a particular pronunciation in colloquial speech often represents another sound in formal or 'correct' speech. As a consequence, the formal sound is occasionally restored over-enthusiastically, for the sake of 'correctness', to names which never contained it. This over-enthusiastic restoration of a sound which did not originally exist in a particular word or name is best termed 'hyper-correction'. It is a form of analogy, due to comparison with other words or names where the same restoration would indeed be valid.

A few examples will clarify the principle. In English names, the ending *-worthy* often developed, quite regularly, into *-ery* in speech, as mentioned earlier; a good instance is seen in the colloquial form *Kennery* 1699, from older *Carneworthy* (now CANWORTHY). There was evidently a consciousness that *-ery* often represented 'correct' *-worthy*: the two pronunciations must have existed side by side, one colloquial, the other formal or emphatic. As a result of that consciousness, the 'correct' *worthy* has occasionally been over-restored to some names which did not contain it originally. CLUBWORTHY was correctly pronounced 'Clubbery' in the nineteenth century (original form *Clobiry* 1322). The ending '-ery' was wrongly thought to be a colloquial form of 'worthy' (by analogy with other names where that was indeed the case), and the name is now written Clubworthy by hyper-correction.

An instance of the same phenomenon in names of Cornish origin is seen in the consciousness of the sound-change (no. (4) above) whereby -*ou*, etc., became -*a*. People were evidently aware that what they pronounced, for instance, as 'Bohurra', 'Perscatha' and 'Trebba' were spelt Bohurrow (Bohortha), Portscatho and Traboe, and that those written forms might be used in 'correct' or formal speech. By analogy with such names, there has been an over-enthusiastic tendency to restore the 'correct' -*o*, even in names where it did not exist before. The early forms of POLPERRO normally end in -*a* or -*e* (*Portpira* 1303, *Porthpire* 1361), evidently representing the neutral vowel by the sixteenth century, 'Polperra'. In modern times that -*a* has wrongly been taken to be a colloquial form of an older -*o* (which had never previously existed in this name), and the form 'Polperro' has arisen; the new ending appears first in *Polparrow* 1748. Similarly with TREVISCOE, the modern form ending in -*oe* has no basis in the older spellings of the name, and can only be explained by assuming a pronunciation 'Trevisca', in which the -*a* was wrongly thought to be a colloquial form of 'correct' -*o*.

This is probably an English phenomenon, rather than a Cornish one. Examples of it occur mostly in the eighteenth century and later. As mentioned earlier, the sound-change responsible, -*ow* becoming -*a*, is also known in English ('sparrer', 'barrer'). There is also a similar change in a name of English derivation, Harrowbarrow. This was originally *Harebere*, 'grey grove', which might have been expected to give a modern form 'Harbeare', or the like. The modern form is probably due to re-interpretation, but hyper-correction may also have played a part.

Owing to the loss of *th* after *r*, some names, especially in the Hundred of Pydar, show hyper-correct restoration of *th* in names which did not contain it previously. There are no certain instances in this book. ROSEWORTHY contains non-original *th*, but it is probably due to analogy with English names ending in -*worthy* (compare HALL-WORTHY), rather than hyper-correction.

Finally, it is just possible that CRIM ROCKS was originally *Cribynn*, 'little crest', and that the modern form is due to the wrong assumption that *Cribynn* was from Late Cornish *Cribm*, from supposed earlier *Crim* (change (6) above). Then the form *Crim* would be a hyper-correction.

7. Re-interpretation

Re-interpretation, often called 'folk-etymology', is the process whereby the users of a word or name change it in order to make it appear to mean something else. An English example, often cited, is the way that 'asparagus' is re-interpreted as 'sparrow-grass'. Such change is particularly liable to happen when a place-name is borrowed from one language into another, as Cornish names were into English. Examples of such re-interpretation would include SEATON (where the new, English meaning given to the name was particularly apt); *Halldrunkard* (see HALLWORTHY), where the presence of an inn may have helped the re-interpretation; and the first part of HERODSFOOT (where the new form is not at all apt, and merely puzzles people). BROWN WILLY and GEORGIA are other examples of names which have been re-interpreted as a result of the transfer from Cornish to English. Sometimes only a part of a name is re-interpreted, as in Herodsfoot, GOLDSITHNEY, and *Porth Island* (an early form of *Porraylan*, the Cornish name for HOLYWELL).

But the process can also happen within a single language as well, and it is not even necessary for the meaning of a name to have been lost for re-interpretation to take place. When *Tingaran* was changed to TRENAR-REN, the first element *tin* (a variant of *din*, 'fort') was re-interpreted to become the common word *tre*, although the name may still have been understood. The unexplained form of the first syllable of KYNANCE might be due to re-interpretation within Cornish, as if it were *ki*, 'dog'. However, there are not many instances of re-interpretation within Cornish in this book, though they do occur.

Re-interpretation has also occurred widely within English. A good example is seen in Twelvewood (the name of the wood at DOUBLEBOIS), which was originally *Twyfeldewode*, 'two-fold wood'. Whatever RED DOWN may mean, it was not 'red down' originally; and WAINHOUSE CORNER formerly had a 'wine-house', not a 'wagon-house' nearby. The change from *Clubbery* to CLUBWORTHY, here ascribed to hyper-correction, could alternatively (or in addition) be attributed to re-interpretation, with people assuming that what they pronounced '-ery' should really be 'worthy'. Indeed, cases of hyper-correction might often be seen as a particular type of re-interpretation. But, in the case of Clubworthy, it is doubtful if people understood the actual meaning of *worthy*, so perhaps it cannot be counted as a true re-interpretation.

There is no means of telling what re-interpretations may have occurred before the date of the earliest forms of place-names. Many names must have a long unrecorded history before the date of their earliest appearances in written documents. But it is useless to speculate on such possibilities. Re-interpretation cannot be assumed unless there is evidence in the spellings, or in parallel names, to show its presence.

Explanation of the entries

Under each entry is given:

(1) The name.

(2) The grid reference. For names appearing on the Ordnance Survey Quarter-Inch map, only a four-figure reference is given. For other names, a six-figure one is usually given. All places in Wales and south-west England (and in most of the rest of England) have S as the first of their two grid letters: in accordance with Ordnance Survey recommendation, this first letter S has been omitted from the grid references of places in Cornwall. Thus Truro, for which the full grid reference is SW8244, appears as W8244.

(3) In brackets, the ancient parish in which the place is located; and the nature of the place being named. The name refers to a habitation unless otherwise specified (hill, coastal feature, antiquity).

(4) The earliest recorded form of the name; and other spellings which may be necessary to demonstrate the derivation, or to illustrate how the modern form arose from the ancient form, or which may be of intrinsic interest in the history of the name. Normally these spellings are sample ones only, and are intended to be typical of the name at various periods. Occasionally there are no others available. It will be clear that there is a shortage, for

instance, when the earliest spelling cited is as recent as the seventeenth century or later. If there is only one or a few medieval spellings available, then the inadequacy is usually pointed out. In such cases, the derivation is less secure, and the entry usually states that the lack of sufficient evidence makes an interpretation difficult or uncertain.

In citing these spellings, I have taken certain liberties, in accordance with the intended nature of the book. I have inserted hyphens in a few particularly long forms, in order to show where they should be divided into their constituent parts: all hyphens appearing in early spellings are editorial additions of this kind. (See, for instance, forms of GOLDSITHNEY and RELUBBUS.) I have normalised medieval *u* and *v* (often used interchangeably), so that the spellings always have *u* for the vowel, and *v* for the consonant. But this has not been done if there is uncertainty whether a *u* or *v* represents a consonant or a vowel. The Anglo-Saxon letters called 'eth' and 'thorn' have been expanded as *th*, both in spellings of names and in citing elements. Among the dates of the spellings, the formula '12th' means 'a document, undated, of the twelfth century'. The formula '1165 (14th)' means 'a document which is dated 1165 but which survives in a later copy of the fourteenth century'. It is very important to observe when the forms are copied ones, for obviously the possibility of corruption is greater in such forms than in those of original documents; or such forms may have been modernised.

The documents which contain these early spellings are often also splendid sources for the history of the places themselves. They may contain mention of a mill, a tinwork, of the owner or tenant, or of the use of the land. Sometimes the information may be relevant for the meaning of the name, and then it has been included along with the early form. Most documents before the sixteenth century are in Latin, and excerpts from those have been translated, between quotation marks. Thus the form 'island of *Aganas*', for AGNES in Scilly, is a translation of Latin *insula de Aganas*.

Many Cornish surnames are derived from place-

46

names, and in the medieval period people often took their names from the places where they actually lived. Thus many of the place-name forms cited here are actually references to people rather than places. When that is so, I have usually given the individual's Christian name as well, to show the fact. I have translated the Christian names from Latin into English. Usually (but not always) the Latin word *de* 'of' connected the two names: Roger de *Boloude* and Simon de *Bodkadwen* mean 'Roger of BE-LOWDA' and 'Simon of BOCADDON'. In a few cases, though only when it is reasonably certain that the man was actually living at the place, I have omitted the personal details for convenience.

(5) A suggested meaning, and the elements which the name contains. Throughout the book, the language of the name is Cornish, unless it is otherwise stated to be English or French (or, in Scilly, possibly Old Norse). However, with derivative names, such as ROSEMULLION HEAD, the second part, where it is very obvious in English, is often ignored. The elements are listed, in their separate languages, at the end of the book, together with all place-names which are suggested to contain them. These derivations are not necessarily all my own ideas: in many cases they have long been recognised, or have been suggested by previous workers such as Gover, Nance and Pool. Cross-references to other names in the book are given in SMALL CAPITAL letters.

(6) Alternative names by which the place has been known at some time are given; and also sometimes the pronunciation where it is relevant, unexpected or interesting. These pronunciations are of course intended as rough guides only. They should be read as if they were ordinary English words, in the reader's own dialect. The stress, most important in Cornish names, is indicated by *italics* in the syllable to be stressed. Thus 'Linkin*horne*' is stressed on the last syllable, and '*Tre*gony' on the first.

(7) Occasionally an incorrect derivation is cited, for refutation. Of the many incorrect derivations which have been given for Cornish place-names in the past, only those which have gained a certain currency are given. In some cases these are derivations given in my own *Cornish*

Place-Name Elements, where fresh evidence, or the suggestions of others, has made a revision necessary. No doubt some of the derivations given in the present book will also need to be revised, as work progresses.

Dictionary of
Cornish Place-Names

St Agnes V8708 (island, Scilly) 'Island of *Aganas*' 1193
(16th), 'island of *Hagenes*, of *Hagenesse*' 1194, *Agnas* 1244,
St Agnes c.1540. It is tempting to see the second part of
this name as Cornish *ynys*, 'island', but such an idea is hard
to sustain. The middle syllable would have been stressed,
so that one would expect a modern form 'Agennis'. But the
middle syllable in *Hagenes* was evidently unstressed, as
shown both by the modern pronunciation and by the spelling *Agnas* 1244. In addition, the vowels in the earliest
form, *Aganas*, are wrong for a name containing *ynys*.
Therefore a Scandinavian name is much more likely, probably 'pasture-headland', *hagi* 'pasture, enclosure for
grazing' + *nes*, with later transference of the name from a
headland to the whole island. Compare a lost 'meadow
called *Hagenesse*' 1213, in Lincolnshire. See NEW GRIMS-
BY for another probable Norse name on Scilly. The prefix
'St' is a late addition (16th-century), not normally used in
local speech, and is due to incorrect analogy with the
names of other islands in the group.

St Agnes W7250 (parish) 'Parish of *Sancta Agnes*' 1327,
Agnette alias St Tannes 1586. The church is dedicated to
St Agnes, a fourth-century martyr in Rome. The Cornish
name of the churchtown was *Bryanek* 1286, surviving as
Bryanick 1884: *bre*, 'hill', + unknown word or name. (Not
'pointed hill', as previously suggested, for the forms do not
allow a derivation from *bannek* 'pointed'.) St Agnes Head
W6951 (coast) was *St Agnes' Head* c.1870.

Albaston X4270 (Calstock) Alice de *Alveveston* c.1286,
Aliveston, Alptone 1303, *Alpeston, Alpiston* 1337. It is not
quite certain that the first two forms belong to Albaston,

though they appear to do so. English, probably personal name + *tún* 'farm'; but the forms (if they all belong here) are too variable to show what personal name is involved.

River Allen x0985—x0071 **(river)** *Layne* c.1470, c.1540, *Laine* 1842, *River Allen* 1888. This river has changed name twice; but the meanings of all three names are unknown. Its name in the historical period was always *Laine*, which is unexplained. Owing to an error in the late 19th century, *Laine* was replaced by *Allen*, a common Celtic river-name also of unknown meaning; the name *Allen* was incorrectly transferred to it from the adjacent River CAMEL, which it had previously denoted. However, farms along the course of the Laine/Allen show that it must previously have been called *Dewi*, though it is never recorded under that name. Trethevey in St Mabyn, x035734, is 'house upon the Dewi' (*Tewardeui* 1086, *ti* [later *chi*]+ *war* + *Dewi*), and Pendavey in Egloshayle, x006712, is 'foot of the Dewi' (*Bendewy* 1284, *ben* + *Dewi*). This, too, is a common Celtic river-name, again of unknown meaning.

St Allen w8250 **(parish)** 'Church of *Sanctus Allunus*' 1261, *Seynt Alun* 1270, *Eglosellan* 1840. The church is dedicated to a saint Alun, of whom nothing is known; there is a Breton saint Alan. *Eglosellan*, the Cornish name of a field at the churchtown, is 'church of St Allen', *eglos* + saint's name.

Altarnun x2281 **(parish)** *Altrenune* c.1100 (14th). 'Altar of St Nonn', *alter* + saint's name. She was believed to have been the mother of the Welsh St David; compare PELYNT, another dedication to her, and the parish of DAVIDSTOW is adjacent to Altarnun. In the 15th century she was believed to be buried here; but Dirinon in Brittany, 10 miles east of Brest, also claims her burial site.

Annet v8608 **(island, Scilly)** *Anec* (*c* for *t*) 1302, *Anete* 1306, *Anet* 1336. Completely obscure. No Cornish word or name in west Cornwall should normally end in -*t*, so that even the language is uncertain.

St Ann's Chapel x4170 **(Calstock)** 'Chapel of *Sancta Anna*' 1500, *Sent Anne is Chapell* (and two wells of St Agnes) 1541. English, self-explanatory; the saint is the mother of the Virgin Mary. But there is no record of the use of the chapel, and its site is uncertain. There was earlier, in the same area, a piece of land 'next to the well of St Andrew' 1347; and it may be that in this name St Ann has replaced St Andrew, the patron saint of the parish church.

St Anthony in Meneage W7825 (parish)　　　*'Sanctus Antoninus* in *Manahec'* 1269, *Lanyntenyn* 1344, *St Antony* 1522. Named from the dedication of the church to the Cornish St Entenin, king and martyr (*Antoninus* in Latin). He is first mentioned in the 10th century (List) as patron saint of St Anthony in Roseland; 'in Meneage' distinguishes this parish from the Roseland one (see MENEAGE separately). In both cases the Cornish name has been rationalised into the English name 'Anthony'. *Lanyntenyn* is *lann* 'church-site' + saint's name; it survives as the churchtown farm, Lantinning.

Antony X3954 (parish) *Antone* 1086, *Anton* 1289, *Antony* c.1540. English, 'Anta's farm', personal name + *tún*. The place-name would normally have developed into *Anton*, but the later form has been influenced by the unconnected Christian name 'Anthony'.

Ashton W6028 (Breage) So found in 1867. A 19th-century village and name; English, presumably 'ash-tree village', or possibly transferred from elsewhere.

St Austell X0152 (parish) 'Church of *Austol'* c.1150 (13th), 'church of *Sanctus Austolus'* 1169 (1235). From the dedication of the parish church. The saint is first mentioned, as patron saint of this church, in the 10th century (List). He was believed to have been a companion and follower of the more famous St MEWAN, and was honoured also at St Méen le Grand in Brittany. St Austell Bay X05 (coast) is so found in 1813.

Baldhu W7743 (Kea) *Baldue* 1748 (a tin mine), 1813. 'Black mine', *bal* + *du*. The incorrect *h* in the modern spelling is due to a misguided belief that putting an *h* into a word makes it look more 'Celtic': compare POLDHU.

Ballowal Barrow W3531 (antiquity, St Just in Penwith) *Ballowall Cairn* 1879. The barrow was discovered and excavated in 1878-79. It is named from the neighbouring settlement of Bollowall W359313; that is found as *Bolawall* 1302, Ralph de *Bolauhel* 1396: probably 'dwelling of Lou- hal', *bod* + personal name.

Barripper W6338 **(Camborne)** *Beaurepere* 1397. French, 'beautiful retreat', *beau repair*. Compare BEREPPER and similar names elsewhere in the county (in the parishes of Mevagissey, Mawnan and Ruan Lanihorne, among others); also in other English counties: Belper in Derby- shire (*Beurepeir* 1231), Bear Park in County Durham (*Beaurepayre* 1267), and elsewhere. The names in Corn- wall have been given a Cornish flavour, with the stress on the second syllable, and their development has been al- tered accordingly.

Bathpool X2874 **(North Hill)** *Bathpole* 1474. English, pres- umably self-explanatory and referring to a pool in the River Lynher nearby.

Bawden Rocks or Man and his man W7053 **(coast, St Agnes)** *The Manrocke* 1587, 'little isle called *Bond*' 1650, *the Man & his Man* 1699, '*Bawden Rocks*, more properly *Boen Rocks*' c.1720, *Boden* 1748, *Boden Rocks or Man and his Man* c.1870. *Bawden* is unexplained. There is a farm called Bawden on the neighbouring coast, W708515, and it is unknown which was named first, the farm or the rock; but as the farm name is not recorded until 1888, it is like- ly to be named from the rock. It might possibly be *bowyn* 'cow', as suggested by *Boen* in c.1720: coastal rocks are often named metaphorically, using animal-words. But, if so, the *d* would be irregular in that word. No other sugges- tion is available; the earliest form shows that it cannot be the common surname Bawden. The alternative name is probably English 'man', personifying the larger and smal- ler rocks (compare BISHOP ROCK); or, less likely, Cornish *men* 'stone'.

Bedruthan Steps W8469 **(coast, St Eval)** *Bodrothan Steps* 1851. Named from the neighbouring farm of Bedruthan W854698. That was *Bodruthyn* 1335, 1431, *Bodrethan* 1657, *Bodrothen* 1717, *Bedrewthan* 1748; probably 'dwell- ing of Rudhynn', *bod* + personal name, though the exact nature of the middle vowel is not apparent from the avail- able spellings.

Belowda W9661 (Roche) Roger de *Boloude* c.1240, *Bolloude* late 13th (14th), *Belleuse* 1302, '*Belowdy*, commonly, and not unproperly, termed *Beelowzy*' 1602, *Belovedy alias Belowsey* 1699; *bod* + unknown word or name, probably a personal name, 'dwelling of Loude'. Note the change of *d* to *s* in 1302 and later; but the archaic written form has survived. The English re-interpretation of the *s*-form, as in 1602, gave rise to a contrasted alternative *Belovely* c.1870.

Bennacott X2992 (Boyton) *Bennacote* 1201, *Bunacote* 1302. English, probably 'Bynna's cottage', personal name + *cot*. Compare Binworthy in Devon, 'Bynna's farm'.

Berepper W6522 (Gunwalloe) *Beauripper* 1443 (19th), *Breepar* 1699. French, 'beautiful retreat', *beau repair*, like BARRIPPER.

Berryl's Point W8467 (coast, St Mawgan in Pydar) *Berryls* Point c.1870. English, no doubt from some surname, perhaps Burrell or Birrell, though no such name has so far been found in the parish.

Bilberry X0160 (Roche) *Billebery* c.1280, *Billibyry* c.1280 (14th). An early English name, 'Billa's mound', personal name + *beorg*. In form, the spellings could equally well indicate Old English *byrig*, dative of *burh* 'fort', as the second word; but as there is no fort nearby, nor an obvious site for one, *beorg* seems more likely, with reference probably to a lost tumulus. Compare CLUBWORTHY and FLEXBURY, where similar conditions apply.

Bishop Rock V8006 (coast, Scilly) 'A rock in the sea called *Maenenescop*' 1302, *The byshop and hys clerkys* 1564, *Bishop* 1689. 'The stone of the bishop', Cornish *men* + *an* + *escop*, later translated into English; but the reason for the name is not known. Probably it was a fancied resemblance in shape: rocks called The Bishop are known elsewhere (e.g. in Breage, named from its shape, Mullion, St Columb Minor, and at Bassenthwaite in Cumberland); they usually have no known connections of church ownership. Some forms (of 1564, for instance) show an extension of the original name, with the surrounding rocks seen as the bishop's 'clerks' or clergymen. The remarkable reference in 1302 is to a woman, Muriel de *Trenywith*

(Trenoweth on St Mary's), and her two daughters, convicted of theft, being marooned there 'until they were drowned by the waves of the sea'.

Bissoe W7741 **(Kea/Perranarworthal)** *Bedou c.*1250, 'wood of *Bedow*' *c.*1260, *Besow* 1480. 'Birch-trees', *besow*. The wood which gave rise to the name does not survive.

Black Head W7716 **(coast, St Keverne)** *Peden due alias Blackhead* 1699. English, self-explanatory; the Cornish name means the same ('black headland', *penn + du*, with late *dn* for *nn*), and is presumably older, so that the English name is a translation.

Black Head X0447 **(coast, St Austell)** *Blake Hedd, Blak-Hed c.*1540. English, as above; but in this case there is no evidence that the name is translated from Cornish.

Blackwater W7346 **(St Agnes/Kenwyn)** *Black water coomb c.*1696 ('Blackwater valley', + *cumb*). English, 'black stream'. This stream also runs through CHACEWATER.

St Blazey X0654 **(parish)** Chapel of *Sanctus Blasius* 1440, *Seynt Blasy* 1525; from the dedication of the church to St Blaise, an Armenian martyr of perhaps the 4th century, invoked particularly for afflictions of the throat. He was also the patron saint of wool-combers, through having been tortured with wool-combs. Until the 16th century, St Blazey was more normally known by its Cornish name of *Landrait* 1169 (1235), *Landrayth* 1284: 'church-site on a strand', *lann + treth*, with mutation of *t* to *d*. The 'strand' is the same one as in TYWARDREATH, but the estuary has since become silted and built upon, so that the tide no longer reaches the church.

Blisland X1073 **(parish)** *Glustone* (*G* for *B*) 1086, *Bloiston* 1177, *Bleselonde, Bliston* 1284, *Blislonde* 1300. English, unknown word or name + *tún* 'farm' and *land* 'land', used as alternative suffixes. The name with *tún* denoted the village or manorial centre, while that with *land* denoted the lands of the manor. In Cornwall these English suffixes were often added to pre-existing Cornish names (see, for instance, HELSTON, KILKHAMPTON, LAUNCESTON and STOKE CLIMSLAND), but the derivation of *Blus* or *Blois*, whether English or Cornish, is unknown.

Bocaddon x1758 (Lanreath) Simon de *Bodkadwen* 1315, *Bocadwen* 1507. 'Dwelling of Cadwen', *bod* + personal name.

Boconnoc x1460 (parish) *Bochenod, Botchonod* 1086 (*d* for *c* or *ch*), Nicholas de *Botkennoc* 1241 (14th), *Boskennec* 1282, *Bodkonok* 1331. 'Dwelling of Conec or Kenec', *bod* + personal name. Note the form of 1282, which shows *bos* from older *bod*; but the more archaic form, lacking the *s*, has survived in this parish name.

Bodieve w9973 (Egloshayle) Henry *Boduff* 1302, *Bodyuf* 1323, *Bodeff* 1425. 'Dwelling of a lord', *bod* + *yuv*. The name also occurs, as Bojea (St Austell) and Bogee (St Ervan).

Bodmin x0767 (borough and parish) *Bodmine* c.975, 1086, *Botmenei* c.1100 (c.1200), *Bodmen* 1253, *Bodman* 1337, *Bodmyn* 1522. 'Dwelling by church-land', *bod* + probably *meneghi*. The exact meaning of *meneghi* in Cornish place-names is uncertain. The derivation depends upon where the stress was in the early period: if the name contains *meneghi*, the earliest form, *Bodmine*, must show the last two syllables (*neghi*) already conflated into one (*ne*), and the stress must have been on the last syllable (original 'Bodmen*eghi*' becoming 'Bodmi*ne*'). Such a stress would regularly have moved forward to the first syllable ('*Bod*-mine': compare LINKINHORNE), which would then explain the loss of the final *e*, and the reduction of the middle, unstressed vowel to *a*, *Bodman* being the commonest spelling in the later Middle Ages. Bodmin Moor x17 is so found in 1813. The name was apparently invented by the Ordnance Survey, and it has unfortunately supplanted the ancient name, which is found as *Fawimore* 1185, *Fowymor(e)* 1347, 1355, surviving as late as *Foy Moor* 1844; English, 'moorland of the River FOWEY', which rises in it: compare Exmoor and Dartmoor, both named in the same way. A Cornish name for the moor, found once, is *Goen bren* 12th (14th); probably 'downs of a hill', *goen* + *brenn*. Bodmin Road Station x1164 (station) is named in keeping with other stations outside their towns, such as GRAMPOUND ROAD, ST COLUMB ROAD, and, in Wales, Builth Road. English, either 'road' in the sense 'railroad', or 'where one alights for Bodmin'.

Bohortha w8632 (St Anthony in Roseland) *Byhurthw* 1284, *Behorthou* 1302. 'Cow-yards', plural of *buorth*. Note the regular reduction of *-ow* to *-a* in the modern form; an alternative spelling still current is *Bohurrow*, retaining *-ow* but with loss of *th*. The pronunciation is 'Bo*hurr*a', with both changes.

Bojewyan w3934 (St Just in Penwith) *Bosuyon* 1302, 1327, *Bojewyan alias Bosuyan* 1699. Perhaps 'dwelling of Uyon', *bod* + personal name; but the form of the personal name is uncertain, and no exact parallel can be found. The modern form shows the *d* of *bod* having become first *s* (already in 1302), then 'dj', as elsewhere in the far west of Cornwall.

Bolingey w7653 (Perranzabuloe) *Velingey* 1566, *Melinge* 1650. 'Mill-house', *melin-ji*. A mill here is mentioned earlier, in 1337. The modern form of the name, with *B*, shows confusion of inital *b* and *m*. This is due to hyper-correct de-mutation of *V* (as in the form of 1566), *v* being the mutated form of both *b* and *m*.

Bolventor x1876 (Altarnun) *Boldventure* 1844. English; the 'bold venture' was the mid-19th century attempt to found a farming settlement in the middle of the moorland.

Bosavern w3730 (St Just in Penwith) *Bosavarn* 1302. Probably 'dwelling of Avarn', *bod* + personal name, though no exact equivalent has been found.

Boscastle x0990 (Forrabury) *Castrum Boterel* 1284, *Castel Botereaus* 1287, *Boterelescastel* 1302, *Botrescastell* 1343, *Boscastel c.*1540. English, 'Boterel's castle'. The earliest form shows the same name, 'castle of Boterel', in Latin, and the second one the same in French. The original name was probably the French one, and it was translated into English by reversing the order of the words. Boterel or Botreaux was a major Norman family in the county, appearing first in 1130; they probably took their surname from Les Bottereaux, in Normandy. The castle itself has almost completely disappeared: all that remains is slight earthworks at X099908.

Boscoppa x0453 (St Austell) Roger de *Boscoppe* 1284, Philip *Boscoppa* 1302; *bod* 'dwelling' (later *bos*) + unknown word or name. Compare the medieval surname *Coppe*,

Coppa, common in Dorset and Devon, and found in Cornwall in 1297 and 1302, though not in the St Austell area. If Boscoppa could be a late name in *Bos-*, formed in the 13th century, it might contain that surname, 'dwelling of a family called Coppa'.

Boskednan w4434 **(Gulval)** Robert (de) *Boskennon* 1327, 1328, *Boskennan* 1597, *Boskednan* 1623. Probably 'dwelling of Kennon', *bod* (later *bos*) + personal name, though no exact equivalent of such a personal name has been found. Note the late Cornish *dn* from earlier *nn*.

Bossiney x0688 **(Tintagel)** *Botcinnii* 1086, *Boscini* 1291. 'Dwelling of Kyni', *bod* + personal name. Note the unusual change of *c/k* to *s* before *i*, presumably due to Norman influence. Bossiney is also unusually far east for a name which shows, in its modern form, *s* for the older *d* of *bod*.

Bosullow, Great w4133 **(Madron)** *Bossowolo-meour* ('great Bosullow') 1517, *Great Bosullow c*.1870; compare, at an earlier date, *Botuolo bichan* 1244 and *Boschiwolou-bigha* 1302 (both 'little Bosullow'). The original name seems to be 'dwelling of a cottage of light', *bod* + *chi* + *golow* (with mutation of *g* to *w*), though it is unclear what that would actually mean. Great Bosullow (denoted with the suffix *meur*, now translated as 'great') is not recorded until 1517; but the addition of *byghan* 'little' in the forms of 1244 and 1302 implies that Great Bosullow existed then too.

Boswinger w9941 **(Goran)** *Boswengar* 1301. 'Dwelling of Gwengor', *bod* (later *bos*) + personal name, with mutation of *gw* to *w*.

Botallack w3632 **(St Just in Penwith)** *Botalec* 1262; probably 'steep-browed dwelling, dwelling on a steep brow', *bod* + *talek* 'steep-browed' (*tal* 'brow' + *-ek*). A personal name, 'dwelling of Talek', is also possible; but the situation of the place, near the cliff, makes the former more likely.

Botusfleming x4061 **(parish)** *Bothflumet* 1259, *Botflumyet* 1291, *Bodflemy* 1336, *Botflemyng* 1348, *Blowflemyng* 1553; *bod* 'dwelling' + unknown word or name. 'Fleming' is a corruption of the original *flumyet*, and *Botus-* a corruption of the original *Bod-*, although *Blow-* is the normal spelling in the early modern period (16th-17th centuries).

Boyton x3292 (parish) *Boietone* 1086. English, 'Boia's farm', personal name + *tún*. Compare Boyton Hall, in Essex.

Braddock x1662 (parish) *Brodehoc* 1086, *Brothac* 1201, *Brothek* 1284, 1317, *Brodok* 1522, *Bradocke* 1563, *Broadoak* 1748. Probably English, either 'broad hook (of land)', *brád* + *hóc*, or 'broad oak', *brád* + *ác*. The church is situated in the middle of a broad spur of land, which might be a 'hook'; and there are four places in Gloucestershire called 'broad oak', providing parallels for the second possibility. But the modern form *Broadoak* could be due to re-interpretation. Either derivation would fit the earliest and the modern spellings well, except for *Brod-* in 1086 where *Brad-* would be expected. The intermediate forms show a transient change of *d* to *th*, as in LITTLE PETHERICK, etc. The reversion to *d* in the modern form is presumably an archaism.

Brane w4028 (Sancreed) *Bosvran* 1323, 1324, *Borrane* 1386, *Brane* 1588. 'Dwelling of Bran', *bod* (later *bos*) + personal name, with mutation of *b* of *Bran* to *v*; *bran* 'crow' is possible but less likely. As well as being a common personal name, Bran was also the name of a Welsh mythological figure associated with hill-forts (Dinas Bran in Wales; compare British *Branodunum*). Such an association could exist here in relation to the nearby hill-fort called Caer Brân 'fort near Brane' (so named in 1754).

Bray Shop x3374 (Linkinhorne/South Hill/Stoke Climsland) *Bray's Shop* 1728. English, 'Bray's workshop'. The surname is found in South Hill in the 16th-17th centuries, and in Linkinhorne in 1621. The place-name apparently did not exist in 1613, when this place was called *Malla downe lane end*, from Tremollet Down nearby, x3375.

Brazacott x2691 (North Petherwin) *Brosiacote* 1330, *Brassacott* 1618. English, 'Brosya's cottage', surname + *cot*. The surname *Brosia*, *Brosye* is found in Devon in 1330-32, and later in Cornwall; it is of unknown derivation and meaning.

Breage w6128 (parish) 'Church of *Egglosbrec*' *c.*1170 (13th), 'church of *Sancta Breaca*' 1264, *Breke* 1522; from the patron saint of the church (sometimes with *eglos*, 'church of

St Breage'). She was believed to have been born in Ireland and to have come to Cornwall with other local saints, including SITHNEY, CROWAN and GERMOE. She seems to be unique to Cornwall, but there is a male St Briac, supposedly Irish, honoured in Brittany, who may be the same. The older pronunciation is 'Braig' (rhyming with 'Haig'), but 'Breeg' (rhyming with 'league') is now common. The church was also sometimes called *Eglospenbro* *c*.1207 (14th), 'church of Penbro' (from a nearby farm called Penbro, 'end of the region', *penn + bro*); but the reason for the church to be so named is a mystery, for Penbro was not the major place of the parish.

St Breock W9771 **(parish)** 'Church of *Sanctus Briocus*' 1259, *Breok* 1522. From the patron saint of the church. He was believed to have been born in Cardiganshire, educated in France by St German of Paris, and to have lived and worked mainly in Brittany; he has dedications in both South Wales and Brittany, primarily at Saint-Brieuc. There was an alternative name of the churchtown, found as *Lansant* 1259, *Nansant* 1291, *Nanssent* 1335, surviving as Nancent in 1841. The forms are ambiguous between *a* and *e* in the second syllable; and that syllable could be either a personal name or an ordinary word. Thus either 'valley of Sant or Sent', *nans* + personal name, or else 'holy valley' or 'valley of saints', *nans + sans* 'holy' or *syns* 'saints' (plural of *sans*). Original *-nt* is preserved. St Breock Downs W9668 (downs) occurs as *St Breock Down* 1813.

St Breward X0977 **(parish)** 'Church of *Sanctus Brewveredus*' *c*.1190, *Seynt Brewerd* 1380, *Semerwert* 1406, *Symon ward c*.1535. From the patron saint of the church. He is mentioned as 'in Cornwall, *Sanctus Branwalarethus*' in the early 12th century, and he was believed to have been the son of a king *Kenen*. He is also honoured in Brittany, Jersey, and elsewhere in Wessex, where his cult is imported from Brittany. Forms such as *Symon ward*, common in the 16th-17th centuries, must be corruptions of *Semerwert*, where 'Saint' has merged with the actual name (the opposite of the process seen in ST LEVAN and VERYAN).

Bridgerule S2702 (parish, Devon) *Brige*, held by a man called *Ruald* 1086, *Brigge* c.1180 (15th), *Briggeroald* 1238. English, 'bridge', *brycg*, distinguished from other places so called by means of a suffix showing the feudal lord.

Brighton W9054 (St Enoder/Ladock) So found in 1888. A 19th-century hamlet, presumably named after Brighton in Sussex, though no connection or reason is known. (The Sussex place was *Bristelmestune* in 1086; English, 'Beorhthelm's farm', personal name + *tún*.)

The Brisons W3431 (coast, St Just in Penwith) *'Bresan island'* 1576, *Breezon Island* 1750. French, 'shoal of rocks, reef', *brisant* (literally 'breaker'), or its plural.

Broad Sound V8308 (coast, Scilly) *The brode sownde* c.1540. English, self-explanatory; *sound* 'strait, sailable channel'.

Brown Willy X1579 (hill, St Breward) *Brunwenely* 1239 (15th), *Brounwellye hill* 1576. 'Hill of swallows', *bronn* + *gwennili*, plural of *gwennol*, with mutation of *gw* to *w*.

Bryher V8715 (island, Scilly) *Braer* 1319, *Brayer* 1336. Probably 'hills', *bre* + *-yer* plural suffix. This would have been the hilliest part of the original single island of Scilly (see ST MARY'S).

Bude S2106 (Stratton) 'Chapels of Holy Trinity and St Michael of *Bude*' 1400. An obscure name. It probably referred originally to the stream here, though the earliest mention of that is *Bedewater* 1587. Later spellings such as *Bede* show that the original *u* was the Cornish *u*-sound, becoming 'Beed', and that the modern spelling with *u* is archaic. This suggests possibly a Cornish word related to Welsh *budr*, 'dirty': compare the River Boyd (Gloucestershire, formerly *Byd* 10th); but the absence of *r* in both names would be odd. If so, then the original stream-name might have meant 'dirty (stream)', but that is very uncertain. Bude Bay S10 (coast) was *Bedebay* 1468, 1470. Bude Haven S2006 (coast) was *Beedes haven* c.1605.

Budock Water W7832 (Budock) *Budock-water* 1884. English, seemingly a 19th-century hamlet, situated on the stream (*water*) near the church: compare CANWORTHY WATER, CHACEWATER, etc. Budock church and parish are

60

named from the patron saint, 'church of *Sanctus Budocus*' 1208, *Plu vuthek* c.1400 (*plu* 'parish' of Budock, with mutation of *b* to *v*), *Bythick* 1727. St Budock was believed to have been born while his mother Azenor, a Breton princess, was floating to Ireland in a barrel; she had been cast adrift when wrongly accused of being unfaithful to her husband. St Budock later floated back to Brittany in a stone coffin, and became bishop of Dol. As well as in Brittany, he is honoured at St Budeaux ('Buddocks') near Plymouth, and at St Botolphs in Pembrokeshire, SM8907. Note the pronunciation shown by the form of 1727.

Bugle X0158 **(St Austell)** So found in 1888. A 19th-century village, which grew up around the inn of the same name. In 1840 the inn, then newly-built, was said to have been named in honour of the prowess of a local bugle-player; it used to have a coaching-horn on its sign.

Burlawn W9970 **(St Breock)** *Bodolowen* 1243, Matthew de *Bodlouen* 1277, Thomas de *Bodeloweyn* 1317. Probably 'happy dwelling' or 'dwelling of Lowen', *bod + lowen* or personal name *Lowen*. The forms with vowels between *d* and *l*, though frequent, probably represent an epenthetic, nonoriginal vowel, so that 'dwelling of an elm-tree' (*bod + elowen*), formerly suggested, is not likely to be right.

Burras W6734 **(Wendron)** *Berres* 1337, *Burras* 1625. Probably 'short-ford', a compound of *berr + rys*: the place is at a stream-crossing. Note the irregular change from *e* to *u* in the first syllable.

St Buryan W4025 **(parish)** 'Church of *Sancta Beriana*' c.939 (14th), *Sancta Berriona*, *Eglosberrie* 1086, *Seint Beryan* 1343, *Burian* mid 15th. From the patron saint of the church. She is first mentioned as *Berion* 10th (List); she was believed to have been Irish and to have cured the son of King Gerent from a paralysing illness; and she is also honoured at Berrien in Finistère. The form of 1086 is 'church of Beryan', *eglos* + saint's name. The name always contained *e*, not *u*, anciently; *u* first appears in the 15th century, and does not become common until the 16th; but it is still correctly pronounced '*Berri*an'.

Cadgwith w7214 **(Ruan Minor)** *Cadgewith* 1748; earlier *Porthcaswith* 1358, *Por Cadgwith* 1699; '(harbour of) a thicket', (*porth +*) *caswydh*.

Caerhays: see under ST MICHAEL CAERHAYS.

Callestick w7750 **(Perranzabuloe)** *Calestoc* 1086, *Kalestoc* c.1250, *Kellestek* 1302. An obscure name; it is unclear whether it is Cornish, or an English one in Cornish guise. The former seems more likely; if so, then it is an adjectival form in *-ek*, but the first element is unknown. (One can hardly suggest *Kelestrek* 'pebbly place', from *kelester* 'pebble', comparing Middle Breton *Calestreuc* 'pebbly place', since that would entail the curious loss of *r*, already by 1086). The spellings of CALSTOCK, an English name with *stoc*, are similar; but the two names are unlikely to be the same.

Callington x3569 **(parish)** *Calwetone* 1086, *Calwinton* 1187, *Calyton* 1306. English, probably 'settlement at the bare-hill', *calu* 'bare-hill' (dative *calwe*) + *tún*, with reference to KIT HILL, which dominates the town. Callaughton, in Shropshire, has the same derivation and closely similar forms. The *ing* in the modern name is non-original; it is seen already beginning to appear in the form of 1187; but later spellings without it are also found. The interpretation of this name was formerly confused by the application to it of forms referring to an Anglo-Saxon manor in the tenth century, called either *Cællwic* or *Cællincg*; but there is no evidence as to where that manor was. However, if it could be shown to be Callington, the English interpretation given above would have to be revised, for the names of the Anglo-Saxon manor are not compatible with it.

Calstock x4368 **(parish)** *Kalestoc* 1086, *Kalistoke* 1208 (17th), *Calestoke* 1265, *Kalstok* 1270, *Calistoke* 1329. English; unknown word or name + *stoc* 'settlement'. The early forms conflict between *Cal-*, *Cale-* and *Cali-*. Sometimes *stoc* can have the sense 'outlying farm, belonging to a parent place nearby'. Chardstock in Devon, ST3104, is three miles from Chard in Somerset; and Basingstoke is two miles from Basing (Hampshire). If *Cal-*, etc., were a shortened form for CALLINGTON, four miles away, then this name could mean 'outlying farm of Callington'. But that is very uncertain.

Cambeak x1396 (coast, St Gennys) So found in 1789. Probably English, 'comb beak', a sharply-crested promontory. Theoretically a Cornish name is possible, 'crooked-point', a compound of *camm* + *pig* (with mutation of *p* to *b*); but *pig* is a rare word, and an English derivation is more likely for a coastal name in this part of the county.

Camborne w6440 (parish) Balcherus de *Camberon* 1182, *Cambron* c.1230 (14th), 1755, *Camborne* 1431. 'Crooked hill', a compound of *camm* + *bronn*. *Camvron* might have been expected, with mutation of *b* to *v* in a compound; but perhaps the *m* preserved the *b* from mutation.

River Camel x1387—w9277 *Camel-* 13th, *Camle-* 1256 (see CAMELFORD), *Camel* 1602, *Camel or Alan River* 1748. An obscure name; the difficulties are increased by the lack of reliable early forms. The name *Camel* originally referred not to the whole river, but only to its uppermost section, which flows through Camelford as far as Trecarne, X0980. It may contain *camm* 'crooked', perhaps with a river-name suffix *-el* or *-ell*; if so, then 'crooked one' simply. Compare Welsh streams called Caman, Camen, and Camedd. 'Crooked estuary', *camm* + *heyl*, will not do, for the name did not refer to the Camel estuary until the 18th or 19th century. The former name of the main river, running from near Roughtor to Wadebridge, was *Alan* 1200, *Aleyn* 1298 (14th). The Ordnance Survey incorrectly transferred this name to the River ALLEN, which was formerly called *Layne*. *Alan* is a common Celtic river-name, but of unknown meaning: there are eight Romano-British rivers called *Alauna*.

Camelford x1083 (Lanteglos by Camelford) *Camelford* 13th, *Camleford* 1256. English, 'ford of the River CAMEL'. The earliest reference is from Layamon's *Brut*, an Arthurian poem based upon Geoffrey of Monmouth's work; *Camelford* is Layamon's substitute for Geoffrey's *Camblan*, where King Arthur's last battle occurred (located in Cornwall by Geoffrey, but clearly derived from the unlocated *Camlann* where Arthur died in the older Welsh

Annals). Layamon must have known of the existing Cornish place, and decided to improve upon Geoffrey's local nomenclature.

Canonstown W5335 (Ludgvan)   *Canons Town* 1839, *Canonstown* 1870. A 19th-century village, named after John Rogers (1778-1856) of Penrose near Helston, canon of Exeter Cathedral. He was an 'energetic landlord', botanist, mineralogist and biblical scholar. His family had long had lands in the parish of Ludgvan, and this village was presumably planned by him.

Canworthy Water X2291 (hamlet, Jacobstow)   *Kennery bridg* 1699, *Kenworthy Water* 1748. A hamlet by the River (*water*) Ottery, below the farm of Canworthy (in Warbstow): compare BUDOCK WATER, etc. Canworthy itself was *Carneworthy* in 1327; English, 'farm' (*worthig*) at an unknown place called *Carn* (Cornish *carn* 'tor'). Note the pronunciation shown in the form of 1699, with reduction of -*worthy* to -*ery*; but the name has now reverted to a more archaic form.

Cape Cornwall W3531 (coast, St Just in Penwith)   *Cap Cornwall* 1699. English, self-explanatory. 'In the eyes of Cornishmen, Cape Cornwall always used to be, and still, in spite of accurate measurements, is held to be the most westerly point in Cornwall' (1879). Its Cornish name was *Kulgyth* 1580 *(18th), The Kilguthe* c.1605; unexplained, perhaps containing *kil* 'nook, corner'.

Caradon Hill X2770 (hill, Linkinhorne)   *Caradon hill* c.1605. Named from the nearby hamlet of Caradon, X2971. This was *Carnetone* 1086, *Carnedune* c.1160 (15th), *Carnedon* 1234. English, 'hill' (*dún*) at *Carn*; that was presumably an older, Cornish, name for the hill, *carn* 'tor, rock'. The earliest form seems to show *tún* 'farm' instead; but that may be an error, since all later forms show *dún*.

Carbis Bay W5238 (village, Lelant)   So found in 1884: a 19th-century village, named from the bay. That in turn was named from the farm of Carbis W524386, *Carbons* 1391, *carr-bons* 'causeway'. The Cornish name of the bay itself is Barrepta Cove: *Parrupter* c.1499, *Porthreptor* 1580 (18th), *porth* + unknown word or name.

Carclew w7838 (Mylor) William de *Crucleu* 1314, William de *Crukleu* 1327. The name looks like 'coloured tumulus', *crug* + perhaps *lyw* (literally 'barrow of colour'); but the meaning of such a name would be unclear. No barrow is known near the house.

Cardinham x1268 (parish) *Cardinan lebiri* c.1180, Robert de *Cardinan* 1194. Cornish *ker* 'fort' + *dinan* 'fort'; the name is repetitive, but presumably the original name was simply *Dinan*, 'fort', with *ker* added later. The name probably refers to Bury Castle x1369, an Iron-Age hill-fort one mile to the north-west. In the form of c.1180, *lebiri* is 'the fort', French *le* added to English *byrig*, dative case of *burh*. It could refer either to Bury Castle again, or to Cardinham Castle, a motte-and-bailey which was the Norman centre of the estate, at x125680. By coincidence, the manor of Cardinham came into the hands of the Dynham family of Devon in the late 13th century, so that the name came to look as if it were 'fort of the Dynham family'; but its name had existed for at least a century before their ownership.

Cargreen x4362 (Landulph) *Carrecron* late 11th, *Kaergroyn /-growne*, *Corgroyn/-growne* 1478. 'Rock of a seal', *carrek* + *reun*. The name was later re-interpreted as if it contained *ker*.

Carharrack w7341 (Gwennap) *Cararthek* 1408, *Carharthek* 1423, *Carharracke* 1590. Probably 'fort of the high-place', *ker* + *ardhek*, adjective of *ardh* 'height' + *-ek*. Note the disappearance of *dh*, and the intrusion of non-original *h*.

Carines w7959 (Cubert) *Crouwortheynys* 1348, *Crowarthenes* 1473. '(Part of) *Crou* near an island'. The original name was of a settlement called *Crou* in 1302 and 1327 ('hut', *crow*). It was split into three parts, and one was named by being 'near an island', *orth* + *ynys*. It is in fact inland, but near marshy ground. The other parts of *Crou* survive as the nearby farms of Colgrease, formerly *Crowgres* 1498, 'middle *Crou*', + *cres*; and Carevick, formerly *Crowarthevycke* 1567, + uncertain word or name.

Carland Cross w8453 (St Erme) So found in 1972. A road-junction named from the adjacent farm, which is called

Cowland 1813, *Carland* 1840. The forms are too late to be of much use. *Cowland* could be English, self-explanatory; but *Carland* might possibly be Cornish *cor-lann* 'animal-fold'. The lateness of the forms encourages the idea that it should be an English name.

Carn Brea w6840 (hill, Illogan) *Carnbree* 1348. 'Tor of a hill', *carn* + *bre*; but the true meaning is probably 'tor above Brea village', even though the village is not recorded until a little later. Pronounced 'Carn *Bray*'.

Carne w9138 (Veryan) *Kern* 1513, *Carne* 1562. Probably *carn* 'tor', here referring to the barrow called Carne Beacon, W912386. King Gerent, the eighth-century king of Cornwall, was believed to lie buried here in a boat. It is curious that one of the largest barrows in the county should be described, not as *crug*, 'barrow', but as *carn*, which normally refers to a natural pile of rocks.

Carnhell Green w6137 (Gwinear) So found in 1813. An 18th- or 19th-century hamlet; English, 'grassy-plot at Carnhell'. The farm of Carnhell itself, W618373, was *Karnhell* 1249. It appears to be 'tor near a hall', *carn* + *hel*; or possibly 'rocky place', *carnel*, from *carn* + *-el*, with non-original *h* added.

Carnon Downs w7940 (Feock) 'Moorland of *Carnon*' 1569, *Carnon Downes* 1683, *Goon Carnon* 1782 (*goen* 'downland' of Carnon). A 19th/20th-century village, built on the moorland which formerly belonged to the group of farms called Carnon nearby. That name first appears as *Karnen* 1284; probably 'little rock', *carn* + *-ynn*, or else 'rocky place', *carn* + *-an*.

Carn Towan w3626 (Sennen) A rock is so found in 1888, and a farm in 1906. The hamlet is even more recent. No doubt 'tor of sand-dunes', *carn* + *tewynn*.

Carnyorth w3733 (St Just in Penwith) *Carnzorgh* 1481, *Carnyorke alias Carnyorth* 1550 (1572). 'Crag of a roebuck', *carn* + *yorgh*. The *z* of the earliest form stands for *y*.

The Carracks w4640 (coast, Zennor) *Carracks* 1748. 'Rocks', *carrek* with English plural.

Carrick Roads w83 (estuary) *Caryk Rood* 'a sure herboro for the greatest shyppes that travayle be the occean' c.1540. English *road* 'a sheltered piece of water for ships; a roadstead'. The original *carrek*, 'rock', from which the Road is named, is the one now called Black Rock at its entrance (W833316, *Black Rock c.*1580). This was formerly called *an garrak ruen c.*1400, 'the seal's rock', *carrek + reun*; compare CARGREEN.

Carthew X0055 (St Austell) *Carduf* 1327, *Carthu* 1367. 'Black fort', *ker + du*, with mutation of *d* to *th*. The final *f* of the first spelling is remarkably archaic.

Castallack W4525 (Paul) Oliver de *Castellak* 1284. Probably 'rocky place' or 'fortified place', the adjective of *castell* 'fort, rock' + *-ek*.

Castle-an-Dinas W9462 (fort, St Columb Major) 'Castle of *Dynas*' 1478, *Castel an dynas c.*1504, *Castell Dennyse c.*1582. 'Fort at Dennis', *castell* + place-name. Dennis itself is a nearby farm, found as *Dynes* 1428; 'hill-fort', *dinas*. It must also have been called *An Dinas* (with *an*, 'the'), the form used in the compounded name. Pronounced 'Castle-Dennis'. The hill-fort featured in Cornish legends. William of Worcester, in 1478, tells that Cador, duke of Cornwall and husband of King Arthur's mother, was killed here; in the next reference, *c.*1504, the Duke of Cornwall is said to have a fort here.

Cawsand X4350 (Rame) *Couyssond* 1405. English; the *u* may stand for either *v* or *w*; the *ys* looks like a genitive singular. Possibly '*Cow*'s sand', where *Cow* (the animal) was the name of some rock by the beach. Compare other coastal rocks called *Cow*, for example *Cow and Calf* (an old name for QUIES), Cow and Calf (St Endellion, W9680, and St Eval, W8370); and, in Dorset, The Cow (Chaldon Herring parish), Cow Corner (East Lulworth) and The Blind Cow (West Lulworth). Cawsand Bay X4450 (coast) is found as *Causet Bay* 1583, *Causam Bay* 1602.

Chacewater W7544 (Kenwyn/Kea) *Chasewater* 1613. English; part of the 'chace' or hunting-ground, on the stream (*water*). Compare Chacewood W7543, nearby. The chace belonged to the manor of Goodern or Blanchland, and is mentioned first in the late 12th century Tristan legend, and later in the Life of St Kea. In both sets of legends, it is a hunting-ground of lords of Cornwall — of King Mark in the Tristan legend, and of the wicked King Teudar or Theodoricus in the saints' Lives.

Chapel Amble w9975 (St Kew) *Amaleglos* 1284, 'church of *Sanctus Aldelmus* of *Ammaleglos*' 1302, *Chaple Amble* 1664. English, 'the part of Amble with a chapel'. The name is translated from the older Cornish name *Ammaleglos*, place-name + *eglos* 'church'. The estate of Amble is found earlier as *Amal* 1086; it seems to mean 'edge, boundary' (Cornish *ammal*), perhaps because it is near the boundary of the hundred of Trigg. At some time before 1284 *Amal* was split into three. *Ammaleglos* was named from the presence of the chapel; the two other divisions were *Ammalmur* and *Ammalgres* 1347, 'great Amble' (+ *meur*) and 'middle Amble' (+ *cres*), now Lower and Middle Amble. St Aldhelm, the patron saint of the chapel, was an Anglo-Saxon bishop who died in 709. He was the first bishop of Sherborne in Dorset (which then included Cornwall in its diocese), and was buried at Malmesbury. He visited Cornwall, and addressed a letter to its king, Gerent, exhorting him to make the Cornish church conform to normal practices. The dedication of this chapel to him is doubtless of much later date.

Chapel Point x0243 (coast, Goran) *Chapelle Land or Point* c.1540. English, self-explanatory. The chapel is mentioned in 1327, but no remains of it are known.

Charlestown x0351 (St Austell) *Charles-Town*, *Charlestown* 1800. English; the port and village were founded (in 1791, it is said) to serve the growing china-clay industry, and were named after their sponsor, Charles Rashleigh of Menabilly (1747-1825). The older Cornish name of the place was Polmear (surviving in the name of Polmear Island, at the entrance to the harbour), originally *Portmoer* 1354, 'great harbour', *porth* + *meur*, contrasted with PORTHPEAN nearby.

Chilsworthy x4172 (Calstock) *Chillesworthy* 1337. English, 'Ceol's farm', personal name + *worthig*.

Church Cove w7112 (coast, Landewednack) English, so found in 1888, from Landewednack church above it.

Chyandour W4731 (Gulval/Madron) *Chyendower* 1504. 'The cottage of the stream', *chi + an + dowr*.

Chysauster W4735 (antiquity, Gulval) 'Ancient British village on the estate of *Chysauster*' 1861. Named from the adjacent farm of Chysauster; that is found as *Chisalwester* 1302, *Chisalvestre* 1313, 'cottage of Silvester', *chi* + personal name. Pronounced 'Chezoister'.

St Cleer X2468 (parish) 'Church of *Sanctus Clarus*' 1212, *Seintclere* 1388; named from the patron saint of the parish church. His main cult is at St Clair in Normandy, where his shrine is a popular object of pilgrimage. He is said to have been born in England, to have lived in north-west France in the 9th century, and to have been 'a martyr of chastity', murdered by the plotting of 'an impious and lewd lady of quality'.

St Clement W8543 (parish) 'Church of *Sanctus Clemens*' 1329, *Clemens* 1522; earlier there was nearby a 'well of *Sanctus Clemens*' *c.*1190 (14th). From the patron saint of the parish church; he was a Roman pope of the first century. There is a legend that he was tied to an anchor and thrown into the sea in the Crimea; as a result maritime sites (see the next entry) were often dedicated to him, and he is the patron saint of Trinity House in London, the organisation in charge of lighthouses. Earlier the church and parish were usually called by the name of the manor, Moresk W852434: *Moireis* 1086, 'church of *Moreis*' 1178 (1523). This is possibly French, *marais* 'a marsh', which would suit the site, though the *o* is against it.

St Clement's Isle W4726 (coast, Paul) 'An islet and a chapel of *St Clementes* in it' *c.*1540. See above. There are now no remains of a chapel here, but one is shown on a 16th-century plan. The island was also called *Moushole Ile* 1587, and it was the reason why MOUSEHOLE was also called *Porthennis*, 'harbour of an island'.

St Clether X2084 (parish) *Seyncleder*, 'church of *Sanctus Clederus*' 1249, *Seyntclether* 1405. From the patron saint of the church. St *Cleder* was believed to have been one of the 24 offspring of King Broccan of Breconshire, according to the Cornish version of the legend; and to have retreated to Cornwall from south-west Wales, where he had previously set up a monastic community. The *th* in the modern form of the name is a secondary development, appearing first in 1405: compare Little PETHERICK, etc. The saint's name appears also in the village of Cleder in Brittany, 14 miles north-west of Morlaix (but its patron saint is St Ke); and, in Cornwall, Ventonglidder in Probus, W901493, is 'holy well' (*fenten*) of St Cleder (with mutation of *c* to *g*); note the preservation of original *d* here, in contrast with *th* in east Cornwall.

Clubworthy x2792 **(North Petherwin)** *Clobiry* 1322, 1330, *Clobery* 1748, *Clubworthy* 1813, *Clubbery* 1842. English, perhaps 'muddy mound', from dialect *clob* 'clod of earth, mud' + *beorg* 'hill'. The spellings could equally well suggest Old English *byrig*, dative case of *burh* 'fort', as the second element; but there is no known fort nearby, and the name probably refers to the hill just to the west of the hamlet, or to a lost tumulus. Compare BILBERRY, etc. The spelling *worthy* is a recent hyper-correct one, and is due to the fact that *-ery* elsewhere often stands for older *worthy* (compare CANWORTHY WATER). The original form is still seen in 1842.

Coad's Green x2976 **(North Hill)** *Coades Green* 1813. English, an 18th- or 19th-century hamlet. The surname is found in the parish in 1660, William *Code*, and again in the 18th century.

Codda x1878 **(Altarnun)** *Stingede-lace* 1239 (15th) (+ English *lacu* 'stream'), *Stymkodda* 1385, *Codda* 1459, 1671, *Codde Fowey* c.1540 (+ river-name). An obscure name. The first word is 'bend', *stumm*; it was dropped from the name in the 15th century. The second one was formerly thought to be a derivative of *coes* 'wood' (older *cuit*); but, since the name is linked in c.1540 with that of the River FOWEY, which rises near the place, it is very tempting to see *codda* as a Cornish equivalent of Welsh *codi* (older *cyfodi*), 'to rise'. If so, then '(bend of) the river-source'. However, there is no record of such a Cornish equivalent to the Welsh word.

Colan w8661 **(parish)** Hamelin of *Sanctus Culanus* 1201, Richard of *Sanctus Colanus* 1205, *Sien Colan* 1302, *Colan*

70

1429. From the patron saint of the church. He may be the same as the Welsh St Collen honoured at Llangollen, in north-east Wales, and also perhaps at two places called Langolen in Brittany. The Welsh saint was believed to have beaten an oriental pagan chief in combat on behalf of the Pope, and to have become abbot of Glastonbury on his return to Britain. But his name has double *ll*, whereas the Cornish and Breton names show single *l*; so a different, unknown, saint may be involved.

Colliford Reservoir x1772 **(reservoir, St Neot)** The reservoir was completed in 1983. It is named from the nearby farms of Colliford (East Colliford X180708); the name is first found as '(ford of) *Colaford*' mid-13th. English, probably 'cool ford', *cól* + *ford*; compare Collaford in Devon (Plympton St Mary parish).

St Columb Major w9163 **(parish)** 'Church of *Sancta Columba*' c.1240, *Saint Colombe the Over* c.1547. Named from the patron saint of the church. She is evidently different from the well-known (male) St Columba of Iona, but little is known of her; she was believed to have been martyred at RUTHVOES nearby. The parish was called 'greater' (Latin *major*), or 'higher' (*over*), in contrast with the next entry. The parishes are adjacent.

St Columb Minor w8362 **(parish)** 'Chapel of *Sancta Columba Minor*' 1284, *Colombe the nether* 1549. 'Smaller' (Latin *minor*) or 'lower' (English *nether*), in contrast to St Columb Major.

St Columb Road w9159 **(St Columb Major)** *St Columb Road Station* 1888. A 19th/20th-century village, which grew up around the railway station; *road* is 'railroad', as in BODMIN ROAD, etc.

Common Moor x2369 **(hamlet, St Cleer)** So found in 1867. A 19th-century village; English, self-explanatory.

Connor Downs w5939 **(Gwithian)** *Conner Down* c.1870; a 19th-century village on former downland. The downs are mentioned as *Conerton Down* 1580 (18th), *Conner Down* 1813; they were named from the lost manor of Connerton. That manor, centred at GWITHIAN, W5841, was *Conarditone* in 1086, *Conarton* c.1155 (16th). The name is obscure.

It evidently contains English *tún* 'farm, manorial centre'. The first word might be an old name of the Red River, which emerges just to the north, for in *c.*1540 that was called *Dour Conor*, 'stream of Conor' (*dowr*); but it is unexplained.

Constantine W7329 (parish) *Sanctus Constantinus* 1086, *Langustenstyn* 1367, *Costentyn* 1441. From the patron saint of the church; some forms are 'church-site of Constantine', *lann* + saint's name, with mutation of *c* to *g*. Little is known of the saint, but he was commemorated as a 'king and martyr'. He may therefore be the same as the sixth-century king of Devon and Cornwall called Constantine, whom Gildas vilified as the 'tyrannical cub of the filthy lioness Dumnonia' who had slaughtered two royal youths at the altar of a church. Welsh pedigrees also mention a royal *Custennyn Gorneu*, 'Constantine the Cornishman'. The correct Cornish pronunciation 'Cos*ten*ton' was still known earlier this century.

Constantine Bay W8574 (coast, St Merryn) *Colstenton Bay* 1699, *Constantine Bay* 1813. Named from the nearby chapel of St Constantine (W865748); it is found as 'chapel of *Sanctus Constantinus*' 1390, *Egloscontantyne c.*1525 (*eglos* 'church' + saint's name). For the saint, see the preceding entry. Note that the Cornish pronunciation of the saint's name was evidently known here, as shown in the form of 1699.

Coombe W9551 (St Stephen in Brannel) *Combe* 1813. English, 'valley', *cumb*.

Coombe S2011 (Morwenstow) *Come* 1439 (15th). English, 'valley', *cumb*.

Coppathorne S2000 (Poundstock) *Copelle horno* 1699, *Coppet Thorn* 1748. English, 'copped (pollarded) thorntree'. The first form is corrupt, for *Copett thorne* or the like.

Cornwall *Cornubia c.*705 (mid-9th), *Cornwalas* 891, *Cornugallia*, *Cornualia* 1086, *Cornwal c.*1198, *Kernow c.*1400. The name in Cornish, *Kernow*, must go back to an original tribal name, *Cornowii*. The name is not recorded in the Roman period in the south-west, but there are tribes elsewhere with the same name. It means 'the horn-people', most likely with reference to the situation of the tribe at the end of a long peninsula, the 'horn' of Britain. *Cornubia* is an artificial latinisation of that name. Later the first syllable of the name was borrowed by the Anglo-Saxons, who referred to the people as the *Corn-Wealas*, meaning 'the *Corn*-Welsh' or '*Corn*-foreigners'. *Wealas* 'foreigners, serfs' was used by the Anglo-Saxons particularly for the Britons, the indigenous inhabitants of the island, of whom the Cornish were one tribe. The curious form *Cornugallia* (variant *Cornugallie*) shows a re-interpretation of the second part as *Gallia* 'Wales'.

Cotehele House x4268 (Calstock) William de *Cotehulle* c.1286, Eustace de *Cotehele* 1305, *Cuttayle* 1602. Probably 'wood on an estuary', Cornish *coes* (older *cuit*) + *heyl*. Most spellings show re-interpretation of the name as if it were English, 'cot-hill', but the stress on the second syllable (pronounced 'Cut*eel*') indicates a Cornish derivation. The banks of the Tamar estuary are still well-wooded here.

Coverack w7818 (St Keverne) *Covrack* 1588. Meaning unknown; probably originally the name of the stream emerging at the cove. Another instance of such a stream-name is seen at Coverack Bridges near Helston, W6630. Note that the name Coverack, on its own, does not appear before 1588; the older name for the cove and village was probably *Porthcovrec* 1262 (*porth* 'cove, harbour'), though it is uncertain whether such forms actually refer to the village or to Polcoverack, a hamlet half a mile inland.

Crackington Haven x1496 (village, St Gennys) *Crakamphavene* 1358, *Crackington Horn* 1813 (*Horn* is a bad spelling for *Hawn*, dialect form of 'haven'). English, 'harbour at *Crak*'. The cove is named from the nearby manor of Crackington, which had two alternative names originally. One appears as *Crachemua* 1086, *Crakemude* 1196; and the other as *Cracumtona* c.1170, *Crakenton* 1181, *Craketon* 1182. Both names are based on an original Cornish name *Crak*, probably meaning 'sandstone', *crag*. To the name the English added alternatively *mútha* 'river-mouth' and *tún* 'farm, manorial centre'. As at KILKHAMPTON, the last part of the manorial name in *-ton* was assimilated to English '-hampton' at an early date. This form 'Crackhampton' was then used (with the dropping of -*ton*) to form *Crakamphavene* (+ *hæfen*), the form of 1358. The name survives locally as 'Cracken Awn', the local pronunciation for Crackington Haven.

Crafthole x3654 (Sheviock) *Croftilberwe* 1314, *Crofthol* 1348, *Croftholburgh* 1420. English, probably 'croft-hill' (hill with enclosed arable land), *croft* + *hyll*. However, the *i* of the earliest form is discrepant, and later spellings show *o* in the second syllable, suggesting *hol* 'hollow' instead of *hyll*. But the place is situated on a hill, so *hyll* is greatly preferable, despite the numerical weight of spellings with *o*. Some early forms (e.g. those of 1314 and 1420) show the addition of English 'borough' to the name. By *c.*1600 the borough had degenerated so that there was a local saying, 'In Crafthole twelve houses and thirteen cuckolds'.

Crane Islands w6344 (coast, Illogan) *Crane Island c.*1870. An obscure name; compare perhaps Crane Ledges (Landewednack), another coastal name. Or the name might be transferred from Crane in Camborne, two and a half miles away (W638399), if the grazing nearby belonged to that place. On the map which supplies the earliest reference, *c.*1870, the names of Crane Island and Samphire Island (W638447) are reversed, so that it is impossible to say which was which originally.

Crantock w7960 (parish) *Sanctus Carentoch*, *Langorroc* 1086, *Seint Karentoc* 1234, 'church of *Sanctus Carantocus* of *Lancorru*' 1302, *Crantocke* 1546. From the patron saint of the church. He was believed to be of royal birth in Cardiganshire; on his way to Cornwall he assisted King Arthur by taming a dragon in Somerset. He also has dedications in Brittany. The Cornish name of the churchtown survives as Langurra, a house in the village; it is 'church-site of Correk', *lann* + personal name, with mutation of *c* to *g*; note the early loss of final *c/k*, as at ST WINNOW. *Correk* may be a pet-form of the saint's name, Carantoc.

Creed w9347 (parish) Thomas de *Sancta Crida c.*1250, *Crede* 1509. From the patron saint of the church. She is first mentioned as patron saint of this parish, in the form *Crite* ('Cride'), in the 10th-century List, but nothing is known of her. Compare SANCREED.

Cribba Head W4022 **(coast, St Levan)** So found in 1888. Probably 'crests, ridges', *cribow*, plural of *crib*.

Crim Rocks V8009 **(coast, Scilly)** *Crim* 1689. Obscure. It is just possible that the name could have been originally *Crybyn* 'little ridge' (*cribynn*, diminutive of *crib*; compare GRIBBIN HEAD). When no longer understood, *Crybyn* might have been wrongly thought to be late Cornish *Cribm* from a supposed original *Crim* (compare Gilly Gabben W686251, 'crooked grove', *kelli + camm*, with mutation of *c* to *g*), and the name might then have been hyper-corrected back to the assumed original form. Otherwise no explanation can be offered.

Cripplesease W5036 **(Towednack)** *Cripples-ease* 1884. A 19th-century inn and hamlet, named from its position near the top of a long hill.

Crowan W6434 **(parish)** *Eggloscrauuen* *c*.1170 (13th), 'church of *Sancta Crawenna*' 1238. From the patron saint of the church. She was believed to have come from Ireland along with St BREAGE and others; she is also honoured in Brittany. The earliest form shows *eglos* 'church' + saint's name.

Crowdy Reservoir X1483 **(reservoir, Davidstow)** The reservoir was opened in 1973. It is on the site of the former Crowdy Marsh, which was *Crowdey Marsh* in 1813; compare '*Crowdy*, upon the moore' *c*.1613 (*moore* meaning 'marsh'). Probably *crow-ji* 'hovel', with preservation of Old Cornish *d* (instead of the later *j*) here in east Cornwall.

Crowlas W5133 **(Ludgvan)** *Croures* 1327, *Croulys* 1361. The change from *r* to *l* in this name is curious. If the *r* is original, then the name is either 'weir-ford' or 'hovel-ford', a compound of *crew* 'weir' or *crow* 'hovel' + *rys*. (The spellings favour *crow*, but the sense and analogies elsewhere would favour *crew*.) However, if the later *l* is correct instead, it is 'hovel-court, hovel-ruins', a compound of *crow* + *lys*. The situation at a stream-crossing makes the 'ford' more likely.

Crow Sound V9213 **(coast, Scilly)** *Crawe Sound* 1570. English, *sound* 'strait, sailable channel'. Crow Rock, at the entrance to the sound, is found as *The Crow c*.1585. It may well be that the Scillonian 'port called *Crowenest*' 1345 was nearby; if so, the rock and sound probably took their names from a cut-down form of that name. (However, there is another Crow Island off Bryher, V869147.) *Crowenest* is English, but the meaning is uncertain: *crow's nest* in its nautical sense is recorded only from 1818, though it occurs in 1604 with the apparent meaning 'a fort placed on a height'. It is a commmon name elsewhere, for instance Crow's Nest, inland in St Cleer X263693, first recorded as *Crows nest* 1699; Crowsnest in Devon, X377919, is first recorded in 1281, and there are, for example, 10 instances in the West Riding of Yorkshire, and several in Cheshire. No doubt the names have some jocular or fanciful sense.

Crugmeer W9076 (Padstow) *Crucmur* 1336, *Crigmeare* 1702. 'Great barrow', *crug + meur*. The form of 1702 shows the pronunciation.

Cubert W7857 (parish) *Sanctus Cubertus* 1269, *Sanctus Cuthbertus* 1305, *Eglos Cutbert* 1402, *St Kibberd c*.1605. Named from the patron saint of the parish church, the 7th-century English St Cuthbert, bishop of Lindisfarne, whose relics are in Durham cathedral; he is also honoured at Gwbert in Cardiganshire. Some forms of the place-name show *eglos* 'church' + saint's name. Just by the churchtown is a farm called Lanlovey W787580, formerly *Lanowyn alias Lanwoven alias Egloscubert* 1622, *Lenowen alias Lanlovey* 1783. It is probably the original Cornish name of the churchtown, but the forms are too late to give a derivation; *lann* 'church-site' + unknown word or name.

Cudden Point W5427 (coast, St Hilary) *Cuddan poynt* 1576. Obscure; *cudynn* 'tress of hair' is possible (though *Kidden* might rather be expected in the modern form), but the meaning here would be obscure.

West Curry X2893 (Boyton) *Great Cory* 1748, 1813, *West Curry* 1842. Compare *Chori* 1086, William de *Kery* 1284, and *Currey, East Correy Parke* 1654. The interpretation of this name is hampered by the lack of definite early references, but it belongs to a group of names of similar form, all found in the south-western counties. Other examples are Cory in Morwenstow, S217161; Cory and Coryton in Devon; and various places in Somerset called Curry. Most

76

have good early spellings, going back to a form *Cory*. The derivation of these names is completely unknown. It has been surmised that they were all originally names of rivers or streams, which is possible.

Cury W6721 **(parish)** *Egloscuri* 1219, 'church of *Sanctus Corentinus*' 1284, *Seyntcorentyn* 1369, *Cury* 1473. From the patron saint of the church; *Cury* is apparently a pet-form of Corentin. He is a Breton saint, patron of the cathedral at Quimper, and is believed to have been the first bishop of Cornouaille. Some forms of the name show Cornish *eglos* 'church' + saint's name (always in the pet-form).

Darite X2569 **(St Cleer)** *Daryet* 1506, *Daryth* 1510 (*c*.1595), *Daryte* 1530 (*c*.1595). An obscure name. There was a Gregory *Daryth* living in the area in 1391, and the surname *Daryte* continues to appear until the mid-16th century (John and William *Daryte*, St Cleer, 1569). It is probable that the place was named from the family, and not the other way round, since the surname is found earlier, by more than a century; but either is possible. However, no explanation for the surname is available, nor does it occur elsewhere. The village was called Railway Terrace for a few years either side of 1900.

Davidstow X1587 **(parish)** 'Church of *Sanctus David* (alias *Dewstow*)' 1269, *Dewestowe* 1313, *Dewstowe* alias *Davystowe* 1423. English, 'holy place (*stów*) of St David'. The name used to contain not *David*, but *Dewy*, the Cornish version of his name, and the pronunciation 'Dewstow' is still known. Dewstow in Monmouthshire has the same derivation. St David is the patron saint of Wales, venerated primarily at St David's, and also in Brittany. The church at ALTARNUN, nearby, is dedicated to his mother.

St Day W7342 **(Gwennap)** *Seyntdeye* 1351, *Sendey* 1398. From the saint: he is widely honoured in Brittany, but nothing is known of him. There is not even any record of St Day being venerated at this place, apart from the place-name. The chapel here, a frequent object of pilgrimage in the Middle Ages, was dedicated instead to the Holy Trinity, and is so mentioned in 1269. The traditional pronunciation, 'St Dye', was still known in 1949.

Delabole x0683 (St Teath) *Delyou Bol* 1284, *Delyoubol* 1302. 'Deli with a pit'. The original name was *Deliou* 1086, surviving as Deli nearby, X085840. This appears to be 'leaves', *delyou*, from *deyl*, but the meaning is obscure. Already in 1086 there were two manors here with the same name; at a later date they were distinguished, one as *Delyou Bol*, 'Deli with a pit' (+ *poll*), now Delabole, and the other as *Delyoumur* 1284, 'great Deli' (+ *meur*), surviving as Delamere, X064830. The 'pit' which gave its name to Delabole probably refers to the great slate quarry here. It must therefore date back over 700 years, to before 1284, since it had already given the name to Delabole by then. The reason for the mutation of the *p* of *poll* to *b* is not clear.

De Lank River x1581—X0873 (river) *Dymlonke, Dymlanke* c.1650 (a holding of land). An obscure name; more early forms are needed. Possibly 'fort of a ravine', *din* + *lonk*, though no hill-fort is known near the gorge through which the river flows.

St Dennis w9558 (parish) 'Parish of *Sanctus Dionisius*' 1327, *Seynt Denys* 1436. From the patron saint of the church, St Denys of Paris, a third-century martyr. But as the church is on a hill-top surrounded by a fort-like structure, the dedication is more likely due to a corruption of Cornish *dinas* 'hill-fort', as first suggested in 1903.

Devoran w7939 (Feock) *Dephryon* 1275, *Deffrion* 1278, *Devrian or Devoran* 1683. 'Waters', *devryon*, the plural of *devr-*, a variant of *dowr*. The village is situated at the point where three streams merge into a wider creek.

Dizzard Point x1699 (coast, St Gennys) *Dazard Point* 1813. Named from the nearby manor of Dizzard, which was *Disart* 1086, 'very-steep (place)', *di-serth*.

Dobwalls x2165 (Liskeard) *Dobwalls or Hogswall* 1607, *Dobbewalles* 1619. English, 'Dobb's walls, Dobb's ruins' from the surname *Dobbe* + *wall* plural. Compare a William *Dobbe*, who held land nearby in Liskeard in 1396 (15th); and, in the next parish, a family called *Dobbe* flourishing in St Neot in the 16th century. Alternatively, as the forms are late, it is just possible that the name is a corruption of nearby DOUBLEBOIS. However, the two places were already distinct in 1627, so the former explanation is much more likely. The alternative name for Dobwalls, *Hogswall*, is now lost; English, seemingly 'pig's wall'.

Dodman Point X0039 (coast, Goran) *Dudman foreland* c.1540, *Dodman* 1564, *Deadman Point* 1699. English, from the surname Dodman, itself from the Old English personal name *Dudemann*. The personal name is found in Cornwall from an early date: *Dudemann*, a merchant, in 1201, and *Dudeman* 1206. More particularly, there was a man surnamed *Dudman* farming in the nearby estate of Bodrugan in 1469, and it must be from him or his family that the headland was named, although the reason is not known. The older Cornish name of the headland appears in the nearby farm of PENARE. Pronounced 'Dedman', through English re-interpretation, as seen already in 1699.

St Dominick X3967 (parish) 'Church of *Sancta Dominica*' 1263, *Seynt Domyneke* 1444. From the patron saint of the parish church, apparently a woman, not the well-known Spanish man who founded the order of Black Friars at Toulouse in the early 13th century. But such a female saint is otherwise unknown. There is also a male saint of the same name honoured in Brittany.

Doublebois X1965 (Liskeard) *Dobelboys* 1293, 'wood of *Doubleboys*' 1337. French, 'double wood'. The wood is now called by the same name translated into English: Twelvewood X2065, formerly *Twyfeldewode* 1375, 'two-fold wood', *twifeald* + *wudu*. Pronounced as English, 'Double-boys'.

Downderry X3154 (St Germans) So spelt 1699, 1706. An obscure name. There is another instance of the same name in the parish of St Stephen in Brannel, W956507; it dates from about the same period (first recorded in 1685). It probably originated as an English field-name, and may be connected with refrains such as 'Derry, derry, down', in folk-songs. The instance in St Stephen appears four years before the unsuccessful siege of Londonderry in 1689, so the names cannot be due to that historical event.

Downgate X3672 (Stoke Climsland) *Downgate* 1840. English, 'gate leading onto the downs'; a 19th-c. hamlet on the edge of Hingston Downs. Compare WIDEGATES, etc.

Dozmary Pool x1974 **(lake, St Neot)** 'The western head of *Thosmery*' c.1241-44 (15th), *Dosmerypole* 13th (15th), '(a lake) upon the summit of *Tosmeri* hill' c.1300. It seems that the name originally referred to the moorland surrounding the lake, and was later transferred to the pool. It is completely obscure, and even unclear whether the name is Cornish or English. The second part is not English *mere*, 'lake', both because of the final *i/y* in the early forms, and because that would not be suitable if the name refers primarily to the hill. The legend that the surface of its water goes up and down like the tides appears already in the reference in c.1300.

Drift w4328 **(Sancreed)** William de *Dref* 1302, *Drift* 1748. At an earlier date there is found *Drek bichan* 1244 (*k* for *f*), *Drefbygan* 1262, 'little Drift' (+ *byghan*). 'The village', (*an*) + *tre*, with mutation of *t* to *d* after a lost definite article. The same name is found in Constantine and Braddock parishes; all three names show preservation of the original *v/f* of *tre* (Old Cornish *trev*). They all also show the late addition of non-original final *t*, giving modern Drift. That is probably an English development; compare dialect 'clift', for 'cliff'. Drift Reservoir W4329 was constructed in 1961.

Duloe x2358 **(parish)** *Dulo* 1283. 'Two pools', *dew* + *logh*; or, perhaps better, 'two Looes', the parish being situated between the two Rivers Looe. 'Black pool', *du* + *logh*, is also theoretically possible, but the former meaning suits the location well. The Cornish name of the churchtown was *Lankyp*, *Lankep* 1286, 'church-site of St Cuby', *lann* + saint's name, from the dedication of the church.

Eastcott x2515 **(Morwenstow)** *Estcote, Escote* 1327. English, self-explanatory; *éast* + *cot*. It is in the north-east of the parish.

Eastern Isles v9414 **(Scilly)** So found in 1892. English, self-explanatory.

East Taphouse: see under T.

Eddystone Rocks x3834 **(coast, Rame)** 'A ship wrecked upon *Ediston*' 1405, 'a rok called *Edestone*' 1478. English, 'eddy stone', referring to sea-currents around the rock.

Egloshayle x0071 **(parish)** William de *Egloshail* 1166, Matthew de *Eglosheil* c.1210. 'Church on an estuary', *eglos* + *heyl*. The same name is also found for PHILLACK and Maker churches. The whole Camel estuary must originally have been called *Heyl*. It is referred to as 'the estuary called *Hægelmutha*' 11th (Cornish *heyl*, with the subsequent addition of English *mútha* 'mouth, estuary'), and as 'the mouth of *Heil* river' 13th (14th); and the name survives at Hayle Bay W9379.

Egloskerry x2786 **(parish)** 'Chapel of *Egloskery*' c.1145 (15th), 'chapel of *Eglescheria*' c.1170 (15th), *Egloskury* c.1280 (15th). 'Church of Keri', *eglos* + saint's name. *Keri* is named as one of the 24 Children of Broccan in the Cornish legend, but nothing else is known of the saint, except that she was believed to be female (from the latinised form *cheria*); if so, she must be different from the (male) saint Cury or Corentin, of CURY parish. Compare the Breton St Quiry in Plounévézel, near Carhaix-Plouguer.

St Endellion W9978 **(parish)** 'Church of *Sancta Endelienta*' 1260, *Endelient* 1439, *Endelyn* 1522, *Delyn* 1543. From the patron saint of the church. St *Endilient* was believed to be a daughter of the Welsh king Broccan, according to the Cornish version of the legend. She was also believed to have been a god-daughter of King Arthur, who helped her when a local lord killed her cow; and the site of the church was determined after her death, when her body was put to be drawn by oxen and she was buried at the place where they stopped. No other dedications to her in Wales or Brittany are known.

St Enoder W8956 **(parish)** *Heglosenuder* 1086, 'church of *Sanctus Enodorus*' 1270, *Enoder* 1522. From the patron saint of the church; he was believed to be male, but nothing else is known of him. Nor has he any dedications in Wales or Brittany, though there is said to be a lost 'monastery' of *Lan-Tinidor* at Landerneau, Finistère.

St Erme W8449 **(parish)** 'Church of *Sanctus Hermes*' 1250 (14th), Geoffrey de *Egloserm* 1345, *Seynt Erme* 1456. From the dedication of the church to St Hermes, a 3rd-century Roman martyr. He is also venerated at ST ERVAN, and also

81

formerly at a chapel in Marazion. But these are the only dedications in the country to this universal saint, and they may have replaced earlier dedications to an unknown Celtic saint. There is a Breton St Hervé, honoured in many parishes, whose name is temptingly similar. *Egloserm* is Cornish *eglos* 'church' + saint's name; it survives as Egloserme, the churchtown farm.

St Erth W5535 (parish) 'Vicarage of *Sanctus Ercius*' *c*.1270, 'parish of *Sanctus Ercus*' 1327, *Seynterghe* 1332. From the patron saint of the church. Nothing is known of him, except that he was believed to have been a brother of St Euny (see LELANT, nearby). However, he may be the same as the well-known Irish St Erc, Bishop of Slane, who was believed to have been a page at Tara and a pupil of St Patrick. If so, this is a very rare instance of a Cornish church dedicated to a genuinely Irish saint. The older Cornish name of the churchtown was *Lanuthinoch* 1204, *Lanuthno* 1269, *lann* 'church-site' + unknown word or name, perhaps a district-name; compare PERRANUTHNOE and also Hennowe (St Ewe). St Erth Praze W5735 is *Praze c*.1870, *pras* 'meadow, pasture'.

St Ervan W8970 (parish) Richard of *Sanctus Hermes c*.1210, 'parish of *Seint Erven*' 1397. The church is dedicated to St Hermes, the same Roman martyr as at ST ERME. But the vernacular form *Erven* strengthens the suspicion that the saint may have replaced an earlier Celtic one; as well as the Breton St Hervé, mentioned under St Erme, there is a Welsh St *Erven* recorded at Llangwm, Monmouthshire, in the 12th century; also a Breton saint *Erven*.

St Eval W8769 (parish) 'Church of *Sanctus Uvel*' 1260, 'church of *Sanctus Uvelus*' 1291, *St Evel* 1525. From the dedication of the church: St *Uvel* is also honoured in Brittany, but nothing is known of him. The Cornish *u* sound should have become long *e*, resulting in the name being pronounced 'eevel'; but the long vowel has understandably been shortened.

St Ewe W9746 (parish) *Sancta Ewa* 1282, *Saynthuwa* 1303, *St Tew alias Ewe alias Ewa* 1650. Nothing is known of this saint, who was believed to be female. She is first recorded, as patron saint of the parish, in the form *Euai* 10th century List. The original two-syllable form of her name, still current in 1650 and later, is also preserved in the name of the churchtown farm, Lanuah (*Lanewa* 1302), *lann* 'church-site' + saint's name.

River Fal w9958—w8331 (river) *fram fæle, to fæle* ('from Fal, to Fal') 969 (11th), *of fæle, to fæle* 1049, *Fale* c.1210 (late 13th), *Vale* 1576. Obscure; the name does not look Cornish, and it may be pre-Celtic. It seems that the pronunciation developed to 'Vale', with a long vowel and voicing of *f* to *v*.

Falmouth w8032 (Budock)

Falmouth Bay w82 (coast) *Falemue* (a port) 1225, port of *Falemuth, Falesmuth* 1234, *Fallmouth villa* 1478. English, self-explanatory, 'mouth of the FAL', river-name + *mútha*. It is usually said that the town is of 17th-century origin, but the reference to a *villa* ('settlememt') in 1478, and surnames such as William *Falemouth* 1403, show that there was already a settlement bearing the name, however small, in the 15th century. Before that date, the references to Falmouth usually designate Falmouth Bay. In its period of growth in the second half of the 17th century, the town was also known by two other English names. One was that of an older settlement in the area, *Smitheck*, first found as *Smythwyk* 1370: English, 'smiths' village', *smith* + *wíc*. The other, 'Pennycomequick', is first found as *Pennicomequicke* in 1646; note also *Penny-come-quick alias Smitheck* 1660. This is also English, a nickname 'get-rich-quick', found elsewhere applied to fields, but here referring to the growing town. (A Cornish derivation, supposedly meaning 'head of the valley creek', is sometimes given for this last name; but there are several good reasons why that derivation cannot possibly be right, and anyway the phrase does not mean that, nor anything else, in Cornish.)

Feock w8238 (parish) '*Fioc* the name of a saint', *Lanfioc, Lamfioc* c.1165 (17th), 'church of *Sancta Feoca*' 1264, 'church of *Seyntfeok*' 1392. From the saint of the church; compare St Fiac in Brittany, but nothing at all is known of him or her. *Lanfioc* (now a nearby farm called La Feock, pronounced 'La*vaig*') is *lann* 'church-site' + saint's name.

Fire Beacon Point X1092 (coast, St Juliot) So found in 1813. English, self-explanatory. Compare two places in Devon called Firebeacon, at Hartland S245202 and Tiverton S957167, recorded from 1400 and 1571 respectively.

Fistral Bay W7962 (coast, St Columb Minor) *Fistral Bay* 1813, *Fistral Bay c.*1870. Obscure; no explanation can be attempted, for lack of earlier spellings.

Flexbury S2107 (Poughill) William de *Flexberi* 1201. English, probably 'flax-mound, mound where flax grows', *fleax* + *beorg*. The spellings could equally well indicate Old English *byrig*, dative case of *burh*, 'fort', as the second word; but no fort is known near the place, nor any obvious site for one. Nor is there a distinctive natural hill, so *beorg* probably refers to a lost tumulus. Compare BILBERRY, etc.

Flushing W8033 (Mylor) *Flushing* 1698, 1699. Like Flushing in St Anthony in Meneage and in New York, this place is named after the port of Flushing (Vlissingen) in Holland. The Dutch place (*Vlisseghem* 1220) is from a personal name *Flisse* + suffix *-inghem*. All transferred cases of the name are ports; Tonkin, in the early 18th century, referred to this place as 'lately built by the Dutchmen'.

Four Lanes W6838 (Wendron) So found in 1872. English, self-explanatory; a 19th-century mining village.

River Fowey X1781—X1251 *Fawe c.*1210 (late 13th), *Fawy* 1241 (early 14th), *Foy* 1576. Apparently 'beech-tree (river)', *faw* 'beeches' + -*i*. Beech-trees are not thought to have flourished in Roman and Dark-Age Cornwall, but the name seems to show their presence in the area of this river. The good stands of them now seen around Golitha Falls on the river, X2268, are planted. The form *Foy* in 1576 already shows the modern pronunciation. Although the river itself is not mentioned until *c.*1210, it had already before 1086 given its name to the manor of Fawton, X1668 (in St Neot), *Fauuitona* 1086; English, 'farm/estate on the River Fowey', river-name + *tún*; and also by the 12th century to BODMIN MOOR, 'Foymoor', where the river rises.

Fowey X1251 (parish) 'Town of *Fawi' c.*1223, *Fowy* 1301, *Foy* 1602. Named from the river on which it stands. Pronounced 'Foy', like the river. The Cornish name of the churchtown was *Langorthou, Langworthou* 1310; this looks like possibly 'church-site of (?) clans', *lann* + (?) *cordhow*, plural of *cordh* 'clan' (with mutation of *c* to *g*), but such an interpretation makes little sense. If the form with *w* is valid, a personal name is more likely.

Foxhole w9654 (St Stephen in Brannel) Found in 1686 (a tin-work) also 1748 (a hamlet); English, self-explanatory.

Fraddon w9158 (St Enoder) *Frodan* 1321, *Frodan wartha* ('upper Fraddon', + *gwartha*) c.1510, *Fraddon woolas or Vradon woollas* ('lower Fraddon', + *goeles*) 1702. Perhaps 'streamlet', *frodynn*, diminutive formed from *fros* (older *frod*) + *-ynn*, or more likely 'place of streams', *frod* + *-an*. Compare the Welsh stream-name Ffrydan, Merionethshire. A modern form *Frozzan* or *Fruzzan* would have been expected, with *d* becoming *z*. The *d* must have been preserved by the influence of written forms. The irregular change of *o* to *a* in the first syllable occurred some time in the 16th or 17th centuries, before 1702.

Freathy x3952 (St John) *Vridie* 1286; compare Roger *Fridia* living in the parish in 1327, and Thomas *Fredea* in the hundred in 1428. It is unknown whether the place-name or surname is the original. If the place-name, it is of unknown derivation. If the surname is the original, it might be compared with the surname Friday, found in Devon in 1332, and elsewhere.

Garras w7023 (Mawgan in Meneage) *Garrows Common* c.1696, *Garras* (a hamlet) 1748. Probably 'rough moorland', a compound of *garow* + *ros*; compare Garris (Gulval), perhaps GARROW TOR, and Garros (Finistère). As a settlement, the place seems to date only from the 18th century, built upon the common grazing-land.

The Garrison v8910 (Scilly) *'The garison* in the Hugh or New Towne' 1652. English, self-explanatory, referring to the fort here. Compare 'the fort which is begun on the Hew Hill', 'the fortifications on the Hew Hill' 1593 (see HUGH TOWN). The main fort was built in 1715-46.

Garrow Tor x1478 (hill, St Breward) *Garross Moors* c.1640, *Garrah* (a farm) 1748. Possibly 'rough moorland', *garow* + *ros*, like GARRAS, with loss of the final *s*. But note also Henry and Roger *Garra* in the parish in 1327, and a place called *Garroy* there in 1353: if those are good forms, the derivation fails. More early references are needed.

St Gennys x1497 (parish)   *Sanwinas* 1086, *Sanguinas* 1086, 'church of *Sanctus Genesius*' c.1160 (15th), *St Ginnes* 1244. From the patron saint of the parish church. There are several international saints called *Genesius*, and already in the 12th century the local saint here was evidently identified with one of them, perhaps (as later) the 3rd-century martyr of Arles. But such an identification could have been a replacement for an earlier local saint of similar name; however, nothing would be known about such a saint. Compare perhaps the Welsh St Gwynws, patron of Gwnnws, in Cardiganshire. The traditional pronunciation of St Gennys is like 'Guinness'.

St George's or Looe Island x2551 (island) ' Island of St Michael of *Lammana*' 13th (1727), 'the isle of *Lamayne*' c.1547, 'island of St Michael' 1576, *St Georges Island* 1602, c.1605, *Looe Island* 1699. The island is always named from St Michael in the Middle Ages, and on most maps throughout the 17th century. It is not known how the change from St Michael to St George came about, though it seems to have been due to the influence of Carew and Norden in the early 17th century. It may even have originated as an error. The Cornish name, *Lammana*, is perhaps *lann* + *managh*, 'church-site of a monk', though that is an odd meaning; it survived as *Lemain* until 1839 on the mainland, but seems to have referred originally to a chapel on the island. Most recently, the island has been named with reference to the town of LOOE nearby.

Georgia w4836 (Towednack)   *Gorga moor*, *The Gorga Craft* (fields) c.1696, *Georgia*, *Georgia Croft* 1841. This was originally the name of an area of moorland, and later given to a 19th-century farm. Probably *gor-ge* 'broken-down hedge'. This place cannot have taken its name from the state of Georgia in America, since that was named from George II in 1732, more than thirty years after the first appearance of this Cornish name; but the state may have influenced the later development of the Cornish name.

St Germans x3557 (parish) *Sanctus Germanus* mid-10th, 994; 'the church of *Sancta* [*sic*] *German*' 11th; 'the church of *S. Germanus*' 1086. There has been much discussion as to whether it was the well-known St Germanus of Auxerre who was the original saint here, or an unknown local saint instead. The problem remains unresolved. There is also an Old Cornish name for the place, *Lannaled*, found only in Latin forms in two documents of the mid-10th (*Lannaledensis*, *Lanaletensis*): *lann* 'church-site' + obscure word or name, perhaps an unexplained district-name, like Allett (in Kenwyn, W7948) and Aleth in Ile-et-Vilaine, Brittany.

Germoe w5829 (parish) ' Chapel of *Sanctus Germoch*' *c*.1176 (1300), *Germogh* 1283, 1312, *Sent Germowe* 1549. From the patron saint of the chapel (with early loss, already by 1283, of the prefix 'Saint', when the name referred to holdings of land in the village). No such saint is known anywhere else. In 1478 he was claimed to have been a bishop; by Leland's time (*c*.1540) he was believed to have been a king who came from Ireland along with St BREAGE. In *c*.1800, or earlier, there was a local saying, *Germow mahtern, Breage lavethas*, 'Germoe was a king, Breage but a midwife', which may relate to some lost story about the two saints.

Gerrans w8735 (parish) *Seint Geren* 1201, 'church of *Sanctus Gerentus*' 1202, *St Gerance* 1578. From the patron saint of the church. He is earlier referred to as *Gerent* 10th List (patron saint of this parish), and as *Gerontius* 12th. It is unknown whether he is the same as the historical Cornish king of the early 8th century called *Gerent*, but very likely so. If not, nothing is known of the saint. Gerrans Bay W83 is so found in 1813.

Godolphin House w6031 (Breage) Edward de *Wotholca* 1166, Alexander *Gludholghan* 1186, *Wulgholgan* 1194, Alexander de *Woldholgan* 1201, *Godholkan c*.1210, *Godolghan* 1327. Obscure; the early forms conflict with one another, and some must be corrupt. *Godolghan* probably best represents the medieval pronunciation. It is unclear whether or not the first syllable contained *l*, though probably not. Probably *go-* 'little', plus an unknown second word, probably of the form *tolghan*, with mutation of *t* to *d*. (The interpretation 'hillock', sometimes given, is invalid, because based upon false analogy with a non-existent Welsh word.) Godolphin Cross W6031 is so found in 1888: a 19th-century village at the cross-roads.

Godrevy Island W5743 (coast, Gwithian) *The rokket Godryve* c.1540. Named from Godrevy, the farm on the mainland nearby. This occurs as *Godrevy* 1297: 'small-holdings, little farms', plural of *go-dre* (go- + *tre*).

Golant x1255 (parish) *Gulnant* 1299, *Golananta* 1342, *Golenance* c.1462, *Gollant* 1478, *Glant* 1635. Probably 'fair in a valley', *goel* 'fair, festival' + *nans* (older *nant*), though the early forms, rather few in number, are not altogether consistent. Many show a vowel between *l* and the first *n*, which would not be expected. If the derivation is right, the vowel must be epenthetic. No fair or festival is recorded at the site. The church is dedicated to St Sampson, and occurs earlier as 'Chapel of *Sanctus Sampson*' 1282. Note that, as expected, the final *-nt* of *nant* did change to *-ns*, as shown in the form *Golenance*; but the archaic *t* has been preserved in the modern form of this parish name.

Golberdon x3271 (South Hill) *Golberton or Goberton* 1620, *Goberdon* 1627, *Golberdon* 1659, 1679, *Golborn* (a hamlet) 1748. An 18th-century village built on former rough grazing-land. The 17th-century forms all refer only to pasture-land, not to a settlement. English, unknown word + probably *dún*, 'hill, downland'. The spellings are too late for the first part to be explained.

Goldsithney W5430 (Perranuthnoe) *Pleyn-goylsithny* 1399, *Goylsithny* 1403, *Golsithny* 1409. 'Fair of St Sithny', *goel* 'fair, festival' + saint's name. The first reference is prefixed by *plen* 'arena, ground' ('ground of the fair of St Sithny'). There is no chapel here devoted to that saint, and the only connection of the place with him is that the fair held here had previously been located in the parish of SITH-NEY: it is called 'the fair of *Merdreseni*' in 1140 (14th), from Merthersithney or Merther in that parish. It was moved from there to Goldsithney (thus giving the place its name) at some time before 1284, when it is found at the new site; but the evidence of its origin remained in the name.

Goonbell w7249 **(St Agnes)** So found in 1813. 'Far downs', *goen + pell*, with mutation of *p* to *b*.

Goonhavern w7853 **(Perranzabuloe)** 'Moor of *Goenhavar*' 1300, *Goonhavern* (a farm) 1748. 'Downs of summer-ploughed land', *goen + havar*. The word *goen* normally denotes pasture, not arable land; so the name presumably refers to an area of rough grazing (*goen*), which had a piece of summer-ploughed land (*havar*) within it or near it. The village is 19th-century.

Goonhilly Downs w7221 **(downs, several parishes)** 'Moor of *Goenhili*' c.1240 (14th), 'pasture of *Gonhely*' 1284, *Gonelgy* 1315. Either 'downs of brackish-water',*goen + hyli* 'brine', or more likely 'downs of hunting', *goen + helghi* 'to hunt'; but few of the early spellings show signs of the *gh* sound which that would require after the *l*.

Gooseham s2216 **(Morwenstow)** Hamund de *Gosham* 1201, Richard de *Gosham* 1297; English, 'goose-meadow', *gós + hamm*.

Gorran Haven x0141 **(Goran)** *Gurran hone* 1699, *Gorran-haven* 1748. The harbour of the parish of Goran; *hone* is dialect *hawn*, 'haven', now converted into the standard word in this name. Gorran Haven is an old village, but until the 18th century it went by its Cornish name, which was *Porthjust* 1374, *Porteuste* 1576, *Porth East* 1792, 'harbour of St Yust', Cornish *porth* + saint's name, from a chapel there dedicated to that saint (note the pronunciation of St JUST as 'east'). The parish and churchtown of Goran itself are found as *Sanctus Goranus* 1086, *Seynt Goran* 1302, *Langoron* 1374, *Laworran* 1717 ('church-site of Goran', *lann* + saint's name, with mutation of *g* to *w*). Named from the patron saint of the parish; he is first recorded as *Guron* 10th (List). Note the pronunciation as 'Gurran' in 1699. St Goron was believed to have lived a religious life at Bodmin, but St Petrock crowded him out, and he moved away to found a new settlement at Goran; however, his well is still known at Bodmin.

Grampound w9348 **(Creed)** *Grauntpount* 1302. French, 'great bridge' (*grand pont*), from the crossing of the River Fal at the foot of the village. In 1297 the 'borough-plots of

Ponsmur' appear; that is the same name in Cornish, 'great bridge', *pons + meur*. It is uncertain whether the French name is a translation of the Cornish, or (more likely) the Cornish a translation of the French. Grampound Road W9150 (Ladock) is so found in *c*.1870, a 19th-century village which grew up around the railway station (compare BODMIN ROAD, etc.).

Great Bosullow: see under B.

Greeb Point W8733 **(coast, Gerrans)** *The Greeb* 1748. 'Crest, ridge', *crib*. The mutation of *c* to *g* may be due to a lost definite article, *(an) grib*; or it may have become fossilised in this word.

Gribbin Head X0949 **(coast, Tywardreath)** *Grebin* 1699, *Gribbin Head c*.1870. Perhaps 'little ridge', *cribynn*, diminutive formed from *crib + -ynn*, with mutation of *c* to *g* after a lost definite article. The older name for the promontory was *Pennarthe* 1525, *Penarth-Point c*.1540: *penn-ardh* 'headland'. Curiously, there was a 'Thomas son of Robert *Grobbin'* living nearby at Polridmouth in *c*.1260; but the surname is not found later, so it is doubtful whether it is connected with the name of the headland. If it were, however, the derivation from *cribynn* would fail; there is no evident derivation for the surname *Grobbin*.

New Grimsby V8815 **(Scilly)** *New*, *Old Grymsey c*.1540, *c*.1585, *Newe*, *Olde Grynssey* 1570, *New*, *Old Grimsbye* 1652. Probably Norse, 'Grímr's island', personal name + *ey*. This would have been an old name for the island of Tresco — or, perhaps better, a Norse name for the whole large island of Scilly, for at the period of the Norse visits Tresco would only just have been separating off from the main island. Other islands along the western seaboard of Britain also have Norse names, such as Lundy ('puffin island') and Anglesey; compare AGNES for another possible Norse name in Scilly. The form *Grynssey*, with *n*, shows a genuine variant: it recurs in various sources. The modern form with *b* (from 1652) is presumably due to confusion with Grimsby in Lincolnshire.

Grimscott S2606 **(Launcells)** Richard de *Grymescote* 1284. English, 'Grim's cottage', personal name + *cot*. *Grim* is here an Anglo-Scandinavian name (used by English-speakers), rather than an Old Norse one.

Grumbla w4029 **(Sancreed)** *Gromlogh* 1503 (for *-legh*), *Grumbler* 1872. '(The) dolmen', *cromm-legh*, with mutation of *c* to *g* after a lost definite article. There are the remains of a barrow here, consisting of 'part of [a] retaining wall of very large stones'.

Gugh v8908 **(island, Scilly)** *Agnes Gue* 1652 (common land belonging to AGNES); *keow*, possibly 'home-field'.

Gulland Rock w8778 **(islet, Padstow)** *The Gull rock* 1576, *Gulland* 1748. English, self-explanatory: 'gull ground'. Many rocks around the Cornish coast have been called 'Gull Rock' at some time in their history, partly no doubt because they would have been of value, the gulls' eggs being gathered for food. In this instance English 'land' was added later to the name.

Gulval w4831 **(parish)** 'Church of *Sancta Welveda*' 1302, 'church of *Sancta Welvela*' 1328, 'church of *Sancta Gwelvela alias Wolvela*' 1413, *Gulvall* 1522. From the patron saint of the church. The earliest spelling of her name, with *d*, is corrupt, and the original Cornish form was probably *Gwelvel*. St Gulval was evidently believed to be female; but nothing is known of her, and she may instead be the same as the Breton St Gudwal, a man. However, that saint, as well as being male, never appears with spellings in *Wel-* or *Gwel-*, and a different saint (unknown, female) is perhaps more likely. The churchtown also had a Cornish name, which appears as *Landicle* 1086, 'church of *Lanestli*' 1261, *Lanystly* 1328, and survived to give Lanisley Common 1888: *lann* 'church-site' + unknown word or name of the form *ystly*.

Gunnislake x4371 **(Calstock)** 'Tin-work at *Gonellake*' 1485, *Gunnalake* 1608, 1614, *Gunnislake* (a copper mine) 1796, 'village of *Gunnislake*' 1828. English, 'Gunna's stream', personal name + *lacu*. Compare the name of a lost place in Linkinhorne, *Gunnecombe c.*1160 (15th), 'Gunna's valley', showing the same personal name + *cumb*. The later intrusion of *s* into Gunnislake may be due to an incorrect re-interpretation of the first part as if it were dialect *gun-*

nis 'crevice in a mine-lode', but its absence in the early spellings shows that that word cannot have been present in the name originally. The village seems to date only from the 19th century.

Gunver Head W8977 (coast, Padstow) So found in 1813. Obscure, for lack of earlier forms. The name looks Cornish, rather than English. One might possibly compare the coastal name Gwynver in Sennen, W3627, which is probably Cornish 'white way', a compound of *gwynn + fordh*; but there it is applied to a long beach of pale sand (WHITE-SAND BAY), which could not apply at Gunver Head. Here it might possibly apply to the dramatic chasm which runs along the foot of the cliff, formed by a line of off-shore rocks.

Gunwalloe Fishing Cove W6522 (coast, Gunwalloe) So found in 1888. English, self-explanatory. Saint Gunwalloe or Winwaloe is first found as patron saint of the church here in 1332, 'chapel of *Sanctus Wynwolaus*'. He is patron saint also of Landewednack, and of Landevennec in Brittany. He was believed to have been born in Brittany of a mother called *Alba Trimammis*, 'white three-breasts', because she bore triplets and grew a third breast to suckle them; he also, as a child, restored his sister's eye when it was pecked out and swallowed by a savage goose.

Gurnard's Head W4338 (coast, Zennor)   *Gurnards Head* 1748. English; from the shape, which resembles the head of a gurnard fish. St Ives fishermen still call the headland *Izner* (*the Isnarl* 1935), which preserves the old name of Chapel Jane nearby (W434382), *Innyall Chappell* 1580 (18th): obscure, possibly *enyal* 'wild, desolate'.

Gweek W7026 (Constantine)   Roger de *Wika* 1201, *Wyk* 1300, *Gwyk* 1358. The meaning of Cornish *gwig* is uncertain: it could be 'forest', like Welsh *gwig*, or 'village', like Old Breton *guic*. Since the Cornish place is a village in a wood, either meaning would be suitable; 'village' or 'trading-post' seems most likely. Or the name could even be Old English *wic* 'hamlet', assimilated into Cornish by turning initial *W* into *Gw*.

Gwennap W7340 (parish)   'Church of *Lamwenep*' (*m* for *nn*) 1199, 'church of *Sancta Weneppa*' 1269, *Seynt Gwenape*

1520. From the patron saint of the church, but nothing is known of her; she may be the saint called *Wynup*, who is listed as one of the 24 sons and daughters of King Broccan of Breconshire in the Cornish version of the legend, although most of those belong in north-east Cornwall. The Cornish name of the churchtown is 'church-site of Gwenep', *lann* + saint's name, with mutation of *gw* to *w*.

Gwennap Head w3621 (coast, St Levan) So found in 1888. In the adjacent parishes of Sennen and St Buryan there were families with the surname *Gwenappe*, *Gwinappe* or *Gwennap(e)* in 1641. They must have taken the surname from the parish of Gwennap originally; but it is not known how or when their surname became transferred to this headland.

Gwenter w7417 (St Keverne) *Wynter* 1263, *Gwynter* 1519. An obscure name; possibly 'windy-land', a compound of *gwyns* + *tir*. If such a compound had been formed when *gwyns* still had its older form *gwynt*, it might have taken the form *Gwyntir*; but such a meaning would not be very convincing. Alternatively perhaps 'fair-water', a compound of *gwynn* 'white, fair' + *dowr*, referring to the stream here; but *Gwenthor* might have been expected for that: compare Gwenddwr in Breconshire, SO0643.

Gwinear w5937 (parish) 'Church of *Sanctus Wynerus*' 1258, 'church of *Sanctus Wynierus*' 1286, *Gwynnyar* c.1535. From the patron saint of the church. According to a 14th-century Life of him by the Breton Anselm, he was the son of a pagan Irish king who came to Cornwall and was martyred, with his 777 companions, by the pagan Cornish king Theodoric. He also has a dedication at Pluvigner in southern Brittany (Morbihan).

Gwithian w5841 (parish) 'Parish of *Sanctus Gozianus*' (z for th) 1327, 'parish of *Sanctus Goythianus*' 1334, *Gothian* 1524, *Gwithian* 1563. From the patron saint of the church, but nothing is known of him; he is also honoured in Brittany. A 6th-century pagan chief in North Cornwall who was converted by St Samson had the same name, *Guedianus* or *Goedianus*, but he need not be the same person. The church is earlier referred to as the 'church of *Connartona*' c.1176 (1300), named from the lost manor of Connerton (see CONNOR DOWNS), which was centred at Gwithian churchtown. Note that the initial *Gw* in this name is not original; it may be due to analogy with GWINEAR, nearby.

Hallworthy X1887 (Davidstow) *Halworgy* 1439, *Haleworthy alias Halldrunkard* 1748. 'Marsh of Gorgi', *hal* + personal name, with mutation of *g* to *w*. The modern form is due to analogy with English names ending in *-worthy*. The alternative name for the place, Halldrunkard, was not due to the inn here, but was a separate place nearby, *Haldronket* 1439, 'marsh of a promontory-wood', *hal* + *troen-goes*, with mutation of *t* to *d*. The final *s* of *troen-goes* was preserved as archaic *t/d* in this east Cornish name.

Halsetown W5038 (St Ives) *Halse Town* 1839, 'built a few years ago by James Halse, Esq., for the accommodation of the miners' 1868. English, self-explanatory. James Halse (1769-1838) was a native of Truro and Member of Parliament for St Ives. It is said that he planned this development in order to secure his parliamentary seat: each house had just enough land to qualify its tenant for the vote, and the tenants were his selected supporters.

Harrowbarrow X3969 (Calstock) Robert de *Harebere* c.1286, *Harebeare* 1327, *Harrobear* 1748, *Harrowburrow* 1813. English, 'grey wood', *hár* + *bearu*; or, if *hár* can mean 'boundary', then 'boundary-wood'. The place is on the parish boundary, bordering with both St Dominick and Callington. Compare Harebarrow, in Cheshire. The modern form of the name is due to re-interpretation.

Hatt X3962 (Botus Fleming) *La Hatte* 1305. English, 'hat', *hætt*, from a fancied resemblance of the nearby hill. The same English name is found in other counties.

Haye X3469 (Callington) Thomas de *Heye* 1327. English, 'enclosure', *hæg*. The same name is found in a good many other parishes; compare HEAMOOR.

River Hayle W6533—W5438 (river) 'River called *Heyl-penword*' 1260, *Heyl* 1265 (15th). 'Estuary', *heyl*, the name for the river-mouth being transferred to the whole river. The first form has suffixed a corrupt spelling of PENWITH, 'Hayle in Penwith'.

Hayle w5537 (Phillack) 'The Port of *Hayle*' 1816, *Hayle* 1824. A 19th-century industrial development, named from the river and estuary on which it stands. In 1813 a single house called *Heyl* occurs across the causeway from the present town, at W546362 in St Erth; it was an independent settlement also taking its name from the estuary.

Heamoor w4631 (Madron) 'The moor called *Hay Moore*' 1663. English, 'marsh (*mór*) at Hea'. Hea is first found as *la Hae* 1277, *Haye alias Anhaye* 1619. '(The) enclosure', English *hæg*, prefixed with French *la* 'the', and later with Cornish *an*. Pronounced 'Hay*moor*'. Compare HAYE.

St Helen's v9017 (island, Scilly) *St Helene* 1564, *Sainte Ellens Isle* 1570. At an earlier date there appears an 'island of *Sanctus Elidius*' c.1160 (15th), 'the island of *Seynt Lyda*' 1478, '*Saynct Lides Isle* ... at her sepulchre' c.1540. This latter name is evidently derived from some saint who was believed to lie in a tomb on the island. He (not she) was believed in 1478 to have been a bishop, and son of a king; but nothing else is known of him. By c.1540 the saint was apparently considered to be female. It is thought that, as a result, he/she was identified with one of the well-known saints Helen, and that the name of the island was corrupted accordingly. Against that theory, at least two sources in the 16th century contain both place-names side by side (*Sainte Ellens Isle*, *Lydes Ile* 1570), suggesting that they were separate places; but that may be an error.

Helford w7526 (Manaccan)

Helford River w72 (estuary) The following forms all refer to the harbour or estuary: *Helleford* 1230, *Hayleford* 1318, *Hailleford* 1347, *Helford haven* 1576. The village itself is not found until a later date: *Haylford*, *Heylford* 1564 (two habitations, to north and south of the estuary), 'towne and haven of *Helford*' 1644, *Helford* c.1689. This name is evidently composed of Cornish *heyl* 'estuary' (which must therefore have been the original Cornish name of the Helford River itself), with the later addition of English *ford* in some sense; but it remains hard to explain. That is partly because of the difficulty of finding a suitable meaning of English *ford*, and partly from the related difficulty of not knowing to what feature the name primarily referred: was *'Heyl*-ford' originally the name of the estuary, or of a water-crossing, or of the village? Most likely the first, since all the early references show it as referring to the estuary. In that case *ford* here must have the sense of 'bay, estuary', even though that is not recorded for the word. *Ford* meaning 'a passage for ships, an arm of the sea', exactly as here, is recorded in dialect in Westmorland in 1891; but there it is presumably influenced by Norse *fjord*, which is not likely in Cornwall. If so, the name means *'Heyl*-bay', and the village must have received its name transferred from the estuary. (Such an explanation seems more likely than a suggestion made by me some years ago, that the name means 'ford beside *Heyl*', and originally referred, not to the estuary, but to the village itself, where there is a small ford across a tributary stream.)

Helland X0770 (parish) *Hellaunde* 1284, *Hellonde* 1285. 'Ancient church-site', a compound of *hen* + *lann*. The same name occurs as a farm-name in Mabe and Probus parishes. In all three cases the second part of the name has undergone re-interpretation, as if it were English 'land'. The dedication of the church is to St Seninan or Synnie (compare SITHNEY).

Helston W6527 (Wendron) *Henlistone* 1086, 'borough of *Helleston*' 1187, Matthew de *Henleston* 1284, *Helston* 1365 (late 14th). 'Ancient court', *hen-lys*, with the later addition of English *tún*, 'farm, manorial centre'. The Cornish form, without *tún* survives as *Hellys* 1396, *Helles* late 17th.

Helstone X0881 (Lanteglos by Camelford) *Henliston* 1086, *Helleslond* 1284, *Helleston in Trigg* 1297. 'Ancient court', *hen-lys*, like Helston, with again the later addition of English words, either *tún*, 'manorial centre', or *land*, 'estate'. Often qualified as 'Helstone in Trigg', to distinguish it from 'Helston in Kerrier'. Contrast LESNEWTH nearby, 'new court': its name suggests that it replaced Helstone as an administrative centre during the Dark Ages.

Hensbarrow Downs W9957 (downs, St Austell) *Hyndesbergh* 1284, 'the Cornish Archbeacon *Hainborough*' 1602. English, 'hind's (female deer's) barrow', *hind* + *beorg*. The barrow can still be seen. Around here was also the tinning

96

area of *Hyndemore* 1261, 1306, 'hind's moor', a name sur-viving at the deserted farm of Henmoor, W970551. Compare also Hen Tor, 'hind's tor', on Dartmoor, SX593653. Cocksbarrow, a 19th-century village situated a mile to the south-west (*Cox Barrow*, a barrow, 1813), must be named as a joke, based on the modern form of Hensbar-row, which shows re-interpretation as 'hen'.

Henwood x2673 (Linkinhorne) *Hennawode* 1327. English, 'hens' wood', *henn* + *wudu*.

Herodsfoot x2160 (Duloe) *Heriott foote*, *Herryottes foote* 1613. English, 'the foot (of a stream) at *Heriard*'. The lat-ter was a nearby place, found as *Heriard* 1490, *Heriod* 1617, *Herod Wood* 1758; Cornish *hir-yarth*, 'long-ridge', with re-interpretation as the biblical 'Herod'. Herodshead, also nearby in Lanreath parish, X200607, occurs as *Bron-heriard* 1284, *Penherierd* 1580; 'hill of *Heriard*', with Cornish *bronn*, 'hill', re-interpreted as *Pen-*, 'head', and translated into English.

Hessenford x3057 (St Germans) 'Mill of *Heceneford*' c.1286, *Hesenford* 1310. English, seemingly 'witches' ford', *hægtesse*, 'witch' (genitive plural *hægtsena*) + *ford*.

Higher Sharpnose Point: see under S.

Higher Town v9215 (St Martin's, Scilly) *Higher Town* 1748. English, self-explanatory; dialect *town*, 'farm'. Com-pare Middle and Lower Town also on the island.

High Street w9653 (St Stephen in Brannel) *High Street* 1748. English, self-explanatory; an 18th-century village high up (500 ft) on former downland. But the sense of *street* here is unclear. The village is at the highest point on a cross-country route from St Austell to Newquay; it might here have been a 'paved road'.

Highway x1453 (Lanteglos by Fowey) *Highway* 1699. Eng-lish, a hamlet on the main road to Bodinnick ferry; compare ST KEW HIGHWAY.

St Hilary w5531 (parish) 'Church of *Sanctus Hilarius*' 1178 (1523), *Sanctus Hillarius* c.1200 (14th), *Hillary* 1524. From the dedication of the church to St Hilary of Poitiers, a fourth-century bishop and vigorous opponent of the Arian heresy.

Holywell w7658 (Cubert) *The Holy Well* 1663. English, self-explanatory. There are two holy wells here, one in a field above the dunes, the other in a cave on the shore. The latter, widely known for its cures, was the more important, and is the one from which the cove is named. The village is entirely 20th-century, a holiday village. Holywell Bay w7659 (coast) was *Holy Well Porth* 1795 (dialect *porth* 'cove'), *Holywell Bay* 1813. The older Cornish name of the cove was *Porth Island* 1630, *Porraylan* 1686, probably 'cove of a little estuary', *porth + heylynn*, diminutive formed from *heyl + -ynn*, re-interpreted as English 'island'.

Hot Point w7112 (coast, Landewednack) *Hot* 1813. Obscure; it looks English, and Hot Cove (1888) is adjacent: turbulent water 'boiling' on the rocks may be an explanation. Compare, however, Carn Haut (coast, Perranzabuloe, w760559), which is presumably a Cornish name.

Hugh Town v9010 (St Mary's, Scilly) *The Hugh or New Towne, the Hugh Port* 1652, *Hugh Town* 1689. English, named from a nearby hill and promontory called *The Hew* c.1585, *the Hew Hill* 1593, *the Hugh Hill* 1652. English, probably *hóh* 'a heel, a spur of land'.

The Hurlers x2571 (antiquity, Linkinhorne) *The Hurlers* 1602, 'two moore stones called *the hurlers*' 1613. Named from the Cornish ball-game of *hurling*, because the circles of standing stones were felt to resemble the players in a hurling-match. In 1675 it was recorded that the stones were 'supposed to be done in memory of some battle. They are now easily numbered but the people have a story that they never could till a man took many penny loafes and laying one on each hurler did compute by the remainder what number they were.'

Illogan w6743 (parish) 'Church of *Sanctus Illoganus*' 1291, 'church of *Sanctus Eluganus* at *Egloshal*' 1302, *Seyntlugan alias Seyntlocan* 1436. From the patron saint but nothing is known of him. In the 15th century he was believed to be buried here. The Cornish name of the churchtown is found as *Eglossalau* 1235, surviving as *Eglish Hallow* 1820; possibly 'church of marshes', *eglos + halow*, plural of *hal*, though that does not make good sense on the ground.

Indian Queens W9159 (St Columb Major) 'A single house called the *Indian Queens*, which is rather a post-house than an inn' 1802; *Indian Queen c.*1870. A 19th-century village, named from the inn around which it grew. The inn was earlier called *The Queen's Head* 1780. 'The Indian Queen' was a popular 18th-century name for inns: compare the Indian Queen (Altarnun), the Queen of India (Gwennap) and the Indian King (Camelford); and, in 18th-century London, at least four inns called the Indian King and at least 18 called the Indian Queen. There is probably no particular reason for such names, and certainly no reason to think that the famous Red Indian queen, Pocahontas, ever visited the Cornish place. She landed at Plymouth in 1616, travelled to London and was buried at Gravesend a few years later. However, there were popular literary and musical works based on her life, and these may have contributed to the use of the phrase for names of inns. (Compare London Apprentice, X0050, similarly named from a popular 18th-century ballad.)

River Inney X1486—X3777 (river) *Æni* 1044, 'water of *Eny*' *c.*1160 (15th), *c.*1195 (15th), 'river of *Innye*' early 17th. Probably 'ash-tree river', from *enn* (plural of *onn*, 'ash-trees') + *-i*, river-suffix. Compare the River FOWEY for a similar name.

Isles of Scilly, see under SCILLY.

St Issey W9271 (parish) *Sanctus Ydi* 1195, *Seintysy* 1362; from the dedication of the parish church. The saint is first mentioned as *Iti* 10th century List (as joint patron saint of MEVAGISSEY); and, in the form *Yse*, he was said to have been one of the 24 sons and daughters of the Welsh King Broccan of Breconshire, according to the Cornish version of the legend. He is also found in the place-name Plouisy, near Guingamp in north Brittany. Near St Issey, and in the same parish, is the hamlet of St Jidgey, which shows the same saint's name in another form, with mistaken division of Cornish *Sans-Ysy*. The reason for this duplication of the name is not known. Presumably St Jidgey was the manorial centre of the parish, and took its name from the older churchtown. The church was certainly at its present site by the late 12th century, when the alternative Corn-

99

ish name of the churchtown is first recorded: 'church of *Egloscruc*' *c.*1190, 'church of Saints Ida and Lydus of *Eglescruke*' 1382, surviving as Egloscrow 1840: 'church of a barrow', *eglos + crug.*

St Ive x3067 **(parish)** *Sanctus Yvo* 1201, *Seynt Ive* 1390 (15th); from the dedication of the parish church. St Ive was believed to have been a Persian bishop who came to convert the pagan English in the Dark Ages; his cult grew up at St Ives (Huntingdonshire) when a buried body was found there in A.D. 1001-02, but it is not known how a dedication to him arose in Cornwall by A.D. 1201. The 13th-century Breton St Yves Helori of Treguier is a different saint, who lived later than the earliest record of the dedication in Cornwall. Pronounced 'Eve'.

St Ives w5140 **(parish)** *Sancta Ya* 1284, *Seint Ive (Baye)* 1346, *Seint Ithe* 1347, *Sent Ia* 1468, *St Ies* 1602; from the dedication of the church. St Ya, a woman, was believed to have been an Irish saint, sister of St Euny and St Erth. She had hoped to cross to Cornwall with St GWINEAR and his companions, but missed the boat, so climbed on a leaf which carried her over to arrive before them. She was also believed to be buried in the church here. The Cornish name of the town was *Porthye* 1284, *Porthia* 1291, 'harbour of St Ya', *porth* + saint's name. The *v* in the modern form is non-original, and seems to have arisen (with a variant in *th*) in the 14th century; the spoken Cornish form of the saint's name was evidently *Ya* (two syllables). St Ives Bay W54 (coast) is found as '*roda* of *Sancta Ya*' 1284 (English *road*, 'roadstead for ships'), and as *Seint Ive Baye* 1346.

Jacobstow x1995 **(parish)** *Jacobestowe* 1270-72, *Yapstawe* 1453. English, 'holy place of St James' (the Apostle, Latin *Jacobus*), saint's name + *stów*. The form of 1453 shows the dialect pronunciation of the place-name.

St John x4053 **(parish)** 'Church of *Sanctus Johannes*' *c.*1160 (13th), *Seynt Johan* 1372; from the dedication of the church to St John the Baptist.

St Just w3731 **(in Penwith; parish)** 'Church of *Sanctus Justus*' 1291, *Seint Just* 1342, *Yust* 1524. From the dedication of the church, but almost nothing is known about the saint.

100

He was believed to be buried in the church here, and has dedications also at ST JUST IN ROSELAND and GORRAN HAVEN. The churchtown is also called (once) *Lanuste* 1396, 'church-site of St Just', *lann* + saint's name; and (at a much later date) *Lafrowda* 1732, surviving at Lafrowda Common nearby (W3831), *lann* + unknown word or name. Often called 'St Just in PENWITH', to distinguish it from the next entry.

St Just in Roseland w8435 (parish) 'Church of *Sanctus Justus*' *c*.1070 (17th), *Seynt Just en Rosland c*.1398; from the dedication of the church to the same saint as in the preceding entry. He is first mentioned as *Iust* 10th List (patron saint of this parish). 'Still popularly pronounced Yust (Youst)' 1887; but the pronunciation also developed to 'east' in some names (e.g. *Portheast*, the Cornish name of GORRAN HAVEN). The Cornish name of the churchtown is Lanzeague, found as *Lansioch* 1204, 'church-site of Syek', *lann* + personal name: compare St Seoc in Brittany. For ROSELAND, see the separate entry.

Kea w8142 (parish) So found in 1813. A name and church-dedication transferred from OLD KEA, where the church was very inconveniently situated right at one end of its long parish. Permission to move the church from there was granted in 1532, but it was not done until 1802, when a 'small and hideous' church was built at the present site; The present building replaced that, in turn, in 1895.

Kehelland w6241 (Camborne) Hervey de *Kellyhellan* 1284, *Kahellen* 1707. 'Grove of an ancient church-site', *kelli* + *hen-lann*; but no ecclesiastical connections of the place are known, either archaeologically or in the documentary record. However, there was a 'round' on the farm, now destroyed. It might have been the site of a Dark-Age cemetery, such as is indicated by the name.

Kelly Bray x3571 (Stoke Climsland) Clarice de *Kellibregh c*.1286, John de *Kellibre* 1306, *Kellebrey, Kellybray* 1337. The earliest form looks like 'speckled grove', *kelli* + *brygh*, but all subsequent ones look like 'grove of a hill', *kelli* + *bre*. The latter seems more likely, with reference to KIT HILL nearby.

Kelsey Head w7660 **(coast, Cubert)** So found in *c.*1870. Named from the nearby manor and settlement of Kelsey, W769599, now abandoned. This was called *Kelse* in 1349, *Kelsey* 1539; its meaning is completely obscure.

Kelynack w3729 **(St Just in Penwith)** *Chelenoch* 1086, *Kellenyek* 1284. 'Holly-grove', *kelynnek*, from *kelynn* + *-ek*. Note the Domesday spelling of the sound *k* with the letters *ch*, as regularly in that source.

Kenwyn w8145 **(parish)** 'Church of *Keynwen*' 1259, *Kenwen* 1270, 'chapel of *Sanctus Keynwynus*' 1342. The name was not considered to denote a saint until the middle of the 14th century, and it probably did not do so originally. It appears to be 'white ridge', *keyn* + *gwynn* (or its feminine form *gwenn*), with mutation of *gw* to *w*. Subsequently the name was equated with that of St KEYNE, patron saint of that parish and of Ceinwen or Llangeinwen, in Anglesey; but at Kenwyn she seems to have been regarded as male.

Kerris w4427 **(Paul)** *Kerismoer* 1301, 1302 (+ *meur*, 'great Kerris'), *Kerres* 1302, 1310. A difficult name. It might possibly be the past participle passive of a hypothetical verb *keri* 'fortify' (derived from *ker* 'a round'); if so, *kerys* could mean 'an enclosed or fortified place', but that is very doubtful. There is an ancient enclosure or fortification nearby, called 'Roundago'.

Kestle Mill w8559 **(St Columb Minor)** *Kestell Mill* 1659, *Kestle Mill* 1717. The nearby farm of Kestle, from which the mill was named, was *Castel* 1194, *Kestel* 1345: *castell*, or its plural *kestell*, probably in the sense 'hamlet', though 'fort' and even 'natural rock' are other possible meanings of the word.

St Keverne w7921 **(parish)** *Sanctus Achebrannus* 1086, *Sanctus Akaveranus* 1201, *Seynt Keveran* 1339; from the patron saint of the church. He is first found, as patron saint of St Keverne, in the form *Achobran* 10th List. Nothing is known of him, though he was wrongly equated in the Middle Ages with the Irish St Ciaran of Saighir. The Cornish name of the churchtown was *Lannachebran* 1086, *Lanhevran* 1504, *lann* 'church-site' + saint's name. The *h* in this form is not an irregular mutation of *k*, but a relic of the original *ch* or *gh* sound in the saint's name (Cornish *Aghevran*). The loss of the initial *A-* in this name was probably due mainly to the equation with St Ciaran; but compare ST NEOT for a similar phenomenon.

St Kew X0276 (parish) *Sancta Cypa* (error for *Cywa*) *c*.962 (14th), *Sanctus Cheus* 1086, *Seint Kewe* 1373; from the patron saint of the church. An alternative name for the churchtown was *Lanhoghou seynt* 1284, 'Lanow of the saints' (*sans*; older *sant*, plural *seynt*). This name refers to Lanow, a nearby farm; it is first recorded as 'a monastery called *Docco*' 7th? (11th), *Lannohoo* 1086: 'church-site of Doghow', *lann* + saint's name. St Doghow was joint patron saint of the place with St Kew; they were believed to have been brother and sister, who came to Cornwall from Gwent in south-east Wales. St Kew Highway, X0375, is called simply *Highway* 1699; a hamlet on the main road, distinguished from others of the same name by the parish in which it lies: compare HIGHWAY.

St Keyne X2460 (parish) 'Church of *Sancta Keyna*' 1291, *Seynt Kayn* 1525. From the patron saint of the church; she was believed to be a daughter of King Broccan of Breconshire, in the Welsh versions of the legend (but not in the Cornish one). She has dedications in Wales also, and the parish church of KENWYN was later considered to be dedicated to her. Pronounced like the biblical 'Cain'.

Kilkhampton S2511 (parish) *Chilchetone* 1086, *Kilcton c*.1175 (13th), *Kilkamton* 1194. The original name was presumably *Kylgh*, Cornish *kylgh*, 'a circle', in an unknown sense: perhaps a lost archaeological feature. At a later date English *tún*, 'farm, estate', was added. The *-ham-* is non-original, and is due to analogy with other English names ending in '-hampton'. The estate of *Kelk c*.839 (late 14th), given to the bishop of Sherborne by the Anglo-Saxon king Egbert, may refer to this place, though that is uncertain. If so, the original Cornish name appears, still uncompounded, in that early reference.

Kilmar Tor X2574 (hill, North Hill) *Kilmarhe rock*, *Kilmare rock*, *Kilmar torr c*.1605. Most likely 'horse's back', *keyn* + *margh*, a name for the ridge, with English 'rock' or 'tor' added later. If so, then *keyn* changed into *Kil-* before

103

the date of the earliest spelling. Alternatively, if that spelling is taken as decisive, the name is 'nook of a horse', with *kil* instead; but that is much less likely, since 'horse's back' is a picturesque name for ridges of hills elsewhere in Cornwall, and also in Wales and Brittany: compare English 'hog's back', with similar meaning.

Kingsand X4350 (Maker/Rame) *Kings sand* 1602. English; probably 'beach (*sand*) of a man or family called King', but the surname has not yet been found sufficiently early in either parish. Compare Richard *Kyng* in St Germans, 1522, and Robert and Thomas *Kyng* in Antony, 1544.

Kit Hill X3771 (hill, Stoke Climsland) *Este kit helle* 1535 ('East Kit Hill'). English, 'kite hill', *cyta* + *hyll*. 'Kite' could refer vaguely to any large bird of prey, such as the buzzard. Compare Kittle in Glamorganshire, *Kitehull* 1360; but Kithill in Devon was originally 'kite's nook', with *healh* instead of *hyll*.

Kuggar W7216 (Grade) Henry de *Coger*, Joan *Cogar* 1324, 'mill of *Cuger*' 1336. This may be an ancient British stream-name, meaning 'winding (stream)', comparable with various rivers elsewhere called Cocker, and also the Coker (Somerset). If so, it would here refer to the stream in the Poltesco valley.

Kynance Cove W6813 (coast, Mullion) *Kinance Cove* 1813. The name occurs earlier as *Penkeunans* 1325 ('head of Kynance', with *penn*), *Kynans*, *Penkynans* 1613. 'Ravine, gorge', *cow-nans*, with reference to the valley which emerges at the cove. The modern form is unexpected: 'Cownance' would have been the natural development. It looks as though the name was re-interpreted as containing *ki*, 'dog'.

Ladock W8951 (parish) 'Church of *Sancta Ladoca*' 1268, *Egloslagek* 1354, *Sent Ladek* 1358, *Ladocke* or *Lazacke* 1596; from the patron saint of the church, but virtually nothing is known of her, and there are no dedications in Wales or Brittany. She is first mentioned, as patron saint of this church, as *Latoc* 10th (List). The form *Egloslagek* shows *eglos* 'church' + saint's name. It also shows the original *d* of the saint's name having become 'dzy' (written *g*);

the authentic pronunciation of the same sound as *z*, 'Laz-
zick', lasted well into this century, but the archaic written
form with *d* has prevailed in this parish name. The *a* is
still short, '*Laddack*'.

Lamorna W4424 **(St Buryan/Paul)** 'Port of *Nansmorno*' 1302,
Nansmornou 1319, *Lamorna alias Nansmorna* 1387. 'Valley' (*nans*) + unknown word or name, most likely a
stream-name *Mornow*: 'valley of (the stream) Mornow'.
The meaning of such a stream-name would be unknown;
possibly from the same derivation as a stream in Monmouthshire, called *Murn* in early Welsh. For that name,
compare perhaps Welsh *mwrn*, 'close, sultry'. Note the re-
ductions of *Nans* to *La-* and of *-ou* to *-a* in the modern form,
and that both of these had already occurred by 1387.

Lamorran W8741 **(parish)** *Lannmoren* 969 (11th), *Lamoren*
1291, *Seynt Moren*, 'parish of *Moren*' 1525. 'Church-site of
Moren', *lann* + saint's name. She is the patron saint of the
church, but nothing is known of her. There is a St Moran
honoured in Brittany. Note the lack of mutation of *m* to *v*
(*Lann-voren* might have been expected); it was probably
the parallel name *St Moren*, or the influence of the ancient
written form, which preserved the *m*.

Landrake X3760 **(parish)** *Landerhtun* late 11th, *Lanrach*
1291, *Larrake* c.1605. 'A clearing', *lannergh*. The earliest
form has English *tún*, 'farm, estate', added. The pronunciation '*Larrick*', as in the form of c.1605, is still known
locally. Compare Larrick in the parishes of Lezant and
South Petherwin, X3078 and X3280, for the same development of the word; and LANNER and MUCHLARNICK for
different developments.

Land's End W3425 **(coast, Sennen)** (Port of) *Londeseynde*
1337, *the Londesende of Engelond* 1427; English, self-explanatory. The name also appears translated into Cornish,
as *Pen an gluas*, *Pen an ulays* 1504: 'the end of the land',
penn + *an* + *gwlas* (with mutation of *gw* to *w*). The English
name is more likely to be the original; in local opinion CAPE
CORNWALL seems to have been the more important headland. An older name for the headland was, in English,
Penwihtsteort 997, 'the tail of PENWITH', place-name +
steort; and, in early Welsh, *Penpenwith* 13th, likewise

meaning 'the end of PENWITH'.

Landulph x4361 (parish) *Landelech* 1086, *Landylp* 1280, *Landilp* 1327, *Landulf* 1440, *Landhilp* or *Landylik* c.1485. 'Church-site of *Dylyk* or *Delek*', *lann* + personal name. Compare St *Dilic* (one of the Children of Broccan in the Cornish version of the legend), St Illick (honoured in St Endellion parish), and a Breton St *Dilecq*; but the church at Landulph is dedicated to St Leonard. The apparent change in this name from *-lek* to *-lp* and *-lf* is unexplained.

Laneast x2284 (parish) *Lanast* 1076 (15th), 'chapel of *Lanast*' c.1170 (15th), *Lanayst* c.1226 (15th), 1342; *lann* 'church-site' + unknown word, maybe a personal name.

Langore x2986 (St Stephen by Launceston) *Langover* 1431, 1463. The lack of earlier forms makes interpretation uncertain, but it is probably 'valley with a stream', *nans* + *gover*, with the common change of *Nans-* to *Lan-*. The hamlet is at the head of a small valley which curves down to the River Ottery.

Lanherne, Vale of: see under VALE OF MAWGAN.

Lanhydrock x0863 (parish) *Lanhideroc* 1201, *Lanhidrek* 1327. 'Church-site of Hydrek', *lann* + saint's name. The saint is unique to this place. His feast-day was kept at Bodmin in the 15th century on May 5th, *Sanctus Ydrocus*; but nothing else is known of him.

Lanivet x0364 (parish) *Lannived* 1268, *Lanivet* 1276. 'Church-site (*lann*) at *Neved*'. *Neved*, meaning 'pagan sacred place', must have been a pre-existing place-name in the area; compare places called Nymet in Devon and *Nemet* (a forest) in Brittany, both with the same derivation. The dedication of the church is unknown.

Lanlivery x0759 (parish) *Lanliveri* c.1170, *Lanlyvri* 1235. Probably 'church-site of Livri', *lann* + personal name, though no exactly suitable personal name is known. Compare a place called *Lanlivry* in Brittany, and the similar Welsh personal name *Llifris*. The church is dedicated to a female St Bryvyth, of whom nothing is known.

Lanner w7139 (Gwennap) *Lannergh* 1327. 'A clearing', *lannergh*. Compare LANDRAKE ('Larrick') and MUCHLARNICK, which show typical east-Cornish developments of the same word, while this name shows a west-Cornish one.

Lanreath x1856 (parish) *Lanredoch* 1086, *Lanreythou* 1266, *Lanretha* 1591, *Lanreth* 1656. 'Church-site of Reydhogh', *lann* + personal name; but the form of the personal name is not quite clear. Compare the early Welsh personal name *Rydoch*, but that shows the single vowel *y* in its first syllable, while most medieval spellings of the Cornish place-name have a diphthong, *ey*. The final consonant may have been either *gh* or *k*. Note the early change from *-och* to *-ou* (compare ST WINNOW), then the reduction of that syllable to *-a*, and finally its complete disappearance in the 17th century. The church is dedicated to an unknown St *Manakneu* (?) and to St Dunstan. Pronounced 'Lan*reth*', with short *e*.

Lansallos x1751 (parish) *Lansaluus* 1086, *Lanselewys* 1291, 'church of *Sancta Ilderna* of *Lansalwys*' 1326. Probably 'church-site of (?) Salwys', *lann* + personal name *Salwys, Selwys* or the like, though no such name is known. The church is dedicated to a female St Ildiern, otherwise unknown; William of Worcester, in 1478, mentions her (or rather him) as a bishop, buried in the church.

Latchley x4073 (Calstock) *Lachesleigh* mid-13th (1619), *Lacchislegh* 1318, *Lacchelegh* 1337. English, 'wetland grove', 'grove of wetland', *læc* + *léah*. Below the village is flat, marshy ground, lying in a bend of the River Tamar.

Launcells s2405 (parish) *Landseu* 1086, Richard de *Lanceles* 1204, *Lanceles* 1244. The spelling in Domesday Book is corrupt, and *Lanceles* best shows the original form; *lann* 'church-site' + unknown word or name, perhaps of the form *seles*, or the like (apparently different from the word or name in LANSALLOS).

Launceston x3384 (borough) *Lanscavetone* 1086 (*c* for *t*), *Lanstavaton* c.1125 (14th), *Lanzaventon* 1176, *Lanceton* 1303, *Lawnson, Lanson* 1478. The original name was *Lann-Stefan*, 'church-site of St Stephen', *lann* + saint's name, with English *tún*, 'estate, manor', added later. In 1086 and earlier it referred to ST STEPHENS, across the valley from Launceston, and not to the present town: that had the English name of *Dounhed*, 'hill-end', *dún* + *héafod*, now revived in the archaic form Dunheved. In 1155 the canons of St Stephens moved across to what is now Launceston, and the name was transferred also. Pronounced 'Lanson', as shown already in 1478. The Cornish form of the name (without the addition of English *tún*) lasted as late as 1602, 'by the Cornishmen called *Lesteevan*'.

Lawhitton X3582 (parish) *Landuuithan* 10th, *Landwithan* late 10th, *Languitetone* 1086, *Lanwitinton* 1188, *Lawittetone* 1260. Probably 'valley of Gwethen', *nans* (older *nant*) + personal name; but *lann* 'church-site' is a possible (though less likely) first element, and *gwydhenn* 'tree' (singular of *gwydh*) a possible second one. As at LAUNCESTON and elsewhere, Old English *tún*, 'estate, manor', was added to an older Cornish name. The two earliest forms show the name before *tún* was added, and it first appears in the spelling of 1086; later it was amalgamated with the last syllable of the original Cornish name (*Landwithan-tun* becoming eventually *Lawit-ton*). The original site to which the Cornish name referred was the farm now called Oldwit, in South Petherwin, X322817: *Yoldelanwyta* 1302, *Olde Lawhytta* 1348, 'old Landwithan'. This place is situated at the head of a valley, but not near the church, thus making *nans* more likely than *lann* in the name.

St Lawrence X0466 (Bodmin) 'House of St Laurence' 1288 (15th), *St Laurence*, 'a pore hospital or lazar house' *c.*1540. There was a leper hospital here dedicated in honour of St Lawrence, a 3rd-century Roman martyr; there were still lepers there in the early 17th century.

Leedstown W6034 (Crowan) So found in 1867. A 19th-century village created by the Duke of Leeds, whose family had married into the Godolphin family and had become major landowners in the area: compare TOWNSHEND.

Lelant W5437 (parish) *Lananta* *c.*1170, *Lalant* 1478. 'Church-site of Anta', *lann* + saint's name. All we know of her is she had a chapel on the rocks at the entrance to Hayle River. The church is dedicated to St Euny ('church of *Sanctus Eunius*' *c.*1170). Note change of *n* to *l*, by assimilation to the preceding *L* (contrast NEWLYN).

Lerryn x1457 **(St Veep/St Winnow)** Gilbert de *Leryon* 1284, 'stream of *Lerion*, bridge of *Leryon*' 1289. An obscure name; the meaning 'waters, floods' is possible, perhaps the plural, *lyryon*, of a Cornish word *lyr*, equivalent to Welsh *llyr*, 'ocean, flood'. Alternatively, compare the name of one of the '28 Cities of Britain' in the 9th century, Old Welsh *Cair Lerion* ('unintelligible and unidentified'); also Middle Breton *Coit-Lerien*.

Lesnewth x1390 **(parish)** *Lisniwen* (for *Lisniwet*) 1086, (hundred of) *Lisniwet, Lisneweth* 1201. 'New court', *lys* + *nowydh*. This suggests a contrast with an 'old court' elsewhere, perhaps HELSTONE.

St Levan w3822 **(parish)** 'Parish of *Sanctus Silvanus*' 1327, *Selevan* 1545, *Sent Levane* 1569; from the patron saint of the church, St Selevan. The name is from Latin *Solomon*, but he was early turned into a St *Silvanus* in official records. As at VERYAN, the first syllable of the spoken name, 'Se*lev*an', was then taken to be the prefix 'saint', so that the name itself became 'Levan'. A saint *Salamun* is first mentioned in a Cornish context in the 10th century (List); he also has dedications in Brittany (*Seleven, Salomon*). Several stories were told locally in the last century about St Selevan and his keenness as a fisherman.

Lewannick x2780 **(parish)** *Lanwenuc* c.1125 (14th), *Lawanek* 1334. 'Church-site of Gwenek', *lann* + personal name, with mutation of *Gw* to *w*. The personal name is equivalent to that of the known Breton saint *Guenoc*; compare also Llanwenog in Cardiganshire. The church is dedicated to St Martin.

Ley x1766 **(St Neot)** 'Cross called *Lay Crosse*' 1515, *Ley* 1698. Presumably English, 'clearing', *léah*; but the forms are too late for assurance. A John *Leye* occurs (unlocated) in Foymoor Stannary in 1436, and such a surname (whatever its origin) could instead have given rise to the place-name. The 'cross' in 1515 was probably a stone monument.

Lezant x3379 **(parish)** *Lansant* c.1125 (14th), *Lassant* 1471. Probably 'church-site of Sant', *lann* + personal name, rather than 'holy church-site' (+ *sans*, 'holy', older *sant*). Compare the earliest form for SANCREED, the Welsh personal name *Sant* (father of St David), and in Cornouaille, Brittany, the place-name *Lan Sent* (now Le Saint).

Ligger or Perran Bay W7556 (coast, Perranzabuloe) *Ligger or Piran Bay* 1813. At the north end of the bay is Ligger Point, also so found first in 1813. It is unknown which is the earlier name, and therefore unknown whether Ligger applies primarily to the point or the bay. Obscure, for lack of early forms. Compare possibly dialect *lig* 'seaweed', or Cornish *cleger* 'cliff, crag' (which would suit Ligger Point), though the loss of the initial *c* would be most irregular. The alternative name, Perran Bay, is taken from the patron saint of the parish: see PERRANZABULOE.

Linkinhorne X3173 (parish) *Lankinhorn* c.1175 (1378), 1259, *Lynkynhorne* 1553. 'Church-site of Kenhoarn', *lann* + personal name. The patron saint of the church, however, is St Mylor; compare MYLOR BRIDGE. Still correctly pronounced 'Linkin*horn*' locally, with the stress on the final syllable; but such a final-syllable stress is often moved forward to the first syllable, resulting here in '*Link*inhorn' (compare BODMIN). The first *i* in the modern form is no doubt due to assimilation to the second. Note, in this east-Cornish name, the lack of the expected mutation of *k* to *g*.

Liskeard X2564 (parish) *Lys Cerruyt* c.1010, *Liscarret* 1086, *Liskyrres* 1298. Probably 'court of Kerwyd', *lys* + personal name. (The suggested name 'court of stags', with *kerwyd* a possible plural of *carow*, 'stag', is much less likely.) A few forms, such as that of 1298, show the expected Middle Cornish pronunciation with -*d* becoming -*s*, but the archaic written form prevailed in this important borough and Duchy manor. Pronounced 'Lis*card*'.

Little Petherick: see under P.

Lizard W7012 (Landewednack) *Lisart* 1086, *Lesard* 1302, *Lesarth* 1323, *Lezard* 1451. 'Court on a height', *lys* + *ardh*. Such a name should have been stressed on the last syllable, so it must be assumed that the modern pronunciation, '*Liz*ard', is the result of a stress-shift, presumably under English influence. Note also the change of -*dh* to -*d*. Lizard Point W6911 (coast) is *le Forlond de Lysard* 1427, *Lyzart poynt* c.1540; it was an important navigational landmark. See PREDANNACK for a possible Cornish name of the headland.

Lockengate x0361 **(Luxulyan)** *Locken Gate* 1748, *'Locking Gate* Toll Gate'* 1839. English, 'lockable gate', for the turnpike toll here.

The Loe w6424 **(pool, Sithney/Wendron)** *La Loo* 1337. 'Pool, inlet', *logh*. Compare LOOE.

Logan Rock w3921 **(coast, St Levan)** *The Logan Stone* 1754. English, 'rocking stone', from dialect *to log*, 'to rock'; but the origin of the term is unknown. It seems to originate in Cornwall, though it was used in Devon and Ireland in antiquarian and travel writings.

Longdowns w7434 **(Stithians/Mabe)** *Long Downs* 1841. English, self-explanatory: a 19th-century hamlet on former downland.

Longships w3225 **(coast, Sennen)** *Langeshipes* 1347, *Longships rock* 1576. English, 'long ship(s)'; not in the sense 'viking ship(s)', for that is a learned, not a popular term, not recorded until 1568 and unlikely to appear in a placename. The name must have been given from a fancied resemblance of the rocks to a long ship or ships. It is unlikely to contain a Cornish word *long*, 'ship' (otherwise unknown), corresponding to Welsh *llong*, with English 'ship' added as a repetitive translation; for the *a* in the first spelling contradicts that and favours English 'long' (older *lang*) instead.

Looe x2553 **(St Martin by Looe/Talland)** *Loo* c.1220 (1320), *Lo* 1237. 'Pool, inlet', *logh*. Until the 16th century the name normally meant East Looe; West Looe is named in Cornish as *Porthbighan* c.1286, and in English as *Westlow* c.1540, *West Loo or Portbyhen* 1622; 'little harbour', *porth* + *byghan*. Looe Bay x2652 (coast) is so found in 1813. For Looe Island see ST GEORGE'S ISLAND.

Lostwithiel x1059 **(Lanlivery)** 'Market at *Lostwetell*' 1194, 'burghers of *Lostuuidiel*' c.1194, *Lostudiel* 1195-98, *Lostwithiel* early 13th. 'Tail of the forest', *lost* + *gwydhyel* 'forest, wooded area', adjective formed of *gwydh* 'trees' + *yel*. Compare WITHIEL for another, independent, instance of the same word.

Lower Sharpnose Point: see under S.

Luckett x3873 **(Stoke Climsland)** *Lovecott* 1557, *Lucot* 1813.
English, probably 'Leofa's cottage', personal name + *cot*.
Compare Luccombe (Wiltshire), from *Lovecombe* 1283. But
earlier forms of the Cornish name are needed.

Ludgvan w5033 **(parish)** *Luduhan* 1086, *Luduan* c.1170,
Ludwan 1201, 'church of *Ludewon*' 1291, *Lusewan* 1454,
Lusvan 1569. Probably 'place of ashes', from *lusow* (older
ludw) + *-an*; the reason would be unknown, but perhaps
from an ancient burial-site found nearby, and now lost.
Note the epenthetic vowel in the form of 1291. The place
was occasionally thought to take its name from a supposed
patron saint of the church ('church of *Sanctus Ludewanus*'
1319), but the saint was evidently invented from the place-
name. Pronounced 'Ludjan' or 'Lidjan'.

Luxulyan x0558 **(parish)** 'Chapel of *Luxulian*' 1282, *Lansu-
lien* 1337, *Luxilyan* 1343. 'Chapel of Sulyen,' *log* + personal
name. The element *lann* 'church-site' occasionally replaced *log* (e.g. in the form of 1337), through analogy with
other names; but *log* is evidently original — the only instance in Cornwall of the common Breton element. In
Brittany, it is generally followed by the name of the patron
saint of the church or chapel; but the church here is dedicated to the universal Saints Ciricius and Julitta. Perhaps
the name of Julitta was suggested by a former dedication,
now forgotten, to the Breton saint Sulien. Pronounced
'Luk*sill*yan', with regular change of Cornish *u* to *i* (compare TRESILLIAN); but in spelling this parish name has
retained the archaic *u*.

River Lynher x2678—x4257 **(river)** *Linar* late 11th, *Liner*
c.1125, *Linner, Lynner* early 17th. This river-name of uncertain meaning has parallels elsewhere, in the River
Lynor in Devon and the river Llynor in Merionethshire,
SJ0538. Several possible derivations have been suggested,
including roots *lei-* meaning 'to flow' and 'to glide'; no definite conclusion is possible. The suffix *-ar* is presumably
the same as in the River TAMAR. Note the pronunciation
with short *i*, shown in the 17th-century spellings; but long
i (as in English 'liner') is now common.

Mabe Burnthouse W7634 (Mabe) *Burnt House* 1813.
English; *Burnthouse* is self-explanatory, but the reason for
the name is not known. There are other instances of the
same name in Cornwall, and one in west Devon, mostly
appearing in the 18th century or later. One of them is close
to Mabe Burnthouse, Burnthouse in St Gluvias, W7636
(first recorded in 1699); so the present one is identified by
being 'in the parish of Mabe'. Mabe itself is found as 'Chapel of *Sanctus Laudus*' 1309 (late 14th), *Lavabe* 1524,
Mape 1549, *St Mabe* 1559: 'church-site of Mab', *lann* + personal name (with mutation of *M* to *v*), with later loss of
lann and restoration of the unmutated *M*. The church, formerly a chapel of Mylor, is dedicated to St Laud or Lo, a
6th-century bishop of Coutances in Normandy.

St Mabyn X0473 (parish) Stephen de *Sancta Mabena*
c.1210, 'church of *Sancta Mabena*' 1266, 'parish of *Sanctus Maubanus*', William *Sent Maban* 1327. From the
dedication of the church; St *Mabon* was believed to be one
of the 24 sons and daughters of King Broccan in the Cornish version of the legend. The saint's gender is variable in
the Latin references, but the majority make it female.

Madron W4531 (parish) 'Church of *Sanctus Madernus*' 1203,
Madern 1310, *Eglosmaddarn* 1370, *Maddron* 1524. From
the patron saint of the church, but nothing is known about
him; compare possibly the male Breton saint Meron (latinised *Mactronus*). However, there is a female Welsh saint
Madrun, who may be identical, venerated at Trawsfynydd,
Merionethshire: if so, the gender changed in the Cornish
tradition. Some forms contain *eglos* 'church' + saint's
name; but the churchtown also had another Cornish name,
Eglos Maderne alias Landythy 1616, surviving as Landithy W452317: *lann* + unknown word or name. The
pronunciation 'Maddern' is still known.

Maidenwell X1470 (Cardinham) *Medenawille* 1347. English, 'the maidens' spring', *mægden* + *wiella*. Similar
names are known elsewhere, notably Maidenwell (Lincolnshire) and Maidwell (Northamptonshire). They may
sometimes refer to a folk custom.

Malpas w8442 (St Clement/St Michael Penkevil) *Le Mal Pas* late 12th (late 13th), Hugh de *Malpas* 1383, *Molpus alias Mopus* 1674. French, 'bad step', with reference to the river-crossing here. The same name occurs elsewhere, for example in Cheshire, Monmouthshire and Cumberland. The name is likely to have been given in the 12th century, and suggests that the river here was regularly, though unpleasantly, crossed at that period. The earliest spellings are from the Tristan poem by the Norman poet Beroul, who relates an episode illustrating the difficulties of the crossing. There is now a foot-ferry. The 17th-century form shows the pronunciation.

Manaccan w7625 (parish) 'Church of *Ministre*' 1259, 'church of *Sancta Manaca* in *Menstre*' 1309, *Managhan* 1395. It is unknown whether the dedication to 'Sancta Manaca' is genuine, or derived from an older place-name. However, there is an early Welsh personal name *Manachan*, and a saint with a similar name is honoured at LANREATH; so this is probably a place-name derived from a church dedication. The lone early vernacular form, *Managhan*, could suggest instead 'place of monks', *managh + -an* (?). This could suit the place, situated as it is within the district of MENEAGE, 'the monkish area'; but it is linguistically improbable. The alternative name of *Ministre* seems to be English *mynster* 'minster church', rather than an equivalent Cornish word. There is no trace, in documents or on the ground, of a former monastic church here.

The Manacles w8120 (coast, St Keverne) So found in *c*.1605; 'rock called *Mannahackles alias Manacles*' 1619; 'pronounced *Meanácles*' 1808. This might be an English name, from the trap which these rocks offer to shipping; but the form of 1619, and the pronunciation given in 1808, if genuine, suggest rather a Cornish stress-pattern. In that case the Cornish derivation 'church stone(s)', *men* (or plural *meyn*) + *eglos*, could well be right. This could be either a fancied resemblance, from their sharpness, or perhaps a reference to the spire of St Keverne church, viewed as a landmark from the sea. Manacle Point w8121 (coast) is *The Manacles poynte* 1576, thus indirectly providing the earliest reference to the Manacles themselves as well.

Man and his Man: see under BAWDEN ROCKS.

Marazion w5130 (St Hilary) John de *Petitmarche*, John de
Parvo Foro c.1220 (14th), *Marghasbigan* c.1265 (14th),
Marhasbean 1532, *Marhasvean* 1591, *Marhasion* 1601.
'Little market', *marghas + byghan*. The late change of the
b to *v*, and its subsequent loss, are irregular. The two earliest references show the same name, 'little market',
translated into French and Latin respectively. The alternative name of the town is Market Jew; this was originally
a separate place adjacent to Marazion, and it is mentioned
as *marcatum ... die quinte ferie*, 'a market on the fifth week-
day', in c.1070 (14th), *Marghasyou* c.1210 (14th),
Marchadiou 1291: 'Thursday market', *marghas + yow*.
References to Marazion are in fact less common than those
to Market Jew in the medieval period, presumably because
the 'little' market was the less important of the two; but
both existed already in the 11th century: 'both the fairs of
the Mount' are mentioned in c.1080 (12th); note also certain fairs 'formerly held at *Marghasbigan*, now to be held
at *Marchadyou*' in c.1265 (14th), and '*Marcasiou* beside
Marcasbyghan' 1310. The two places were merging by
c.1600: *Marhasion alias Marghasiewe* 1601.

Marhamchurch s2203 (parish) *Maronecirche* 1086, *Mar-*
wenecherche 1275, 'church of *Sancta Merwenna* alias
Marwenchurch' 1400, *Marwynchurche alias Marham-*
churche 1417. English, 'church of St Marwen', saint's
name + *cirice*. She was believed to be a woman, one of the
24 sons and daughters of King Broccan according to Cornish tradition; but in fact she could be the English St
Merwenn (*Merewenna* in Latin), 10th-century abbess of
Romsey in Hampshire, under a Cornish guise.

Markwell x3658 (St Erney) *Ælmarches wylle* late 11th,
Adam de *Markewelle* 1199. English, 'Ælmarch's spring',
personal name + *wiella*. The personal name is unusual,
possibly a hybrid composed of late Old English *Æl-* + Old
Cornish *march*. Note how the interpretation of the name
would be impossible if the 11th-century form were lacking.

Marshgate x1591 (St Juliot/Otterham) *Marsh Gate* 1748.
English, self-explanatory: 'gate at (or leading to) a marsh';

compare DOWNGATE, etc.

St Martin w7323 **(parish; in Meneage)** 'Chapel of *Sanctus Martinus*' 1342, *Sent Martin yn Meneck* 1549. From the dedication of the church to St Martin of Tours, the 4th-century Gaulish bishop. But an alternative name was 'parish of *Sanctus Dydminus*' 1327, 'church of *Sanctus Martinus* alias *Dydemin*' 1385, apparently a dedication to a completely unknown male saint, Dydemin or similar.

St Martin x2555 **(parish; by Looe)** *Martistowe* c.1220 (1320), 'church of *Sanctus Martinus*' 1282, *St Marten by Loo* 1516. From the dedication of the parish church to St Martin of Tours, as above. The earliest form is English, 'St Martin's holy place', saint's name + *stów*.

St Martin's v9215 **(island, Scilly)** *Seynt Martyns* c.1540, *St Martines Isle* c.1540; from the dedication of the church. This island is probably the place in Scilly which was earlier called *Bechiek* (error for *Bre-*) 1319, *Brethiek* 1336, *Brechiek* 1390, probably meaning 'place with arms', '(island or district) of promontories', the adjective of *bregh* 'arm' + *-ek*, with reference to the convoluted coastline along the north side of the island.

St Mary's v9111 **(island, Scilly)** 'Church of *Sancta Maria* of *Heumor*' (error for *Hennor*) c.1175 (13th), 'island of *Sancta Maria*' 1375, *Seynt Mary island* 1478. From the dedication of the church. *Heumor* in the earliest reference is a corrupt form of the original name which denoted the single land-mass formed by all of northern Scilly, before it sank and became sub-divided into the present islands. This name is also found as 'island of *Ennore*' 1193 (16th), 'castle of *Enoer*' 1306, 'island called *Enor*' 1372. Probably 'the ground, the land', *an* + *dor* (Old Cornish *en* + *doer*, becoming *En-nor*), meaning 'the main land-mass'. The name became obsolete after the feature to which it referred was subdivided. St Mary's Sound v8809 **(coast)** is *St Mary Sownde* c.1540: English *sound* 'strait, sailable channel'.

St Mawes w8433 **(St Just in Roseland)** 'Town of *Sanctus Maudetus*' 1284, 1302, *Seint Mauduyt* 1342, *Lavousa, Lavausa* 1445, *Seynt Mausa* 1467, *St Maws, St Mausa alias La Vousa* c.1540. From the patron saint of the chapel. He

116

is a saint venerated widely in Brittany, where he was believed to have come from Ireland. In Breton the original form of the name seems to have been *Maudith*, regularly becoming *Maudez*. The best way to reconcile the forms of the Cornish name with the Breton one would be to suppose that the *t* of the Cornish forms stood for *th* (meaning 'Sanctus Maudethus', 'St Maudyth'). In later Cornish that would regularly have become *Mauseth* (which is not found), then *Mausa*, as shown in the form of 1467. But this scheme would be happier if forms such as *Maudethus* and *Mauseth*, showing the *th*, were actually found. The Cornish name of the town is shown by the forms preceded by *La-*, representing 'church-site of Mausa', *lann* + saint's name. Compare the Middle Breton place-name latinised as *Lanna Maudeti*.

Mawgan W7025 (parish; in Meneage) *Scanctus Mawan*, *Santmauuant* 1086, *Sanctus Mauganus* 1206, *Seynt Mowgan in Maneke* 1470. From the patron saint of the church. He is venerated in Wales as St Meugan, particularly in south-west Wales, where a chapel of his was still a centre for pilgrimage in the late 16th century; and in Brittany as St Maugan or Mogan. He occurs as *Maucan* in the 10th-century List, already as patron saint of the Meneage church. He is also portrayed as a wise man, living in South Wales, in Welsh saints' Lives and in Geoffrey of Monmouth's *History of the Kings of Britain*, where he encouraged King Vortigern to believe the strange tale of Merlin's conception; he later became bishop of Silchester.

St Mawgan W8765 (parish; in Pydar) 'Church of *Sanctus Mauchanus* of *Lanherno*' 1257, Maurice de *Seyntmogan* 1284, 'church of *Sanctus Mauganus*' 1291, *Mawgan* 1543. From the dedication of the church; see the preceding name. The saint was honoured in Exeter as *Sanctus Maucannus* in *c*.1100, probably because the dedication at St Mawgan in Pydar already existed. In the Middle Ages the church was often referred to as the 'church of Lanherne', the name of the adjacent manor and evidently of the churchtown: see VALE OF MAWGAN OR LANHERNE. Mawgan Porth W8567 is English, dialect *porth* 'cove'. It is a translation of the older Cornish name, *Porthmawgan* 1755, Cornish

117

porth + saint's name. Earlier still it was called *Porthglyv-yan* 1331, from the nearby farms called Gluvian; an unexplained name, probably that of the stream which emerges here. Note also Thomas *Porth* in the parish in 1327, and *Porth* (a place) in 1419, *Porth in Mawgan* 1659.

Mawla w7045 (St Agnes) *Maula* 1302, 1316, 1327. Completely obscure, despite the consistent early spellings. It is unlikely to be a compound in *le*, 'place', for that ought to be spelt *-le* at the date of the earliest forms.

Mawnan w7827 (parish) 'Church of *Sanctus Maunanus*' 1281, 1291, *Seynt Maunan* 1398. From the patron saint of the parish church, but nothing is known about him. Mawnan Smith W7728 is *Mawnan smith* 1699: compare 'a smith at Mawnan' *c.*1645; probably from a smithy at the cross-roads here (compare SHOP), though a family called Smith is also possible.

St Mellion x3865 (parish) 'Church of *Sanctus Melanus*' 1259, *St Melyn* 1544, *Millians* 1553. Named from the patron saint of the church, the Breton or Frankish St Melaine, 6th-century bishop of Rennes. During his reign there, two British priests came to work in Brittany, introducing insular-Celtic practices to the country. With two other Gallic bishops, St Melaine wrote a letter (still extant) to the priests, threatening to excommunicate them. See MULLION for another dedication to the same saint.

Menabilly x1051 (Tywardreath) Hilary de *Menabilyou* (?) 1354, *Mynabile* 1525; *Mynnybelly alias Mennebile* 1573. Uncertain, for lack of early forms. The lone medieval form, that of 1354, is an uncertain reading. The name could be 'stone of colts', *men* + *ebelyow* (?), plural of *ebel*, though the form of the plural of that word is not certain.

Meneage (district) *Manech c.*1070 (14th), *Manahec* 1269, *Menek* early 16th. 'Monkish (land)', *managhek*, *managh* 'monk' + *-ek*. The district must already have been so called in the tenth century, when it appears as part of the name *Les-manaoc* 967 (11th), now the farm of Lesneage (St Keverne, W770220), 'the court (*lys*) of the Meneage'. The district was never of any administrative significance during the historic period, and its limits are therefore slightly uncertain; but it is generally considered to incorporate the five parishes of ST KEVERNE, ST MAWGAN in Meneage, ST MARTIN in Meneage, MANACCAN, and ST ANTHONY in Meneage. The monastic significance of the name is uncertain: it may refer to the presence of several Celtic monasteries in the district (say, at St Keverne, St Anthony and Manaccan?), though St Keverne is the only place here which certainly had one. Later, from *c.*1070 onwards, much of the area was owned by the monastery of Mont St Michel, and later St Michael's Mount; but that cannot explain the name, since the Meneage was already so called when they acquired it, and apparently as early as 967. Pronounced 'Me*nayg*' or 'Me*neeg*' (compare BREAGE).

Menheniot x2862 (parish) *Mahiniet* 1260, *Mahenyet* 1318, *Mahynyet* 1362 and normally in the 14th-15th centuries. The *n* in the first syllable (*Men-*) appears first in *Menhynyheth* 1342, and after that sporadically, with increasing frequency in the 16th century and becoming standard in the 17th; forms without it lasted as late as *Mehenett* 1553. It is clearly not original to the name, but is due instead to analogy with other names starting *Men-*, perhaps helped by infection from the second syllable. This means that explanations requiring that letter, such as 'monastery of St Neot' (*Meneghi-Nyot*), are invalid. The name is 'land of Hunyad' or 'land of Hynyed', from *ma* 'a plain' + personal name, perhaps of the form *Hunyad*. The spellings would prefer a personal name *Hynyed*, but no such name is known. The undulating uplands comprising the parish are not really a 'plain', but the senses of *ma* are not precisely known; the meaning here may be 'plateau' or 'fertile district', or possibly 'territory'. The lands are locally reckoned among the most fertile in the county.

Merrymeet x2766 (Menheniot) *Merrymeet* 1699. English, 'pleasant meeting-place': a fairly common name for places where several roads meet. Compare Merrymeet at Whiddon Down, Devon (SX693927, so found in 1765), and Merrymeeting in Blisland, Camborne and Gwennap parishes. The names might be thought to suggest former public-houses at the places; but in fact there does not seem to be any record of inns at them.

St Merryn w8874 (parish) *Sancta Marina* 1259, 'church of *Sancta Maryna*' 1342, *Seynt Meryn* 1379. From the patron saint of the church. Modern writers have equated her with St Marina, an early saint of Asia Minor who, as a child, was smuggled into a monastery by her father when he became a monk; she subsequently lived all her life as a monk, except for five years' penance after being accused, and found guilty, of fathering the child of a local innkeeper's daughter. But the saint here is more likely to be the Celtic saint Merin or Meren, honoured in Wales and Brittany, though he was considered to have been male, whereas the Cornish saint was traditionally female.

Merther w8644 (parish) *Eglosmerthe* 1201 (*-e* for *-er*), *Eglosmerther* 1302, 1327, *Merther* 1549, *St Murther* 1569. The churchtown farm is still called Eglosmerther; but the original name must have been *Merther*, 'place claiming relics' (*merther*), with *eglos* added later ('the church at *Merther*'). The patron saint, named as Coan in a few documents (e.g. in 1511), is unique to this church; it is presumably his remains which were honoured here. 'St Murther' no doubt arose from a misunderstanding of *Eglosmerther*.

Mevagissey x0145 (parish) *Meffagesy* c.1400, 'church of *Sanctae Meva et Ida*' 1427, *Meva and Issey alias Mevagissey* 1639, 1737. From the dedication of the church to two saints, Meva and (*hag*) Issey. They are first named, as patron saints of this church, as *Memai* and *Iti* (pronounced 'Mevai' and 'Idi') in the 10th-century List. Nothing is known of the former, who has no other dedications; for the latter, see ST ISSEY, though the saint was here thought to be female, but there usually male. The older name of the churchtown and parish was *Lammorech* c.1210, *Lammorek* 1259, surviving as Levorrick: 'maritime church-site', *lann + morek* (adjective of *mor* 'sea' + *-ek*), or 'church-site of Morek', *lann* + personal name. Mevagissey Bay X04 (coast) is so found in 1813, and is described in c.1540 as 'a sandy bay, wither to fischar bootes repair for a socour'. The port and harbour were called *Porththilly* 1327, *Porthiley alias Levorick* 1694; perhaps 'cove of brine', *porth* + possibly *hyli*.

St Mewan W9951 (parish) 'Church of *Sanctus Mawanus*'
1291, 'church of *Sanctus Mewanus*' 1297, *Seynt Mewen*
1380, 1397. From the dedication of the church. St Mewan
is well-known in Brittany; he was believed to have been an
aristocrat of south-east Wales, related to St Samson, and
to have accompanied the latter to Brittany, where he
founded a monastery (now St Méen) and received dona-
tions of land from the local ruler, Judicael. He is first
mentioned as patron saint of the Cornish church in the
10th-century List, in the form *Megunn* ('Mewinn'). The
early spelling in diocesan records is usually *Mewanus*,
where the *a* is unexpected; but the later vernacular forms
show a more accurate version of the name.

St Michael Caerhays W9642 (parish) 'Chapel of *Sanctus
Michael* of *Karihaes*' 1259, *Lanvyhayll* 1473-1478. From
the dedication of the church to St Michael the Archangel;
the second form shows *lann* 'church-site' + saint's name
(with mutation of *m* to *v*). The parish is distinguished from
other dedications to the same saint by the addition of the
name of the manor, now Caerhays Castle W941416. As well
as *Karihaes* 1259, this is found as *Karieis*, *Caryheys* 1297,
Kerihayes 1313. A baffling name; it must be considered
along with various Breton places called Carhaix. The most
important is Carhaix-Plouguer (Finistère), an ancient tribal centre at an important cross-roads; the others are less
ancient (16th-century or later). The forms of Carhaix are
similar, but not identical, to the Cornish ones: *Caer Ahes*
1084 (12th), *Karahes* 12th. Note the discrepancies, whereby the Cornish name has *-yhaes* or *-yheys*, while the Breton
one has *-ahes*, so it is not even certain that the two names
are identical; but the similarity is too great to ignore. Despite much discussion, there is no agreed explanation for
Carhaix. It is even uncertain whether it contains *ker*
'camp, fort' (also 'village' in Breton), but the probability is
that it does not. One recent explanation is that the name
means 'drivable road', but that is very uncertain. Previous
explanations for the second part included 'field', and 'Ahes,
a princess who had ancient tracks built'. None of these is
very satisfactory, and the two names, Carhaix and Caerhays, remain a mystery.

St Michael Penkevil W8542 (parish) 'Church of *Sanctus Michael* of *Penkevel*' 1261, 1264. From the dedication of the church; distinguished by the addition of the name of the medieval manor, Penkevil W867409. This is first found as *Penkevel c.*1210; probably 'horse's head', *penn + kevyll*, though the second element is uncertain. The reason for such a name is unknown, but place-names meaning 'head of (some particular) animal' are quite common, most often perhaps due to a fancied resemblance of a piece of land to that animal's head. The area including the manor is on a promontory between two tidal rivers, so the name may contain *penn* in the sense 'headland'.

St Michael's Mount W5129 (island) '*Sanctus Michael* beside the sea', mid-11th (12th), 'the mount of *Sanctus Michael* of Cornwall' *c.*1070 (14th), *Mount Mychell, le Mont Myghellmont* 1478, *Seynt Mychell Mount* 1479. Self-explanatory; according to William of Worcester in 1478, St Michael was believed to have appeared here in A.D. 710, one of his three ancient apparitions. The Mount and its priory were given to Mont St Michel in France, though it is uncertain when that happened — either by Edward the Confessor in *c.*1030, if the first reference is from a genuine charter, or by Robert, Count of Mortain, in *c.*1070. The reason for the donation was presumably the similarity of the two sites. It is not known whether there was a Celtic monastery at the site before its donation to Mont St Michel. In antiquarian writings, the Mount is given a Cornish name, *Cara Clowse in Cowse*, 'The Hoare Rocke in the Wood' 1602; *Carrack Looes en Cooes*, 'a hoary or venerable rock in the wood or Forest' late 17th: 'grey rock in the wood', *carrek + loes + yn + coes*. But there is no evidence that this was a genuine place-name, and it is probably an antiquarian coinage.

Michaelstow X0878 (parish) 'Church of *Sanctus Michael* of Hellesbiri' 1279, Thomas de *Mihelstou* 1311, '*Stouwe* of *Sanctus Michael* by *Hellisbiri*' 1315, *Michestouwe* 1327. English, 'St Michael's holy place', saint's name + *stów*. The farm of Mixtow in Lanteglos by Fowey (X129529) has the same derivation, and similar early forms easily confused with those of Michaelstow. The place from which the church was named in some of the references is Helsbury, X088798, and the church is mentioned earlier as 'church of *Hellestone*' 1260 (see HELSTONE, nearby). Helsbury is named from the same Cornish *Hen-lys* 'old court' as Helstone, with the addition of English *burh* 'fort', referring to the hill-fort of Helsbury Castle, X0879.

Millbrook X4252 **(Maker)** *Milbrok* 1342. English, 'stream with a mill', *myln* + *bróc*. The site of the mill is not now known, though its existence is implied in 1602.

Minions X2671 **(Linkinhorne/St Cleer)** *Mimiens borroughe* 1613 (*m* for *nn*, '*Minniens* barrow'), *Minions* (a village) 1897. A 19th-century mining-village, named from a nearby tumulus now called Minions Mound, X260711. The derivation of the name is obscure; it is tempting to see it as containing *men* 'stone', with reference to the nearby stone circles called THE HURLERS; but it is hard to see how the name could contain either singular or plural (*meyn*) of that word. English *minion* 'a darling, a lover' is used in various transferred senses, including 'a small type of gun' (16th-17th centuries), and 'a type of peach' (17th-18th centuries), and it may be some use of that word which is present here. Minions village was earlier called *Cheesewring Railway* 1888, from a railway leading to the quarry at Cheesewring, X2572. The latter name was *Wringcheese* 1602, *Cheswring Rock* c.1605: English, 'cheese-press', from the remarkable natural tor here.

St Minver W9677 **(parish)** 'Church of *Sancta Menfreda*' 1256, *Seynt Mynfre* 1374, *Minver* 1543. From the patron saint of the church. St *Menfre* was believed to be one of the 24 children of King Broccan of Breconshire, according to the Cornish version of the legend. Stories about her were still locally current in the 16th century; she repudiated the devil's unwanted attentions by throwing her comb at him.

Mitchell W8654 **(St Enoder)** *Meideshol* 1239, *la Medeshole* 1284, 1325, *Medschole* 1401. English, seemingly 'maid's hollow', *mægd* + *hol*. The 'hollow' would be the dip in the main road where the village lies; the interpretation of the first part as 'maid' is not certain, but the word would fit the available spellings, and no other English word or name presents itself.

Mithian w7450 (St Agnes) *Mithien* 1201, *Mithian* 1298. A completely obscure name, despite the consistent early forms. It looks Cornish rather than English, and is clearly an ancient name; but no Cornish, Welsh or Breton word is known that could explain it.

Morvah w4035 (parish) *Morveth* 1327, 1337, 'chapel of *Sanctae Brigida et Morvetha*' 1390, *Sancta Morpha* 1435. 'Sea-grave', a compound of *mor* + *bedh* (with mutation of *b* to *v*). There is a farm called Merthyr beside the church, W401354: it is 'place with a saint's relics', *merther*. This confirms that a saint's grave was revered here, but the name of the saint is unknown: 'St Morveth' is due to a re-interpretation of the place-name. William of Worcester in 1478 recorded that '*Sanctus Morianus* martyr' was buried in the parish of *Sanctus Morianus*, above the sea-shore west of Penzance. This unidentifed place probably refers to Morvah. If so, it further confirms the meaning 'sea-grave', and it may also give a unique indication of the saint's name. The church is dedicated to St Bridget of Sweden (founder of the Bridgettine order of nuns), who died in Rome in 1373 and was canonised in 1391.

Morval x2656 (parish) *Morval* 1238. A completely obscure place-name. It looks like a compound of which the first part could be *mor*, 'sea', and the church is situated close to the head of a tidal creek; but no plausible explanation for the second part presents itself.

Morwenstow s2015 (parish) Lucy de *Morwestewe* 1201, *Morwennestohe* 1273, *Morwenestowe* 1284, 1291, '*Sancta Morwinna*, virgin, lies in the church' 1478. English, 'St Morwenna's holy place', saint's name + *stów*. She was believed to be one of the 24 sons and daughters of King Broccan of Breconshire, according to the Cornish version of the legend. Locally she was believed to have helped the parishioners build the church by carrying up a stone for the font from the shore on her head, and by showing the correct spot for the church; and in 1478, apparently, she was believed to be buried here.

Mount w7856 (Perranzabuloe) So found in 1841. English, a 19th-century hamlet, situated half-way up a long hill.

Mount X1468 **(Warleggan)** So found in 1839. English, a 19th-century hamlet situated 500 feet up on former downland. The nearby farm of Mount Pleasant (X145681) is rather older (so found in 1612; self-explanatory), and *Mount* may be simply an abbreviated version of that name.

Mount Edgcumbe X4552 **(Maker)** 'Peter Edgcombe of *Monte Edgcomb* within the countye of Devon' 1579. (This part of Maker parish was formerly in Devon.) The house was built by Sir Richard Edgcumbe, starting in about 1547, and was named after the family. Their previous seat was COTEHELE, and the family surname comes ultimately from the hamlet of Edgcumbe, just over the River Tamar in Devon, X398791.

Mount Hawke W7147 **(St Agnes)** *Mount Hawk* 1813. An 18th/19th-century mining village, named from a local family which first appears with Thomas and Mary Hawke, living in the parish in 1758.

Mountjoy W8760 **(Colan)** Ralph *Meyndi* 1277, *Meyndy* 1284 (1602), *Munjoy* 1735. 'Stone-house', *meyn-ji* (older *meyndi*), with English re-interpretation by analogy with names such as Mount Pleasant.

Mount's Bay W52 **(coast)** *Le Mountesbaye* 1354; English, named from ST MICHAEL'S MOUNT.

Mousehole W4626 **(Paul)** *Pertusum muris* ('hole of a mouse') 1242, *Musehole* 1284, *Mousehole* 1302, *Mowssel*, *Mowssal* 1580 (18th). English, 'mouse-hole', *mús* + *hol*. The name refers to a large cave nearby in the cliffs (The Mousehole, W468257). Compare Mousehole, inland in Devon (SS569090; first recorded in 1330). Near to the Cornish village was a place called *Portheness* 1267, '*Porthenys* beside *Mosehole*' 1310; 'harbour of an island', *porth* + *ynys*, with reference to ST CLEMENT'S ISLE at its entrance. This was later used as a Cornish name for Mousehole itself (*Moushole called Porthennis* late 17th). Pronounced 'Mowzle' (rhyming with 'tousle'), by natural development, as seen already in 1580: compare ROUGH TOR for a similar pronunciation of an English name.

Muchlarnick X2156 **(Pelynt)** *Lanher*, *Lanner* 1086, *Muchele Lanrak* 1307, *Michellarniak* 1415: 'great Larnick'.

The original simple name was Cornish *lannergh* 'clearing' (compare LANNER); the place was later divided, and the two parts were distinguished by the addition of Middle English *muchel* 'great' and *lutel* 'little' (*Lyttyllavracke*, with *v* for *n*, 1525, now Little Larnick X223553).

Mullion W6719 (parish) Peter of *Sanctus Melanius*, of *Sanctus Melanus* c.1225 (14th) and 1241 (14th), 'church of *Sanctus Melanus*' 1262, 1309, *Seynt Melan* 1284, *Eglosmeylyon* 1342, *Moullian* 1569. From the patron saint of the church: see ST MELLION for details of him. Some forms of the place-name show *eglos* 'church' + saint's name. Mullion Cove W6617 (coast) is so found in c.1870. It is also still called by its Cornish name, Porth Mellin, 'cove of a mill', *porth* + *melin*; there was a mill here in 1840 (compare PORTMELLON). Mullion Island W6617 (coast) is so found in 1813, but was earlier called in Cornish *Inispriven* c.1540: 'reptile island', *ynys* + *pryvenn*, probably a fanciful name from its shape. It is also called *Gull Rock* 1699, 1748: compare GULLAND ROCK.

Mylor Bridge W8036 (Mylor) So found in 1745; the place is earlier referred to as *Ponsnowythe* 1562, *Penowith* 1699; 'new bridge', *pons* + *nowydh*. The same name occurs translated as *New bridge* in 1597. Probably 'New' was dropped from the translated name, giving *Bridge* simply (though that is not found), and the parish name was then added to distinguish this *Bridge* from others elsewhere. The parish of Mylor is named from the patron saint of the parish church: he is first mentioned in association with the Cornish parish as *Meler* in the 10th-century List, and he was believed to be a Cornish or Breton prince. When he was a child, his hand and foot were chopped off and replaced with silver ones which grew with him; he was later martyred. He is venerated also at Linkinhorne and at Amesbury (Wiltshire), and in Brittany.

Nancegollan W6332 (Crowan) John *Nansecolon* 1327, *Nansegollan* 1620. 'Whetstone valley', *nans* + *igolenn*. The meaning is unclear: perhaps a valley where whetstones were obtained from a quarry. Pronounced 'Nansy-*goll*an'. The early spellings, and the modern pronunciation, show that 'the valley of the hazel-tree' (which would be *Nans an gollen*, from *collen* 'hazel-tree') is not a possible interpretation.

Nancledra W4935 **(Towednack)** *Nanscludri* 1302, 1343, William de *Nanscludry* 1327, *Nicledera* 1699, *Nancledry* 1748. Probably 'valley of Clodri', *nans* + personal name. If so, then the *u* of the early forms represents Cornish *o*, not *u*, and the *e* of the later forms is an irregular development. Alternatively, if the personal name were *Cludri* with *u*, the later *e* would be a regular development; but there would be less justification for suggesting such a personal name. Pronounced 'Nan*cledr*y' or '*Cledr*y'.

Nanpean W9655 **(St Stephen in Brannel)** *Nanspian* 1332. 'Little valley', *nans* + *byghan*, with unvoicing of *b* to *p* by the *s* of *Nans*.

Nanstallon X0367 **(Bodmin)** *Lantalan* 1201, *Lantallen* 1284 (1602), *Nanstalen* 1392. Either 'valley of Talan', *nans* + personal name, or, more likely, 'valley of the river Alan', *nans* (older *nant*) + river-name, with later re-interpretation of *Nant-alan* as *Nans-talan*. *Alan* was the former name of the River CAMEL.

Nare Head W9136 **(coast, Veryan)** *Penare Point* c.1540, *Nare Head* c.1870. Named from the nearby farms called Pennare, W9238, with subsequent loss of the unstressed first syllable. The farms are found earlier as *Pennarde* c.1100 (14th), *Penhart* 1238: 'headland', *penn-ardh*, with later loss of final *dh*.

Nare Point W8025 **(coast, St Keverne)** *Nare Poynt* c.1605. As with the preceding name, the headland is named from the nearby farm, Penare W795245, with loss of the unstressed first syllable. The farm was earlier *Pennarth* 967 (11th): 'headland', *penn-ardh*.

Navax Point W5943 **(coast, Gwithian)** *Navax Point* c.1870. Obscure, for lack of earlier forms. An area of rough grazing, inland from the point, is called The Knavocks W5943 (*Knavocks* 1838). It is uncertain to which feature the name originally referred, the downs or the point, but it seems more likely to belong to the downs. If so, the name Navax might possibly be 'the summer-land', *an* + *havek*, with English -s added later. The headland may formerly have had another name, *the Ulffes* 1580 (18th): compare WOLF ROCK.

St Neot X1867 (parish) *Sanctus Anietus*, clerics of *Sanctus Neotus* 1086, *Senniet* early 12th (14th), *Sanctus Neotus* 1201, *Seynt Nyet* 1284. Thereafter *Neotus* is standard in Latin, but the original *Niot* lasted in vernacular forms into the 17th century, and in speech (rhyming eventually with 'riot') to the mid-20th. From the patron saint of the parish church. He was believed to have been a relative of the Anglo-Saxon King Alfred (who died in 899), and to have been a monk of Glastonbury who came west to found a monastery here. Later his relics were removed to St Neots in Huntingdonshire. The earliest reference to the saint is probably the name *Nioth* in the 10th-century List. Note the transient initial *A-* in one of the forms of 1086: a similar phenomenon occurs in some words beginning with *n* in early Welsh. There was also an alternative name for the place, found as *Neotestou, Nietestou* 1086, *Neotestoce* mid-11th (12th): English, saint's name + *stów* or *stoc*; but it seems not to have survived beyond the 12th century.

Newbridge W4231 (Sancreed/Madron) *New Bridge* 1839. English, a 19th-century hamlet at a bridge on the parish boundary. But there is also a Cornish name for the area, appearing as *Hallentacken* 19th/20th century, and still current as Hallantacka: *hal* 'moor/marsh' + *an*? + unknown word.

New Grimsby (Scilly): see under G.

Newlyn W4628 (Paul) *Nulyn* 1279, *Lulyn* 1290, 1302, *Nywelyn* 1337. Apart from the earliest form, *Lulyn* is the standard spelling until the mid-14th century. Probably 'fleet-pool, pool for a fleet of boats', a compound of *lu + lynn*. The doubt arises because *lu* properly means 'army', and the sense 'fleet' is found only once, in the Old Cornish phrase *luu listri* 'fleet', literally 'army of boats'. However, in the compound *lu-lynn* (literally 'army-pool'), the sense 'fleet' would have been implied without any need to specify 'of boats', so the meaning 'fleet-pool' for the name is probably valid. The change of the initial *L* to *N* is unusual, but clearly shown in the spellings: contrast LELANT.

Newlyn East W8256 (parish) 'Church of *Sancta Niwelina*'
1259, *Seint Neulin* 1270, *Eglosnyulyn* 1415, *Nulyn* 1543,
Newlyn East 1884. From the patron saint of the church.
She was believed to have been martyred nearby by her
father, a king. One form shows Cornish *eglos*, 'church',
preceding the saint's name. The current map form is 'St
Newlyn East', an incorrect modernism. The prefix 'St' was
dropped increasingly often from the 16th century onwards,
and its absence was standardised in the 19th century. It
was only after it had been dropped that the suffix 'East'
was required, in order to distinguish the place from NEW-
LYN in Paul, of different derivation. If 'St Newlyn' is used,
as a deliberate archaism, then 'East' is otiose. Newlyn
Downs W8354 (downs) is *St Newlin downe* early 17th.

Newmill W4534 (Madron/Gulval) *Mulfra Newe Mill* 1621,
Newmill 1748. English, self-explanatory. In the early ref-
erence it is listed with *Mulfra Mill* and *Mulfra Stampinge
Mill;* all belong to the hamlet of Mulfra nearby at W454347.
The latter is found as *Moelvre c.*1250: 'bare-hill', a com-
pound of *moel* + *bre*, with mutation of *b* to *v*.

New Mills W9052 (Ladock) *Melynewyth* (a corn-mill) 1364,
Melenowith alias New Myll 1596. A translated name,
starting as Cornish 'new mill', *melin* + *nowydh*, later rendered into English.

New Polzeath: see under P.

Newquay W8161 (St Columb Minor) *Newe Kaye* 1602, *New
Key* 1748, *New Quay alias Towan* 1813. English, self-explanatory. The construction of a quay here is mentioned in
1440, and the name presumably originated at that date:
'the construction and maintenance of *a keye* on the sea-
shore at *Tewen blustry*'. The latter name is an alternative,
Cornish, name of Newquay, surviving as Towan Blistra
1906. It is first found as *Tewynplustri* 1308, and consists
of *tewynn*, 'sand-dune(s)' + unknown second word: perhaps a Cornish equivalent of Breton *pleustriñ*, 'to work,
busy oneself'. Another derivation is sometimes given, 'harbour of boats', from *porth* + *lystri*, plural of *lester*, with
supposedly *Porth-lystry* becoming *Perlystry* and then
Plystry. This is not possible, first, because *porth* would not

have become so completely reduced to *P-* without trace at so early a date, and secondly because the vowel in the penultimate syllable is always *u* in early forms, never the *i/y* which that derivation would require. It is unclear whether the alternative name of Newquay in 1813, *Towan,* is a shortened version of Towan Blistra, or a separate placename in its own right: see TOWAN HEAD. Newquay Bay W8162 (coast) is found as *New Quay Bay* 1813.

Newtown in St Martin W7423 (St Martin in Meneage) *Newtown* 1870. English, a 19th-century hamlet.

North Hill X2776 (parish) *Henle* 1238, *Northindle* 1260, *Northinle* 1270, *Hulle* 1276, *Northulle* 1275, 1291, 1311. A difficult name; the early spellings are at variance with one another. The original name seems to have been *Henle* or *Hin(d)le.* This was changed early to 'hill' (*Hulle*) by reinterpretation, and 'North' was added in contrast to SOUTH HILL, 4 miles to the south-east. But *Henle* or *Hin(d)le* itself presents problems. It is unlikely to be Cornish, 'ancient place', a compound of *hen + le.* Assuming it to be English, *Hindle* might be 'hinds' wood or clearing', *hind + léah.*

North Petherwin, North Tamerton: see P and T.

North West Passage V8411 (coast, Scilly) *The North West Channell* 1689. English, self-explanatory.

Old Kea W8441 (Kea) *Sanctus Che* 1086, *Landighe* 1086, *Kee* 1440. The original site of the church dedicated to St Kea. He was believed to have sailed to Cornwall from Ireland in a granite trough, founded a community here, and then to have gone on to Brittany, where he died at Cleder after making a return trip to Britain in an attempt to make peace between King Arthur and Modred. The form *Landighe* contains *lann* 'church-site' + *to-* 'thy' (used in pet-forms of saints' names) + *Ke* (with mutation of *k* to *g*); the name survives as Landegea, the name of the churchtown farm; the same name occurs in Devon (Landkey), North Wales (Llandygai, Caernarvonshire) and, lost, in Somerset (*Lantokai,* an old name for Leigh-on-Street). The parish church was resited at KEA in 1802. According to Doble in 1929, 'Old people still pronounce *Kea* as *Kay*'.

Otterham x1690 (parish) *Otrham* 1086, *Oterham* 1231, 1291. English; the village is situated near the head of the River OTTERY; so it is probably 'river-meadow or enclosed land (*hamm*) on the River Ottery', rather than an independent name, 'river-meadow frequented by otters', *oter* + *hamm*.

River Ottery x1788—x3486 *Otery* 1284, *Atery* 1522, *Atrye* 1538. English, 'otter-river', *oter* + *éa*. Compare the River Otter (Somerset/Devon), formerly *Ottery*. The later forms with *A* are an irregular development, and the name has now reverted to its expected form.

Padstow w9175 (parish) *Sancte Petroces stow* 981, *Petrocys stow c.*995, *Patristowe* 1318, 1343, *Patrikestowe* 1326, *Padristowe* 1350, *Padstowe* 1525, *Padstowe otherwise Petherickstowe* 1686. English, 'holy place (*stów*) of St Petrock (Pedrek)'. The *a* is due to an attempt to equate St Petrock with St Patrick, as shown in some spellings; but the true saint continued to be known locally, where *Pedrek* became *Petherick*. There were also two other names for Padstow. The first is *Eldestawe* 1201, *Aldestowe* 1249, *Oldestowe* 1337; English, 'old holy place', *eald* + *stów* ('old' in contrast with Bodmin, where St Petrock's monastery was removed to). The second is *Languihenoc* 1086, *Lanwethenek* 1350, *Lodenek c.*1540, *Laffenake c.*1600; Cornish, 'church-site of Gwethenek', *lann* + saint's name, with mutation of *Gw* to *w*. St Gwethenek is first found as *Geuedenoc* 10th (List). The Life of St Petrock gives a story to explain the name: the site at Padstow was founded by Gwethenek, who decided to move elsewhere after St Petrock arrived. St Gwethenek was still honoured in Bodmin in 1478. Padstow was raided by Vikings in 981, and it may have been as a result that the main site of the monastery was moved to Bodmin, though Padstow remained important. Padstow Bay W9279 (coast) is *Patystoo havyn* 1478, *Padstow haven* 1576; it is earlier referred to as 'the estuary called *Hægelmutha*' 11th (see EGLOSHAYLE).

Par x0753 (St Blazey/Tywardreath) *Le Pare* 1573, *the Parre* 1665, *Par* 1748. No doubt originally *porth*, '(the) harbour', though conclusive evidence is lacking. On the west side of the estuary there is a settlement called Porth, X074530 (*Porth* 1354); *Par* may be a divergent development of that name, with normal loss of *th* in later Cornish.

Park Head w8470 (coast, St Eval) So found in *c.*1870; from the nearby farm of Park W849709, so found in 1813 (now deserted). The farm perhaps took its name from a former deer-park here, though none is recorded. Near to the headland there is a farm called Pentire, first found as *Pentir c.*1210: 'headland', *penn tir*. This must have been an older, Cornish, name for the point itself, but it is not recorded as such; compare PENTIRE in Crantock and St Minver. In 1699 the headland was called *Pencarne Point*, but that may be a corrupt form.

Paul w4627 (parish) 'Church of *Beatus Paulus*, of *Sanctus Paulinus*' 1259, 'church of *Sanctus Paulus* of *Breweny*' 1323, *Pawle* 1437, *Paul alias Paulyn* 1717. From the patron saint of the church, St Paul or Paulinus; he was believed to have been born in Wales (where he is venerated in Carmarthenshire), and to have founded monasteries in Brittany, notably at St Pol-de-Léon and on the Ile de Batz. The alternative name for the churchtown, *Breweny*, survives as Brewinney W456270; it is *bre* 'hill' + unknown word or name.

Pelynt x2055 (parish) *Plunent* 1086, *Plynt* 1478, *Plenynt alias Pelynt* 1577. 'Parish of Nennyd', *plu* + saint's name. The saint is mentioned as *Sanctus Nunet* (male) in 1442, but was more generally considered to be St Nonn, the mother of St David. However, a male St Nynnid is known in Wales, notably at Eglwys Nynnid, Glamorganshire, and it may be that the same saint was the original one at Pelynt also. The saint's name survives locally at St Nun's Well X224564.

Penare w9940 (Goran) *Pennarth* 1284 (1602), *Penhard* 1303, *Penarth* 1306, *Pennare* 1547. 'Headland', *penn-ardh*, referring to the promontory now called DODMAN POINT.

Pencarrow Head x1550 (coast, Lanteglos by Fowey) *Pencarowe c.*1482, *Pencarrow* 1748. 'Stag's head', *penn* + *carow*, a fanciful name taken from its two-horned appearance from the sea.

Pendeen w3834 (St Just in Penwith) Ralph de *Pendyn* 1284 (1446), *Pendyn* 1306, *Pendeen* 1588. 'Headland of a fort', *penn* + *din*. The name now refers primarily to a 19th-century mining-village. Originally it must have referred to the nearby headland now called Pendeen Watch, W3735 (English *watch* 'look-out place'), but no promontory-fort is known there. The medieval references are to the habitation now called Pendeen House, W383354; and by 1846 the simple name had been transferred to the mining-village.

Pendennis Point w8231 (coast, Budock) 'Castel on *Pendinas*' c.1540. 'Headland of a fort', *penn* + *dinas*. The castle here was built by Henry VIII in 1540-43; but the name is unlikely to have arisen as a result of that. It therefore implies an earlier promontory-fort, presumably Iron-Age; but no trace of such a structure survives.

Pendoggett x0279 (St Kew) *Pendeugod* 1289, *Pendewegoys*, *Pendouket* 1302, *Pendoget* 1467. 'The top of two woods', *penn* + *dew* + *coes* (older *cuit*), with mutation of *c* to *g*. Note the form of 1302, which shows the change of final *d/t* to *s*; but the older form with *t* prevailed, as normally in east Cornwall. The village is situated on a watershed at the head of two wooded valleys.

Penhale Point w7559 (coast, Perranzabuloe) So found in 1813. Penhale Sands W7657 (dunes) is so found in 1888, but was earlier *Piran Sands* 1813 (from the patron saint of the parish, St Piran), and the sands are implied at a much earlier date also (see PERRANZABULOE). Both take their names from the nearby farm of Penhale W763583 (now lost in Penhale Camp); it was *Penhal* 1327, 'head of the marsh', *penn hal*. The farm was situated at the upper end of a marshy depression.

Penhalvean w7137 (Stithians) *Penhalvyhan* 1319. 'Little Penhale', from a pre-existing *Penhal* + *byghan*. *Penhal* is so found in 1327; 'head of the marsh', *penn hal*. 'Little' is in contrast with Penhalveor W709373 nearby, *Penhalmur* 1319 (*meur* 'great').

Penjerrick w7730 (Budock) *Penhegerik* 1327, *Pennanseyryk* 1333, *Pensyryke* c.1525; *penn nans* 'head of a valley' + unknown word or name, probably the name of the stream in the valley. This could be a word *eyrik*, corresponding to Welsh *eirig* 'warlike, fierce'. Other Welsh stream-names end in *-ig*, corresponding to Cornish *-ik*. In the earliest form, *Penheg-* must stand for 'Penez-' ('Pene*zerr*ik'), with the loss of the second *n* of *nans*. It is probably too early for the *g* to stand for the full 'dj' which developed later in this name and others; compare *-lagek* 1354, for LADOCK.

Penkevil: see under ST MICHAEL PENKEVIL.

Penlee Point x4448 (coast, Rame) *Penleigh* 1337, *Penlee poynt* 1602. 'Headland of a slab-stone', *penn + legh*. The same coastal name occurs at the other end of the county, in Paul parish, W473269.

Penpillick x0756 (Tywardreath) Laurence de *Penpelic* 1302, *Penpillyk* 1389. 'Little Penpell', place-name + *-ik*. Penpillick is a quarter-mile from Penpell in Lanlivery parish, X075566, and similar pairs of names are found elsewhere. Penpell itself occurs as *Penpel c.*1194, and may be 'far end', *penn + pell*; it is at the southernmost tip of Lanlivery parish.

Penpol w8139 (Feock) William de *Penpol* 1275. 'Head of the creek', *penn poll*.

Penpoll x1454 (St Veep) Robert de *Penpol* 1327. 'Head of the creek', *penn poll*.

Penrose w8770 (St Ervan) *Penros* 1286. 'End of the moorland', *penn ros*, perhaps here meaning 'end of the hill-spur'. The hamlet is situated near the end of a two-mile ridge of land between streams.

Penryn w7834 (St Gluvias) *Penryn* 1236 (1275), *Penrin* 1259, 'harbour of *Peryn*' 1337. 'Promontory', *penn rynn* (literally 'end of a point'). The town lies on a ridge between two valleys. The form of 1337, with loss of the first *n*, is frequently found at least until 1602, and represents a local pronunciation 'Pe*rin*'.

Pensilva x2969 (St Ive) *'Pensilva* is comparatively a new village, chiefly inhabited by miners' 1868. A 19th-century mining-village with an invented name, formed by the arbitrary addition of the prefix *Pen-* to a pre-existing name in the area. The moorland here was called *Silva Down* in 1840; it is possibly to be compared with names in Devon

134

and Dorset containing English 'silver', and usually referring to streams. If so, the spelling -a for -er would be unusual, but not unique: compare TREVISCOE. But in this instance there is no obvious stream for the name to refer to, and *Silva* may have some other, unknown, derivation.

Pentewan X0147 (St Austell/Mevagissey) *Bentewoin* 1086, *Bentewyn* 1297, *Pentewen, Pentowyn* 1327. An awkward name. The first word is *ben* 'foot', with later re-interpretation to *Pen*. At first sight the name appears to be 'foot of the sand-dunes', *ben* + *tewynn*, but there are problems in such a meaning. For one thing, it makes poor topographical sense (the settlement is *above* the beach, and one sited below sand-dunes is inherently improbable); for another, the name should be connected with the nearby farm of Towan, X014491, and with the associated manor of Tewington (*Deuuintona* 1086, *Tewinton* 1181, *Tewyn* 1337). For these names a connection with *tewynn* 'dunes' is topographically unlikely. It seems most probable that *Tewyn* was an old name of the St Austell River, which emerges at Pentewan. This river would then, as elsewhere, have given its name to the farm of Towan situated beside it, and thus to the manor of Tewington. Pentewan would then make good sense as 'the foot of the river Tewyn'. The meaning of such a river-name would be uncertain, but compare the river Tywynni in Breconshire. For that name, Welsh *tywyn* 'radiance' and *tewyn* 'ember, torch' have been compared, giving the possible meaning 'bright, shining river'; the suggested river-name *Tewyn* might contain a Cornish equivalent.

Pentire W7861 (Crantock)

West Pentire W7760 (Crantock) *Pentir, Pentirbighan* ('little Pentire', + *byghan*) c.1270, *West Pentire, Pentirevean* 1813. 'Headland', *penn tir*, used for each of the two promontories which flank the mouth of the estuary here. Unqualified forms seem to refer to West Pentire, while Pentire at W7861, the eastern one, is the former Pentirevean, 'little Pentire', as shown by the map of 1813.

Pentire Point W9280 (coast, St Minver) *Pentyr* 1284, *Pentire point* 1576. 'Headland', *penn tir*. The nearby farm of Pentire W935802, named from the headland, is found as

Pentir c.1230, 1297. It was later subdivided, and part of it was called *Pentireglas* 1585, now Pentireglaze W943798; 'green Pentire', +*glas*. The latter name was also borrowed to give the former name of New POLZEATH.

Penwith (see HAYLE, ST JUST, and LAND'S END) This name first appears in names for Land's End, Old English *Penwihtsteort* 997 ('tail of Penwith', + *steort*, 'tail'); and in early Welsh *Penpenwith* 13th, likewise meaning 'the end of Penwith'. Penwith itself evidently denoted the whole Land's End peninsula. Its derivation is uncertain; it probably means 'end-district', from Cornish *penn* 'head, end', and the same word -*wedh* as is seen in Cornish *fin-wedh*, Breton *fin-vez*, and Welsh *di-wedd*, all of which mean 'end'.

Penwithick X0256 (St Austell) *Penwythyk* 1357. Probably 'top of the patch of trees', *penn* + *gwydhek*, the adjective formed from *gwydh* + -*ek*. The mutation of *gw* to *w* is presumably due to a lost definite article before *gwydhek* (*Penn an wydhek*).

Penzance W4730 (Madron) Nicholas de *Pensans* 1284, *Penzaunce* 1582. 'Holy headland', *penn* + *sans* (compare Holyhead, Anglesey). Here the name is presumably due to the chapel of St Mary situated on the ridge, first mentioned in 1327, and named as 'chapel of Blessed Mary' in 1379.

Perranarworthal W7738 (parish) 'St Peran' c.1260, 'church of *Sanctus Pieranus* in *Arwothel*' 1388, *St Peran Arwothal* 1543. From the patron saint of the church (see PERRANZABULOE). To the saint's name, *Piran*, was added the name of the manor, *Arwothal*, in order to distinguish this parish from the two other parishes of St Piran, PERRANUTHNOE and PERRANZABULOE. The manor was earlier *Arewethel* 1181, *Arwothel*, *Arwoythel* 1284; 'beside the marsh', *ar* + *goethel*, with mutation of *g* to *w*.

Perran Bay: see under LIGGER BAY.

Perranporth W7554 (Perranzabuloe) *St Perins creeke* 1577, *Perran Porth* 1810. English dialect *porth* 'harbour, cove': a 19th-century mining village, 'the port of St Piran's parish'. Pronounced 'Perran-*porth*'.

Perranuthnoe W5329 (parish) 'Church of *Sanctus Pieranus*' 1348, 'Church of *Sanctus Pieranus* of *Udno*' 1373.

From the patron saint of the church (see PERRANZABU-
LOE), and distinguished from the other parishes of the
saint by the name of the manor, *Uthno,* whose meaning is
obscure. It was earlier *Odenol* 1086, *Hutheno* 1235, *Udno
parva* 'little Uthnoe' 1308. The name survives at the farm
of Ednoe-Vean W541297 (+ *byghan,* 'little'): Uthnoe Veor,
'great Uthnoe', with *meur,* was the name of the churchtown
in 1839. Compare Hennowe (St Ewe, W991460: *Udno*
1328) and the second part of *Lanuthno* (= ST ERTH).

Perranzabuloe W7752 **(parish)** 'The canons of *Sanctus
Pieranus* hold *Lanpiran*' 1086, *Sanctus Piranus* 1195,
John de *Lanberan* 1303, *Seynt Peran* 1336, *Peran in Zabu-
lo* 1535, *St Piranes in the sandes* c.1540. From the patron
saint of the parish, with the suffix 'in the sand' or Latin *in
sabulo,* to distinguish it from the other two parishes of the
saint. The Cornish name, very poorly attested, was *Pirran
in Treth* 1425 (18th), *Peran kreth* (*k* for *t*) c.1605 (*treth*
'sand, beach'). The saint is earlier recorded, perhaps as
Pierguin 10th (List), and certainly in the name *Carn Peran*
960, on the bounds of the parish (*carn* 'tor'). The forms of
the saint's name are variable, but *Piran* seems to be the
best form. The forms of 1086 and 1303 show *lann* 'church-
site' + saint's name (with mutation of *p* to *b* in 1303). The
probable outline of the old churchyard has been found on
the site of the Norman church at W771564; that was abandoned because of drifting sand in 1804, when the present
church was built. The sands (now called PENHALE SANDS)
had been troublesome since at least 1280.

Little Petherick W9172 **(parish)** 'Parish of *Sanctus Petro-
cus Minor*' 1327, 1334, *Pedrok minor alias Nasenton* 1535,
Lyttell Peddrocke 1553, *Petherocke alias Nansenton* 1563.
From the dedication of the parish church to St Petrock ('Pedrek'); *minor* or 'Little' is in contrast with the adjacent
PADSTOW. Note the change (16th century?) from *d* to *th* in
the saint's name: compare BRADDOCK, ST CLETHER,
NORTH and SOUTH PETHERWIN, and QUETHIOCK. The
older name of the parish was *Nanfonteyn* 1281; 'valley of
a well', *nans* + *fenten.*

North Petherwin X2889 **(parish)** 'Church of *Sanctus
Paternus* of *Pidrewina*' 1171 (13th), *North Piderwine* 1259,

North Petherwyn 1524. 'Blessed Padern', from the patron saint of the church, St Padarn (in Welsh) or Paternus (in Latin) + *gwynn* 'white, blessed' (with mutation of *gw* to *w*). *Padern wynn* 'Padern the blessed' evidently became *Paderwyn* before the twelfth century, but the change of *a* to *i* in the first syllable is not readily explained: compare *Peternus* (a member of the Cornish royal family in the Breton *Life* of St Turiau), showing a similar change. The identity of St Patern at North and South Petherwin is not certain. There was a 6th-century bishop of Vannes with the name, and a bishop of Avranches at about the same date. The Cornish saint and St Padarn, who is widely honoured in south Wales, may be the same as one of those. Note the change from *d* to *th* in both North and South Petherwin, as also in LITTLE PETHERICK, etc.

South Petherwin X3081 (parish) 'The parish of a saint called *Paer* in the French language' *c*.1200, *Suthpydrewyn* 1269, *Pitherwyne* 1275, 'chaplain of *Sanctus Paternus* of *Piderwyne*' *c*.1293 (15th), *Sowth Pythewyn* 1522. From the dedication of the parish church to St Padern: see NORTH PETHERWIN. In the earliest reference, *Paer* is an inexact French rendering of *Padern*, made by Peter of Cornwall, who for some reason chose not to give the usual name of the saint, although he must have known it.

Phillack W5638 (parish) 'Church of *Sancta Felicitas*' 1259, and normally to the 15th century, *Felok* 1388, *Seynt Felleck* *c*.1530, *Phillacke* 1613. From the dedication of the church to a saint *Felek*, of whom nothing at all is known. The Latin forms are due to an attempt to equate this saint with one of the several saints called Felicity; but the patron saint of this parish is earlier found as *Felec* 10th (List), and he or she remained so called locally, as shown in the later forms. Note, too, that the *Ph* of the modern spelling is a 17th-century innovation, and that the name was formerly always spelt with *F* (compare PHILLEIGH). The churchtown was also called *Egglosheil c*.1170 (13th), *Egloshayle* 1842, 'church on an estuary', *eglos* + *heyl* (compare EGLOSHAYLE).

Philleigh W8739 (parish) 'Church of *Sanctus Filius* of *Eglosros*' 1312, *Fili* 1450, *Phillie* 1613. From the dedication of the parish church to a St *Fily*, of whom nothing is known. He is first found, as patron saint of this parish, as *Filii* 10th (List). The personal name is also known in Wales and Brittany, though no church dedications occur, except for one or two uncertain instances in Brittany. As at PHIL-LACK, the spelling with *Ph* is an innovation, probably of the 17th century. The alternative name of the churchtown was *Eglossos* 1086 (-*sos* for -*ros*), *Egglesros* 1257, surviving as Eglosrose: 'church of a moorland', *eglos* + *ros*, or possibly 'church of ROSELAND (*Ros*)', although it is not known that Philleigh ever served such a function in the district.

Pillaton x3664 **(parish)** *Pilatona* 1086, *Piletone* 1086, 1259, 1273, *Pilatone* 1272. 'Farmstead of stakes, of posts', English *píl* + *tún*.

St Pinnock x2063 **(parish)** 'Church of *Sanctus Pynnocus*' 1284, 1291, *Seint Pynnok* 1385. From the dedication of the parish church, but nothing is known of the saint. A *St Pinnuh* is mentioned in a Breton list of saints of the 11th century; but he has no Breton dedication, so that mention may actually be a reference to the Cornish saint.

Playing Place w8141 **(Kea)** *Kea Playing Place* 1813 (an antiquity), *Playing Place* 1884 (a residence). English, self-explanatory. The 20th-century village has grown up near a circular arena, which must have been used for performing the Cornish dramas or for games. Slight traces of the arena survive at W814419.

Polapit Tamar x3389 **(Werrington)** *Poolapit Tamer* 1625. English, seemingly 'pool-pit', 'hollow with a pool', *pól* + *pytt*. But a nearby place called Bullapit, X322897, has a much older name, *Bulapit* 1149 (15th). That name is 'bull's hollow', *bula* + *pytt*, and it is possible that Polapit, which does not appear until the 17th century, might be a corruption of the older name. It is unclear why it was felt necessary to add the name of the River TAMAR to this name, unless possibly in contrast with Bullapit.

Polbathick x3456 **(St Germans)** *Polbarthek* 1365, *Polve-thick* 1699, *Polvathick* 1748; *poll* 'pool' ÷ unknown word or name, perhaps a stream-name *Barthek*. If so, compare the

Cornish and Welsh names cited under TREBARTHA. The village is at the head of a tidal inlet, and *poll* here probably has the sense 'creek'. The loss of *r* in the modern form is curious, and so is the transient change of *b* to *v*.

Poldhu Point W6619 **(coast, Mullion)** *Poljew Point* 1888. Named from the adjacent Poldhu Cove W664199. The latter was *Polsewe* 1533, *Poll jew* 1699, *Poljew* 1813. 'Dark cove', *poll* + *du*. Note the correct *j* in older spellings, showing the pronunciation; the modern *dh* is incorrect (compare BALDHU).

Polgooth W9950 **(St Ewe/St Mewan)** 'A tynework called *Polgoyth*' 1500-01. Either 'pool of a goose' *poll* + *goedh*, or 'pool of a water-course', *poll* + *goeth*. The former makes more immediate sense; but since this seems to be the name of a tin-work originally, the 'water-course' may be preferable, and *poll* may here have the sense 'pit'.

Polkerris X0952 **(Tywardreath)** *Polkerys* 1585, *Polkeryes*, *Polkerries* c.1605; *poll* (here 'cove') + uncertain second element: *kerys* 'fortified' is possible, but it is not clear in what sense it is a 'fortified cove'. Or instead one might compare, in Wales, Pwll Ceris, a whirlpool in the Menai Straits, spelt *Polkerist* 10th (c.1100), which may contain a personal name *Cerist*. But the lack of early forms makes it impossible to interpret the Cornish name with any assurance.

Polmassick W9745 **(St Ewe)** *Ponsmadek* 1301 (14th), 'mill of *Polmasek*' 1469. 'Bridge of Madek', *pons* + personal name, with early corruption of *pons* to *Pol-*. Note the standard change of *d* to *s*.

Polperro X2050 **(Lansallos/Talland)** *Portpira* 1303, *Porthpera* 1355, *Porthpire* 1361, *Porthpyre* 1391, *Polpera* 1522, *Polparrow* 1748. Probably 'harbour of Pyra or Pyre', *porth* + personal name, but the exact form of the latter is uncertain: the spellings are inconsistent between *e* and *i/y* in the middle syllable, and between *a* and *e* in the final one. Not *pur* 'clean', or a derivative, for lack of spellings with *u*. Note the 16th-century change of *porth* to *Pol*; and the final *o* of the modern form is a hyper-correction, first seen in the form of 1748.

Polruan x1250 (Lanteglos by Fowey) *Porruwan* early 13th, *Porthruan* 1284, *Polruan* 1292. 'Harbour of Ruveun', *porth* + personal name. Note the change of *porth* to *Pol*, already in 1292, and the early vocalisation of the *v* in *Ruveun* to *w*; this happened also when the same name occured as that of a saint and parishes: see RUAN LANIHORNE and RUAN MINOR.

Polyphant x2681 (Lewannick) *Polefand, Polofant* 1086, *Polefant, c*.1170 (1476). 'Toad's pool', *poll + lefant*. Unusually, the stress in this name has moved to the first syllable, and it is now *'Polyphant'*.

Polzeath w9378 (St Minver) *Pulsath baye c.*1605, *Polzeath* 1748. Probably 'dry cove', *poll + sygh*, presumably meaning one which dries out at low tide; but earlier spellings are needed. New Polzeath w9379 is a 20th-century holiday village, so named in 1972; previously it was called Pentireglaze 1906, 1964, a name borrowed from a nearby farm (see PENTIRE POINT).

Ponsanooth w7537 (St Gluvias/Stithians/Perranarworthal) 'Bridge called *Pons an Oeth*' 1521, *Ponsewoth* 1555, *Ponsonwoth Mills* 1582. Probably 'the bridge of the water-course', *pons + an + goeth*, but 'the bridge of the goose' (*goedh*) is also a possible meaning; with mutation of *g* to *w* in either case.

Porkellis w6933 (Wendron) *Porthkelles* 1286, 1337. Apparently 'hidden entrance', *porth* (here inland, so in the sense 'gateway, entrance') + *kellys* 'lost' (perhaps meaning 'hidden'). But the meaning of the whole is uncertain; possibly 'hidden pass', for the place is at the point where a road crosses over a low ridge.

Portgaverne x0080 (St Endellion) *Porcaveran* 1337, *Portkaveran, Porte Kaverne* 1343; *porth* 'cove, harbour' + unknown word or name. The second element occurs also in the nearby farm of Tregaverne (*Tregaveren* 1284). A word *cavran* or *cavren* is required, but no such word is known. It might instead be a name *Gavran*, literally 'young goat'. This could be either a stream-name (compare streams called Gafran in Caernarvonshire, Merionethshire and Pembrokeshire), or a personal name. If so, then 'cove of the stream Gavran' or 'cove of a man Gavran'. In that case the early forms would show unvoicing of *g* to *c*/*k* by the *th* of *Porth*; and Tregaverne would fail to show the expected mutation of *g* to zero. Pronounced 'Port*g*ayvern' (middle syllable as in 'raven').

Porthallow W7923 **(St Keverne)** *Worthalaw, Werdalau* (*W* for *P*) 967 (11th), *Porthaleu* 1333, *Porthalla* 1748. 'Cove of the *Alaw*', *porth* + stream-name. The meaning of *Alaw* is uncertain. There is an identical river name in Anglesey, and there are two Continental river-names *Alava*, which may be Gaulish. The Welsh stream-name has been explained as Welsh *alaw* 'water-lilies'; but the Cornish stream is not a likely place for water-lilies in abundance, and some other meaning would be preferable. Pronounced 'Pralla', by regular developments whereby the *th* is lost and the *-ow* reduced to *-a* (as seen in 1748).

Porthcothan Bay W8572 **(coast, St Merryn/St Eval)** So found in *c*.1870; from the nearby hamlet of Porthcothan W863720 (St Merryn). This was *Porkehuuson* (?) *c*.1242, *Pordgohoython* 1295 (14th), *Porthkehothon* 1298, *Porthcoythan* 1423. The reading of the earliest form is doubtful; *porth* 'harbour, cove' + uncertain second word. It looks like the plural of a Cornish word corresponding to Welsh *cyhoedd* 'proclamation; public'; but 'cove of proclamations' would make little sense.

Porthcurno W3822 **(St Levan)** *Porthe Cornowe* 1580 (18th), *Port-Curnoe c*.1605. 'Cove of horns or corners', *porth* + *corn* plural; but the meaning is unclear. The early references are to the cove alone; the village is a 20th-century one which grew up around the 19th-century telegraph station here.

Porthleven W6225 **(Sithney/Breage)** *Port-levan c*.1605. 'Smooth harbour', *porth* + *leven*; but it may be that *Leven*, 'smooth one', was originally the name of the stream which emerges here; if so, then Porthleven is rather 'harbour of the stream *Leven*'.

Porthmeor W4337 **(Zennor)** 'Mill of *Pordmur*' 1304, *Porthmur* 1313, *Porthmeor* 1720. 'Great cove or harbour', *porth* + *meur*.

Porth Navas W7527 (Constantine) *Porhanavas* 1649, *Porranavas* 1729. Probably 'the cove of the sheep', *porth + an + davas*, with *porth* regularly becoming *Por-*, and *an davas* becoming *an navas*.

Portholland W9541 (St Michael Caerhays/Veryan) *Portalan* 1288 (*c.*1300), *Porthallan* 1379, *Porthsalen* 1576, *Porthollon* 1699; *porth* 'cove, harbour' + unknown word or name, perhaps a name (*Alan*) for the long stream which flows south to emerge at East Portholland. Such a river-name is of unknown meaning: compare the River CAMEL for other examples. If so, then 'cove of the river Alan'. Note the curious *s* found in local spellings in the 16th century; it is evidently not original, and did not survive. Pronounced 'Port-*holl*and', with replacement, as often, of *porth* by English 'port'. The replacement of *a* by *o* in the modern form (appearing in 1699) is unexpected.

Porthoustock W8021 (St Keverne) *Portheustech* *c.*1255, *Pordeustek* *c.*1290, *Porthowstock* 1543, *Proustock* 1699; *porth* 'cove' + unknown word or name. A word *eustek* might mean 'nightingale', but 'nightingale's cove' seems rather unlikely, and the birds are scarcely recorded in Cornwall. More likely it might be a personal name, 'cove of Eustek', though there is no evidence for such a name. Pronounced 'Prowstock' according to Henderson, with the common reduction of *porth* to *Pr-*: compare PORTHALLOW.

Porthpean X0350 (St Austell) Andrew de *Porthbyhan* 1297, John de *Portbian* 1307, *Porpighan* 1337. 'Little harbour', *porth + byghan*, with unvoicing of the *b* to *p*. Note the loss of the *th* of *porth* by 1337. The place was named in contrast with Polmear ('great harbour'), the Cornish name of CHARLESTOWN.

Porth Reservoir W8662 (reservoir, Colan) The reservoir was built in 1960. It is named from the hamlet of Porth or St Columb Porth W8362, two miles away at the foot of the valley. This was *Porthe* in 1284 (1602): *porth* 'cove, harbour'.

Porthtowan W6947 (Illogan/St Agnes) *Porthtowan* 1628. 'Cove of sand-dunes', *porth + tewynn*. Nearby is the farm of Towan (St Agnes, W697483: *Tewyn* 1316, *Towan* 1699, 'sand-dunes'), and it may be that Porthtowan means rather 'the cove at Towan'. Note that, although there was a tin-stamps here in 1628, the village is 19th-century.

Port Isaac W9980 (St Endellion) *Portusek* 1337, *Porthissek*, *Portissek* c.1540, *Porthtyseke* 1576; *porth* 'harbour' + uncertain word or name. More early spellings are needed. If the lone medieval form is to be trusted, the original vowel was *u* (pronounced /y/), not *i/y*, so that *ysek*, the adjective of *ys* 'corn', is then not possible. Moreover, it is unclear whether the *t* in most later forms is due to early replacement of *porth* by *port* (as elsewhere: see PORTHOLLAND), or is there because the second element started with *t* (*Porth-tusek*). Thus the second word might be *usek*, the adjective of *usyon* 'chaff' (but that makes poor sense), or *tusek*, the adjective of *tus* 'people' (which is little better). Port Isaac Bay X0081 (coast) is so found in c.1870. The correct pronunciation 'Port*izz*ick' is still known locally.

Portloe W9339 (Veryan) *Porthlowe* c.1653, *Portlow*, *Porlow* c.1690. Probably 'harbour of an inlet', *porth* + *logh*. Note the replacement of Cornish *porth* by English *Port-*.

Portmellon X0143 (Mevagissey/Goran) 'Mill of *Porthmelen*' 1469. 'Mill cove', *porth* + *melin*. It is unclear whether the mill in question is Galowras Mill, three-quarters of a mile up-stream from the cove, or some lost water-mill nearer to the cove, or even a tidal mill.

Portquin W9780 (St Endellion/St Minver) Adam de *Porquin* 1201, *Porthguyn* 1297. 'White harbour', *porth* + *gwynn*. The exact meaning is uncertain; usually such names refer to the colour of the sand. Note the loss of *th* of *porth*, with unvoicing of *gw* to *qu*, already by 1201. Port Quin Bay W98 (coast) was better spelt *Portquin Bay* c.1870; compare *Portguin haven*, *Portguin cove* c.1605.

Portreath W6545 (Illogan) *Porthtreath* 1495 (17th), *Porth treyth* 1495 (1866), *Portreath* 1582. The two earliest spellings are copies of the same entry in a lost manuscript, so one of them must be wrong. In either case the name is 'beach cove', *porth* + *treth*. But nearby was a habitation called *Treath* in 1699, 'beach', and it may be that Portreath means rather 'the cove at Treath'.

Portscatho W8735 (Gerrans) *Porthskathowe* 1592. 'Harbour of boats', *porth* + *scath* plural; *scath* is thought to mean a particular type of boat, 'large rowing-boat', so the harbour would be one specialising in that sort of boat. Pronounced 'Per*scatha*' (or 'Scatha' simply), with normal reduction of final *-ow* to *-a*, and of *Porth* to 'Per' (compare PORTHAL-LOW); but the map-form shows instead the common replacement of *Porth* with English *Port*.

Portwrinkle X3553 (Sheviock) *Port Wrickel* 1605, *Porth Wrinkle* 1699, *Portwrincle* 1748. An obscure name. It must be considered along with that of Trewrickle nearby, X356545; this was *Trewikkel c.* 1190 (13th). The two names contain respectively *porth* 'cove' and *tre* 'farmstead' + unknown word or name.

Poughill S2207 (parish) *Pochehelle* 1086, *Pochewell* 1227, *Poghawell* 1284, *Poffill c.* 1605. English; the first element could be *pohha* 'pouch', or the personal name *Pohha*: compare Poughill (Devon) and Poughley (Berkshire). The second element is also in doubt: if the form of 1086 is to be trusted, it was originally *hyll* 'hill', but all other early forms indicate instead *wiella* 'well, spring', and the earliest form is probably corrupt. If so, then the name is either 'Pouch-spring' (meaning a spring in a hollow) or 'Pohha's spring'. Pronounced 'Poffil' , as indicated by the 17th-century spelling.

Poundstock X2099 (parish) *Pondestoch* 1086, *Pundestok*, *Puntestok* 1201, *Pounstok* 1525. English, 'settlement with an animal-pound', *pund* + *stoc*.

Praa Sands W5828 (Breage) *Parah or Prah* 1714, *Pra*, *Pra Sand* 1813, *Prah Sands* 1888. Obscure, for lack of earlier forms. The available spellings and the pronunciation (like 'pray') would be compatible with a derivation from an original name *Porthwragh* (not recorded), meaning 'the hag's cove', *porth* + *gwragh*. Such a name would regularly have become *Porah*, then *Prah*, through reduction of *Porth*. There was a cove called *Polwragh* somewhere in the area in 1331. If that were an early form of Praa, then the name was originally 'the hag's pool', *poll* + *gwragh*, and the later forms would be due to subsequent replacement of *poll* by *porth*. But the identification is uncertain. Both *Polwragh* and the hypothetical *Porthwragh* would show mutation of *gw* to *w* following a lost definite article.

Praze-an-Beeble W6335 **(Crowan)** *Praze-an-beble* 1697, *Praze* 1699. 'The meadow of the conduit', *pras* + *an* + *pibell*, with mutation of *p* of *pibell* to *b*.

Predannack Wollas W6616 **(Mullion)** *Bridanoc* 1196, *Predannek* 1284, *Predennek Wooles* 1339. 'Lower Predannack', with *goeles*, in contrast to Predannack Wartha nearby at W668167 ('upper Predannack', with *gwartha*). Predannack itself means 'of Britain, the British one', the adjective (with *-ek*) of Cornish *Predenn* or *Bredenn*, 'Britain' (from *Britannia*). Such a name would presumably mean '(headland) of Britain', probably referring not to Predannack Head W6616, but to the LIZARD POINT, 4 miles to the south-east. From its navigational importance, it could have been called 'the British one, (the headland) of Britain'. If so, the name must have been transferred from the headland to the settlements at an early date. Pronounced 'Pradnick' (*Pradnek c*.1740), although 'Pre*dann*ick' would have been expected. This may have arisen through a hypothetical form 'Pre*dad*nick' (with regular late Cornish *dn* from *nn*), and subsequent simplification.

Probus W8947 **(parish)** 'The canons of *Sanctus Probus* hold *Lanbrebois*' 1086, 'church of *Sanctus Probus*' 1123 (1379), *Seynt Probus* 1466, *Lamprobus Mill* 1759. From the dedication of the parish church to a St Probus. Nothing is known of him; he is first found, as patron saint of this parish, in the form *Propus* 10th (List). It is unlikely that the saint of this parish is one of the various universal saints called Probus; but one of the same name was honoured at Sherborne in the Middle Ages. Some forms for Probus contain *lann* 'church-site' + saint's name.

Quethiock X3164 **(parish)** *Quedoc* 1201, *Quedyk* 1289, *Quethek* 1535. Probably 'wooded place', Old Cornish *cuidoc* (Middle Cornish *coesek*, *coes* + *-ek*). If so, the original Old Cornish *d* was changed, by the 16th century, to *th*, as elsewhere (compare LITTLE PETHERICK, etc.). Pronounced 'Quithick'.

146

Quies W8376 **(coast, St Merryn)** So found in 1813. Possibly Cornish *gwis* 'female pig, sow': compare other Cornish and English examples of rocks in the sea called by words for animals. The rocks at Quies were themselves called *Cow and Calf alias So. Rock* 1699; the latter alternative is obscure (*South Rock* would little make sense here).

Rame X4249 **(parish)** *Rame* 1086 and subsequently. A completely obscure name. One would like the name to refer to Rame Head, the promontory which the parish occupies and which is such a notable landmark; but no such derivation is available in either Cornish or English. In Old High German there is a word *rama*, meaning 'post, frame, barrier', and it has been suggested that, if a corresponding word existed in Old English, it could be present in this name; the meaning could refer to the promontory-fort on Rame Head. But that is tentative, and the name remains unexplained. Rame Head X4148 (coast) is found as *Ramyshed* 1405, *Ramehed c.*1540: English, *head* 'headland'.

Rame W7234 **(Wendron)** *Raan* (?) 1556, *Rame* 1650. The reading of the first form is uncertain. Compare Mary *Rame* and Anthony *Rame*, married in the parish in 1580 and 1644. The surname is rare, and it is unknown whether the place was named from the family, or the family from the place. *Rayne* is a commoner surname (in east Cornwall and elsewhere in England), and it too occurs in the parish in 1641. It is possible that *Rame* is a variant or corruption of *Rayne*; in that case, the place would have been named from the family. Otherwise no derivation can be suggested. There is no known connection whereby this place might have been named after the older RAME near Plymouth.

Red Down X2685 **(hill, Egloskerry)** 'Pasture in *Richadune*' *c.*1233 (15th), *Rydun* 1536, *Ryghdon* 1550, *Reghdon* 1551, *Reddowne* 1582. English, but clearly not 'red down', though the forms are too variable, and mostly too late, to say what the first element may be. The second word is *dún* 'hill, downland'. The shape of the hill is similar to that at Rightadown in Devon, SS4203, which is 'straight hill', *riht* + *dún*, referring to a long narrow hill; that is possible here too, but the early spellings of the Cornish name, such as they are, do not support such a derivation for it.

Redmoor X0861 **(Lanlivery)** 'Moor called *Redemor*' 1301, *Redmore* 1748 (a farm). English, 'red marsh', *réad + mór*.

Redruth W6941 **(parish)** *Ridruth* 1259, 1324, *Redruth* 1302. 'Red ford', *rys* (older *rid*) + *rudh*. Objections have been raised against such a derivation. One might have expected both elements to show their later forms here in west Cornwall, giving *Resreeth*, but that is not found. The objections fail, however, because archaic spellings are especially frequent in parish-names (compare SANCREED, LADOCK, etc.). A few spellings such as *Rysdruth* 1361, *Resdruyth* 1391, and *Reesdruth* 1435, show the *d* trying to change, but they are only sporadic compared with the commoner forms lacking *s*. (In fact, *d* seems always to be preserved before *r* in west Cornwall: note Bodrifty, Bodriggy, and Bodrivial, and the lack of any counter-examples of *Bosr*-.) Similarly, forms such as *Ridreth* 1333, *Rydryth* 1342, and *Unyredreth* 1563 (+ St Euny, the patron saint of the church), probably show that the name was indeed pronounced 'Red*reeth*'; but the pronunciation 'Red*rooth*' has prevailed, influenced by the archaic spelling. The meaning 'red ford' is secure. In this area, such a feature might have been due to mining-waste: compare the Red River, 2 miles to the west, a name found from *c*.1790 (formerly called *Dour Conor*: see CONNOR DOWNS).

Rejerrah W8056 **(Newlyn East)** *Hryd worwig* 960, John *Roswyrou* 1327, *Rosworou* 1409, *Rosworra* 1630, *Rejorrow*, *Rejorre c*.1690. Probably 'ford of Gorvoy', *rys* (older *rid*) + personal name, with mutation of *g* to *w*. There are discrepancies between the 960 form and later spellings; but the identification is quite secure. The final -*ou* in the medieval forms (as in 1327 and 1409) is best explained as due either to analogy with other names ending in -*ou*, or as hyper-correction (-*worvoy* could regularly have become -*woro*, hyper-corrected to -*worou*). The modern form then shows regular reduction of -*ow* to -*a*. In the middle syllable, note the curious change from *o* (960, 1409, etc.) to *e* in the modern form (the *y* of 1327 is aberrant): compare NANCLEDRA. Most forms, except for the earliest, suggest *ros* 'moorland' rather than *rys* 'ford'; but the location, the earliest spelling with final *d*, and the later change of *s* to *j* (a change not

148

found with *ros*) all show that it is actually *rys*. In the earliest spelling, note the initial voiceless *Hr*, like Welsh *rh*.

Relubbus W5631 (St Hilary/St Erth)   Walter *Reyglubith* 1249, John de *Pons-releubes* 1298 ('bridge of Relubbus', *pons*), *Resleubes* 1355, Robert de *Rellehoubes* 1355, *Reloubys* 1357; *rys* 'ford' + unknown word or name. The same second element recurs independently at Trelubbas W665296, seven miles away (*Trelaheubes* 1319, *Trelehoubes* 1337). No suitable personal name, *Lehoubed* or the like, is recorded in Welsh or Breton.

Retew W9256 (St Enoder)   *Retewe* c.1546; *rys* 'ford' + uncertain word or name. The lack of secure medieval spellings makes this name hard to interpret with assurance, and there is also a danger of confusion (through the similarity of written *n* and *u*) with forms of Retyn W884587, three miles away on the other side of the same parish. Based on the available spellings, it might be 'black ford', *rys* + *du* (with assimilation of older *Rid-du* to *Retew*); or, less likely, 'thick, muddy ford', *rys* + *tew* 'fat, dense'.

Rilla Mill X2973 (Linkinhorne)   *Rillamulle* 1399. English, 'mill (*myln*) belonging to Rillaton'.   Rillaton itself, X2973 half a mile away, was *Risleston* 1086, *Rillectona* 1130, *Ridlehtuna* c.1155 (15th), 'ford of a flat-stone', *rys* (older *rid*) + *legh*, with Old English *tún* 'farm, estate' added later. The mill took its name from the original Cornish *Rid-legh*, without the added English word. The 'ford' in the name was probably the River Lynher crossing at Rilla Mill itself. Note the early change of *rid* to *Ris* already in 1086, and the more archaic *Rid* in the mid-12th century.

Rinsey W5927 (Breage)   *Renti* 1086, *Rendy* 1244, *Rensy* 1367, *Ringie* 1660. Apparently 'point-house' (a compound of *rynn* + *chi*, older *ti*), that is 'house on a point of land'. Rinsey is situated just inland from Rinsey Head, W589269, which must be the 'point' implied in the name. Note the Old Cornish spelling of 1086, with *t* written for 'd'. The *g* in 1660 shows the later change of *s* to 'dj'; but the older *s* has survived in the written form.

Rivers Allen, Camel, Fal, Fowey, Hayle, Inney, Lynher, Ottery, Seaton, Tamar, and Tiddy: see under A, C, F, etc.

The Road V8912 (coast, Scilly) *Roade* 1689. English, *road* in the sense 'a sheltered piece of water for ships, a roadstead': compare CARRICK ROADS.

Roche W9859 (parish) Ralph de *Rupe* 1201, *La Roche* 1258, 'Seynt Michel de *Rock*' 1478, *Roach* 1748. French, *roche* 'rock', from the prominent granite tor now called Roche Rock, W991596. The name was often translated into Latin *rupes*, 'rock', and in 1478 into English. *Seynt Michel* refers to a medieval chapel on the rock, not to the parish church (which is dedicated to an unknown St *Gunand*, 1294). The form of 1748 shows the pronunciation, like English 'roach'. There are other places named with French *roche* in England and Wales.

Rock W9375 (St Minver) 'Ferry of *Blaketore*' 1337, *Black Rock* 1748, *Rock House* 1813. English; the original name was 'black crag', *blæc* + *torr*; by 1748 *torr* had been replaced with *roke* 'rock', and then 'Black' was deleted altogether from the name.

Rose W7754 (Perranzabuloe) *The Rose* 1697; probably Cornish *ros* 'moorland'.

Roseland W83 (district) This comprises the parishes of St Anthony in Roseland, GERRANS, ST JUST in Roseland and PHILLEIGH. It is found as *Rolland* 1201, *Roslande* 1259, *Ros* 1261: originally Cornish *ros*, here in the sense 'promontory', with English *land* added later. Compare the peninsula of Rhos in Pembrokeshire, SN0014. Note also Eglosrose, the alternative name of Philleigh; that name could mean 'the church of Roseland', though it is not known that Philleigh ever served that function.

Rosemullion Head W7927 (coast, Mawnan) *Rosmilion poynte* c.1605, *Rosemullion Head* 1813; named from the nearby farm of Rosemullion W789279. The farm occurs as *Rosmylian* 1318, *Rosemullian* 1562: 'headland of Milyan', *ros* + personal name, or (less likely) 'headland of clover', *ros* + *melhyon*. The modern *u* is an irregular development, apparently dating from the 16th century.

Rosenannon W9566 (St Wenn) Peter de *Rosnonnen* 1326. 'The moorland of the ash-tree', *ros* + *an* + *onnenn*.

Roseworthy w6139 (Gwinear) *Ritwore* 1086, *Redwori*, *Reswori* 1289, *Rosworthy* 1580 (18th), *Rudgewery* c.1605. Probably 'ford of *Gorhi*', *rys* (older *rid*) + personal name. The *th* in the modern form is non-original, and may be due either to hyper-correction, or to analogy with English names in *-worthy*. However, the authentic pronunciation 'Rezurry' or 'Zurry' is still known.

Rough Tor x1480 (hill, St Breward) *Roghetorr*, *Rowetorr* 1284, *Rowtor* 1478. English, 'rough crag', *rúh* + *torr*. Pronounced 'Rowter' (to rhyme with 'doubter'). Compare Rough Tor, Devon, SX6079.

Round Island v9017 (Scilly) *Rownd Ylond* c.1540. English, named from its shape.

Row x0976 (St Breward) So found in 1888. A 19th-century hamlet; English, presumably a 'row' of cottages.

Ruan Lanihorne w8942 (parish) *Lanryhorn* 1270, *Lanrihoerne* 1297, 'parish of *Sanctus Rumonus* of *Lanyhorn*' 1327, *Ruon alias Laryhorin* 1535, *Ruan Lanhorne* 1569. From the patron saint of the parish, St Ruan or Rumon; distinguished from the two other parishes with the same patron saint (see RUAN MINOR) by the name of the manor, Lanihorne. That name is 'church-site of Rihoarn', *lann* + personal name. St Ruan, *Rumon*, is first found as patron saint of this parish in the 10th century (List). The Cornish saint Rumon is probably different from the Breton saint Ronan (honoured at Locronan), with whom he was formerly identified; nothing is known of him, except that his relics were removed from here to Tavistock Abbey, of which he was also the patron saint.

Ruan Minor w7215 (parish) 'Church of *Sanctus Rumonus Parvus*' 1277, *Rumon le meinder* c.1395, *Rewan Minor* 1543, *Ruan Vean* 1569. From the patron saint of the parish (see RUAN LANIHORNE). Latin *Minor* 'smaller' is to distinguish this from the adjacent parish of Ruan Major W703164 (larger in area, though smaller in population); the same is also expressed with Latin *parvus* 'little', French *le meinder* 'the lesser', and Cornish *Vean*, from *byghan* 'small'. Ruan Major was 'church of *Sanctus Romonus*' in 1208.

Rumford w8970 (St Ervan) *Rumford* 1699. English, either a meaningful place-name, 'wide ford', *rúm + ford* (compare Romford, Essex), or from the surname Rumford (itself derived from Romford in Essex). The disadvantage of the first explanation is the late appearance of the name. It is uncertain whether *rúm* 'roomy, wide' would have been used as an adjective so late (it is found until *c*.1635, but mainly in Scots). However, the surname Rumford appears not to be recorded in Cornwall in the 16th-17th centuries. Moreover, the place is at a stream-crossing; so the 'wide ford' is the more attractive alternative.

Rumps Point w9381 (coast, St Minver) *The Rumps* 1813. English, so named from its shape as seen from the sea. Compare The Rumps in Surrey.

Runnel Stone w3620 (coast, St Levan) *Renaldstowe* (*w* for *n*) 1580 (18th), *Rundleston* 1695. English, 'rock with a water-channel', *rynel + stán*. But it is hard to see quite what this means; perhaps *rynel* 'runnel, streamlet' here means 'tidal current'.

Ruthernbridge X0166 (Bodmin/St Breock) 'Bridge of *Ruthen*' 1412, *Rothyn brygge* 1518, *Ruthan Bridge* 1748. English, named from the stream which runs under the bridge; its name is found as *Rodan* (a wood) 1200, *Roethon* (a habitation) 1310, 'water of *Ruthen*' 1412. Probably from a Cornish word *roeth*, equivalent to Welsh *rhwyth* 'juice, liquid', with a suffix *-ynn* or *-an*; the Welsh word itself occurs as a stream-name, Rhwyth, in Carmarthenshire. If that is right, the Cornish stream-name would mean simply 'liquid one'. Note the non-original *r* in the modern spelling, *-ern-*.

Ruthvoes w9260 (St Columb Major) *Ruthfos* 1298, *Ruthas* *c*.1696. 'Red bank', a compound of *rudh + fos*. The form of *c*.1696 shows the pronunciation (rhyming in standard English with 'brothers'). There was a story that St Columb, the virgin, was martyred here, which might have been connected with the redness of the bank; Henderson says, 'curiously enough the hamlet lines the sunken road, the sides of which are red with manganese'.

Saint, St: see under next word.

Saltash x4158 (St Stephen by Saltash) 'Borough of *Esse*' 1201, *Aysh* 1284, *Asshe* 1297, *Saltehasche* 1302, *Ayssheburgh*, *Salte Ayssh* 1386, *Ayshe* 1563. English, originally simply *æsc* 'ash-tree'; compare 22 places called Aish, Ash or Ashe in Devon, with similar early spellings. *Esse*, said to be 'the old name of Saltash', is only a Norman spelling of *Ash*. This particular 'Ash', or part of it, was then separately identified by its production of *salt*: note Saltmill Creek nearby (coast, x4259), 'mill called *Saltmyll*' 1556.

Samson v8712 (island, Scilly) 'Island of *Sanctus Sampson*' c.1160 (15th), *Sampson* c.1585, *Sampsons Ile* 1652. Presumably from a chapel on the island dedicated to the saint, probably St Samson of Dol. There is no historical record of such a chapel, but there are possible archaeological remains of one. Compare St Sampson on Guernsey, in the Channel Isles.

Sancreed w4229 (parish) 'Church of *Eglossant*' c.1176 (1300), 'church of *Sanctus Sancretus*' 1235, 'church of *Sanctus Sancredus*' 1291, *Egglossanres* 1443, *Sanckras* 1580 (18th). From the dedication of the parish church; some forms show *eglos* 'church' + saint's name. St Sancred was believed to have killed his own father by accident, and in contrition he lived as a swineherd; he was as a result revered for curing diseases in pigs. The first form implies an alternative form *Sant* for the saint's name: compare LEZANT (*Lann-Sant*). Note that *Sancred* became 'Sancraz' in speech, as expected, and that this pronunciation lasted into the 20th century; but the archaic written form prevailed in this parish name, as at REDRUTH and elsewhere.

Sandplace x2456 (Morval) *Placeae sabulonis* ('sandingplaces') 1326 (15th), *Sandplace* 1667. English, 'place for bringing sand'. It has been suggested that boats would have brought coastal sand to be unloaded here and put on the fields; seaweed was similarly brought, for the same purpose, until about 1914.

Isles of Scilly Classical spellings, from *Silumnus*, *Silimnus* 1st century onwards, are too corrupt to be of any practical use. *Sulling* c.1160 (13th), *Sully* 1176 (13th),

Syllingar (Norse plural) *c.*1200 (late 14th), *Sylly* 1460, *Iles of Scillye* 1568 (1652), *Sillan* late 17th. A difficult name. One suggestion is that it is derived from that of the pagan Celtic goddess *Sulis*, honoured at Bath and connected with fire and/or water, and identified with Minerva (Athena) by Classical writers. Some Romano-British remains on the islands could be interpreted as suggesting that there was a shrine here in her honour. Whether or not that is right, the precise form and later development of the name are full of difficulties, owing partly to the conflicting spellings. The name may have been subjected to Norse influence, and the ending -*y* might be from Norse *ey* 'island', added to the older Cornish name. There was a variant in -*ing*, which also may be Norse in origin; the late Cornish name *Sillan* might be derived from it. The *c* is non-original, added in the 16th-17th centuries in order to differentiate the name from English 'silly'.

Scorrier W7244 **(Gwennap)** *Scoria* 1330, *Scorrier* 1748. Latin, 'mining-waste', *scoria*. The Latin word was occasionally used in English (e.g. by John Trevisa in 1398), but it is believed never to have become naturalised. However, it must have been current in the south-west, for it appears as a surname at Stoke Climsland, in east Cornwall, in 1297, Warin and Ralph *Scoria*, and 1337, Thomas *Scoria*; and perhaps also in the place-name Scarhill in Devon, SX674941 (*Scoriawell* 1333).

Seaton X3054 **(St Germans/St Martin by Looe)** *Seton Bridge* *c.*1540, *Seythen* 1601, *Seaton* 1602, *Sythian c.*1605: a bridge and village named from the river on which they stand. The river forms the boundary between the two parishes (and thus between the ancient hundreds of East and West). The settlement was already on both sides of it in *c.*1605. The River Seaton, X2670—X3054, is found as *Setthul* (corrupt form) early 13th (15th), *Seychym* (error for *Seythyn*) 1302, *Seythin* 1396 (1593), *Setoun Ryver c.*1540, *Seaton* 1602. Evidently a Cornish name has been made to appear like an English one, partly because the village is indeed a 'sea-town', on the coast. The original *Seythyn* is of uncertain derivation. It has been suggested that it might be 'river full of pot-holes', from Cornish *seth* 'pot' with a suffix *-ynn*. Alternatively it might be from *seth* 'arrow', with the same suffix, but the meaning would be unclear ('swift river', perhaps?). In Wales there are rivers called Saith (Cardiganshire) and Saethon (Caernarvonshire), probably connected with Welsh *saeth* 'arrow'.

Sennen W3525 (parish) 'Parish of *Sancta Senana*' 1327, *Senan* 1524, *Zenning* 1697. From the patron saint of the parish church. She is always female in Cornish records; but there is a male Irish saint of the same name, who was believed to have made a pilgrimage to Rome, and to have founded churches in south-west Ireland. If the Cornish saint has changed sex, she could be the same as the Irish one. But a female Welsh name is also found, latinised as *Senana*; so this could instead be a local Cornish saint, otherwise unknown. Sennen Cove W3526 may be the place called *Porthe Gone Hollye* (read *Hellye*), in Whitesand Bay in 1580 (18th), perhaps the *porth* 'harbour' for Ganilly, in Scilly, V9414; the village is later called Whitesand Cove in 1813 (from WHITESAND BAY on which it lies) and Sennen Cove in 1838.

Seven Stones W0524 (coast, Scilly) *Seven steen* 1584, *Seven stones* 1588, 'The Seven Stones ... may have taken their name, from their lying in a cluster, like the Seven Stars in the heavens; or more probably, from their being generally about seven of them dry at low water spring tides' 1792. English, self-explanatory. The earliest form is a Dutch translation.

Seworgan W7031 (Constantine) *Reswoethgen* 1302, *Sewothgan alias Seworgan* 1614, *Savorgan* 1661. 'Ford of Goedhgen', *rys* + personal name, with mutation of *G* to *w*. The name has undergone considerable change. Note the loss of the unstressed first syllable (already by 1614), the unusual change of *th* to *r* (also by 1614), and the unusual change of *w* to *v* by 1661 (and still current: pronounced 'Se*v*ur*gan'*).

Sharpnose Point, Higher S1914

Sharpnose Point, Lower S1912 (coast, Morwenstow)
*Upper, Lower Sharpnose Point c.*1870. English, self-explanatory, *scearp* + *nós*. Or, since the spellings are so late,

'nose' might be a replacement for *næss* 'promontory' (with the same overall meaning): if so, compare Sharp Ness (Kent) and Sharpness (Gloucestershire).

Sheviock X3755 (parish) *Savioch* 1086, *Sevioc* 12th (13th), *Shevioke* 1259. Probably 'strawberry-place', *sevi* + *-ek*. Alternatively, compare Savick Brook (Lancashire), a stream-name of unknown meaning.

Shop W8773 (St Merryn) *Parkens Shop* 1748. English, 'Parken's workshop', surname + *shop*. The surname is found in the parish (though not necessarily dwelling at this place) at least from 1525, Richard *Parkyn*. Note that both this village and the next one are located at road-junctions, a common site for blacksmiths' workshops.

Shop S2214 (Morwenstow) So found in 1840. English, 'workshop, smithy', as preceding name.

Shortlanesend W8047 (Kenwyn) *Shortlane end* 1678, *Shorts Lanes End* 1716, *Shorts Lane End* 1748, 1813. English; either self-explanatory, 'end of the short lane' or, more likely (since the forms in *Shorts* predominate), compare William and Roger *Shorte* in the parish in 1569. Very close by was *Penfounder* 1547, *Penfounder alias Penvounder* 1695, 'the end of the lane', *penn* + (*an*) + *bownder* (with mutation of *b* to *v*). If the *Shorts* forms are correct, the English name may be an expanded translation of the Cornish one, 'the Short family's part of (*Penvounder* or) Lane's End'.

Siblyback Reservoir X2371 (reservoir, St Cleer)   The reservoir was completed in 1969; it is named from the nearby settlement of Siblyback, X234726. This was *Cibliback* 1567, *Sibliback* 1590: English, the *bæc* 'ridge of land' of a family called *Sibyly*; one such family is found in the district in 1419. The surname is also found elsewhere (e.g. *Sibilye* 1327 Dorset, *Sibilie* 1332 Devon), and is derived from the woman's name *Sibley* (*Sibilla* in Latin). The 'ridge' of the name is probably the hill called Siblyback Moor X2373, just north of the settlement; compare other places in Cornwall called Bake, 'ridge', in St Germans, X3258, and Pelynt, X1854. On the modern map the reservoir is wrongly called 'Siblyback Lake Reservoir', as if there had been a lake here before the reservoir was built.

Sithney w6328 (parish) 'Church of *St Sythninus*' 1230, William de *Merthersitheny* 1230, *Seynt Sitheny* 1379, *Seynt Synney* 1554. From the patron saint of the parish church. He is also venerated at Guisseny on the north coast of Brittany, where he is the patron saint of mad dogs (chosen by the saint himself, in preference to being the patron saint of young women); and where there are good local legends about him. In 1478 he was believed to be buried here at Sithney, and *Merthersitheny* 1230 is *merther* 'place with relics' + saint's name; the name survives as Merther w634292, a farm by the church. The festival formerly held here moved to GOLDSITHNEY before 1284, but that place-name continued to show that its origin lay in this parish.

Smith Sound v8608 (coast, Scilly) *The Smeth sownde, The Smythes sownd* c.1540. English, *sound* 'strait, stretch of water'. Compare the islets of Great and Little Smith, at the entrance to the sound: *The Smyth* c.1585, *Great Smith*, *Little Smith* 1689. Presumably from the surname Smith, though no personal association is known.

South Hill x3272 (parish) *Suthhulle* 1270, *Suthhynle* 1306, *Southille* 1327. A difficult name, to be considered along with NORTH HILL, 4 miles to the north-west. Unlike that place, South Hill always appears with the geographical prefix; and there is only a single form with *n*, that of 1306. There is no obvious feature shared by the two places (except for a ridge-way running between the two), and the parish of Linkinhorne lies in between. The best explanation is that South Hill was a daughter-settlement of *Hindle* (North Hill), named after it with 'South' (and 'North') added to distinguish between the two. That is preferable to the idea of South Hill being an independent 'hinds' wood', *hind* + *léah* (if that is the derivation of North Hill). As with the parent name, South Hill was early re-interpreted as containing English 'hill'.

South Petherwin, South Wheatley: see **P** and **W**.

Start Point x0485 (coast, Tintagel) *Start* 1841, *Start Point* c.1870. English, *steort* 'tail (of land), promontory'.

Stenalees x0157 (St Austell) *Stenaglease alias Stenylease* 1621. This name has to be considered with that of Stennagwyn, three and a half miles away (St Stephen in Brannel, W964549). Both consist of *stenek* 'tin-place' (*sten + -ek*), with the addition respectively of *lys* 'court' and *gwynn* 'white, fair', in order to distinguish the two places. But the meaning of 'court' here would be unknown: the place is not of administrative significance. It is possible that some other word is involved instead, possibly *glas* 'grey-green'; if so, then 'green Stennack', contrasted with Stennagwyn 'white Stennack'. But the forms, such as they are, indicate 'Stennack with a court'.

St Stephen W9453 (in Brannel; parish) 'Church of *Sanctus Stephanus' c.*1166, 'church of *Sanctus Stephanus* in *Branel'* 1291, *Seynt Stevyns* 1478, *Eglostephen* 1578. From the dedication of the parish church to St Stephen, the first martyr, who was stoned to death in Jerusalem in about A.D. 35. The form of 1578 shows *eglos* 'church' + saint's name. This parish was distinguished from the other parishes of the saint by the addition of the manor name: Brannel W956518 was *Bernel* 1086, *Brenel*, *Branel* 1201, an unexplained name, probably an adjective in *-el*. There was also an alternative Cornish name of the churchtown, *Eglosshellans* 1293, surviving as *Egloshellens* 1838, probably 'church of *Helans', eglos* + saint's name, showing a lost Celtic dedication of the church.

St Stephens X3285 (by Launceston; parish) 'The canons of *Sanctus Stefanus'* 1086, 'the upper church of *Sanctus Stephanus* of *Lanstaveton'* 1259, *Seint Stevenys* 1413. From the dedication of the parish church: see above. This place was the original site of *Lann-Stefan* 'church-site of St Stephen', the name which gave rise to LAUNCESTON after the addition of English *tún* and a move of site across the river. After the move of the priory in 1155, there were two 'churches of St Stephen' at Launceston, this older one on the hill and the new one by the ford. Hence 'the upper' in the reference of 1259, to distinguish between them.

St Stephens X4158 (by Saltash; parish) 'Church of *Sanctus Stephanus* of *Seint Estevene'* 1270, 'vicarage of *Sanctus Stephanus* by *Saltasshe'* 1355. From the dedication of the parish church (see above); distinguished from the two other churches by its location beside SALTASH.

Stibb S2210 **(Kilkhampton)** Geoffrey *Stybbe* 1327, *Stibb* 1606. English, *stybb* 'tree-stump'. Compare two instances of the same name in Devon, Stibb Cross SS4215, and Stibb in Ermington parish.

Sticker W9750 **(St Mewan)** *Stekyer* 1319, *Stykker* 1389. Probably 'tree-stumps', *stekyer*, a plural formed of *stok* 'tree-stump' + -*yer*, with vowel-affection of *o* to *e*. Note the 'wood of *Stekyer*' in *c*.1395.

Stithians W7337 **(parish)** *Sancta Stethyana* 1268, 'Church of *Sancta Stediana*' 1282, *Seint Stethyent* 1353, *Seynt Stedyan* 1478, *Stethyans* 1524. From the dedication of the parish church to a St Stithian (*Stediana* in Latin), but nothing is known of her, and nothing remotely resembling the personal name is known in Wales or Brittany. The final *s* of the modern form is odd: it might be descended from the *nt* in 1353, if that is genuine; but no other medieval forms of the name show it. Stithians Reservoir W7136 was constructed in 1965.

Stoke Climsland X3674 **(parish)** 'Church of *Stoke*' 1266, *Stok in Clymeslond* 1302. English, 'outlying farm (*stoc*) in the manor of Climsland'. The name of the manor was added in order to differentiate this *Stoke* from various parishes in Devon (Stoke Canon, Stoke Damarel, Stoke Fleming). The manor was earlier called *Clymes tun* mid-11th, *Clismestone* 1086, *Climeston* 1194 (all referring to the manorial centre at Climsom X369742), and *Climeslande* *c*.1215-1220 (referring to the whole estate). English *tún* and *land* were added to an older name *Climes*; note also Oldclims nearby (X373752), *Oldeclynes* (*n* for *u*?) 1337, perhaps the original manorial centre. The meaning of *Climes* is entirely unknown: there is nothing like it in Welsh or Breton.

The Stone W5526 **(coast, St Hilary)** So found in 1748. English, self-explanatory.

Stratton S2306 **(parish)** *Strætneat* *c*.880 (11th), *Stratone* 1086, *Stratton* 1187. The earliest form shows that this is a Cornish name, despite its English appearance: English *tún* has been added to an older name meaning 'valley (*stras*, earlier *strad*) of the River Neet'. The river-name itself has conflicting early spellings: *Neh(e)t, Neet, Neth* 13th; it is now called either the River Strat (a back-formation from 'Stratton'), or the River Neet (which seems to be an antiquarian revival, for the name is not found after the 13th century). Its derivation is obscure. A comparison with Irish *necht* 'clean' has been suggested; or, instead, one could compare the river Nedd ('Neath') in south Wales, itself obscure. It is uncertain, too, whether Stratton is a cut-down form of a hypothetical *Strætneat-tun*, with English *tún* added to the whole older name. This seems unlikely in view of the second form, of 1086, and perhaps the first syllable alone of the Cornish name was preserved and had *tún* added to it, *Stræt-tun*. Note that, if it were not for the earliest reference, one would assume that this was entirely an English name, since the forms from 1086 onwards have that appearance.

Summercourt w8856 (St Enoder) *Somercourt* 1711 (1738). English, but the meaning of the name is unclear. There is an important fair here in September, mentioned from an early date: (Roger de) *Longaferia* 1227, *La Lunge feire* 1234, 'fair of *Langchepyng*' 1351; English 'long fair', *lang* + *feire* or *cíeping* 'market'. The fair is long in shape, being laid out along the main road. It would be satisfactory to think that 'summer court' might refer to this fair; but 'court' is not recorded in that sense. The name should mean 'court-yard used in summer': compare *Le Somer Yerde* 'the summer yard' 1516 at Newton, St Neot.

Talland Bay x2251 (coast, Talland) So found in 1813, and earlier referred to as *a crikket betwixt Poulpirrhe and Low* ('a creek between Polperro and Looe') in *c.*1540. Named from the parish church of Talland (X228516), which is found as 'church of *Tallan*' *c.*1205 (early 14th), *Tallant* 1440. The name seems probably to be a compound, 'hill-brow church-site', *tal* + *lann*. A saint was subsequently invented from the name, *Sanctus Tallanus* 1452, but this is rare and late, and the older dedication was to St Katherine, the early martyr of Alexandria.

Talskiddy w9165 (St Columb Major) *Talschedy, Talskydy* 1297, *Talskedy* 1300. Possibly 'hill-brow of land-clearance', *tal* + a Cornish word corresponding to Breton *skidiñ* 'to clear land'; less likely 'brow of shadows', *tal* + *skeudi*, plural of *skeus* 'shadow' (older *skeud*). Compare perhaps Tolskithy (Illogan, W6841), *Tolskithey* 1748.

River Tamar S2615—X4357 *'Tamaros* river' *c.*150 (11th), *Tamaris c.*700 (13th), *Tamur c.*984, *Tamer* 997, late11th, and generally to *c.*1870; *Tamar River* 1748. An ancient river-name, formed from a root *tam-*, which occurs in many other river-names in Britain and Europe (Thames, Tavy, Tambre in Spain, Tammaro in Italy, etc.). One suggestion is that this root meant simply 'to flow' (the river-names thus meaning 'flowing one'), but that is very uncertain. For the suffix *-ar*, compare the River LYNHER; but the modern spelling in *-ar* seems to be an artificial revival of the classical form. The 19th-century spelling *Tamer* was preferable, showing the pronunciation. Lower Tamar Lake S2911 (reservoir, Kilkhampton/Devon) is referred to as 'the reservoir' 1821, 'Reservoir' *c.*1870, *Bude Canal Reservoir* 1888. It fed the Bude canal, which was opened in 1823. Upper Tamar Lake S2812 (reservoir, Kilkhampton/Devon) was completed in 1975.

North Tamerton X3197 (parish) *Tamert' c.*1162 (15th), Peter de *Tamerton* 1180, *North Tamerton* 1620. English, 'estate (*tún*) on the river Tamar', with 'North' added later to distinguish it from Tamerton Foliot near Plymouth. But the two parishes, lying in different counties, were not normally confused, and the distinguishing word is rare until the 19th century.

East Taphouse X1863 (St Pinnock) *Ye East topp House* 1675, *Easter Taphouse* 1699. English *tap-house* 'an alehouse'. 'East' is in contrast with Middle and West Taphouse (in Braddock, X1763 and X1563), first found as *Taphouse c.*1533. Until the 19th century this area was moorland, and these would have been isolated inns for travellers on the highway from Liskeard to Lostwithiel, like Jamaica Inn (on Bodmin Moor) and INDIAN QUEENS.

Tean V9016 (island, Scilly) 'Island of *Sancta Teona' c.*1160 (15th), 'island of *Sancta Theona*, virgin' 1193 (16th), *Tyan c.*1540. From the patron saint of the chapel here, of which remains survive. There is a male person called *Teon* mentioned in early Welsh saints' pedigrees; Geoffrey of Monmouth made him into a bishop of Gloucester, who became Archbishop of London after King Arthur's time. If the Scillies saint had changed sex, there might be some connection; otherwise nothing is known of her. Pronounced as a disyllable, 'Teean'.

St Teath x0680 (parish) 'Church of *Sancta Tetha*', *Egglostetha* c.1190 (17th), *Seynte Tetha* 1525, *St Etha* 1549. From the patron saint of the church. She was believed to have been one of the 24 sons and daughters of the Welsh king Broccan, according to the Cornish version of the legend, where her name is given as *Tedda* in the vernacular. Compare Landeda in Brittany (north-west of Brest), and a 9th-century Breton priest called *Tedei*, whose name is the same as that of the Cornish saint. One early form shows Cornish *eglos* 'church' + saint's name.

Temple x1473 (parish) 'Causeway of *Templum*' 1241 (15th), *Temple* 1284, 'the chapel of *Temple*, which formerly belonged to the Templars' 1335. From the ownership of the place by the Knights Templar. Their estate here is mentioned, but not named, at an earlier date, 'one land on *Fawimore*' (BODMIN MOOR) 1185.

The Brisons, **The** Carracks, **The** Garrison, **The** Hurlers, **The** Loe, **The** Manacles, **The** Road, **The** Stone: see B, C, G, etc.

Threemilestone w7844 (Kenwyn) *Three Mile Stone* 1884; a 19th-century hamlet named from its position three miles outside Truro.

Tiddy, River x2869—x3657 *Tudi* late 11th, *Tody* c.1317, *Tyddie* early 17th. An obscure name. The medieval spellings in *o* show that the *u* of the first form is Cornish *o* rather than *u*, so that *tus* 'people' (older *tud*) cannot be compared. The name no doubt contains the river-name suffix -*i*, added to an unknown stem. The change from *u/o* to *i/y* in the first syllable is also unexplained.

Tideford x3459 (St Germans) Ruald de *Tutiford* 1201, *Tediford brigge* 1345, *Todisford* 1378, *Tidiford* 1813. English, 'Ford over the River TIDDY'. By coincidence, the river is tidal up to the bridge. That fact, and the misleading modern spelling, have led to the misconception that the name is English 'tidal ford'; but the constant *i* in early spellings (and as recently as 1813), and the pronunciation 'Tiddy-ford', show the correct derivation.

Tintagel X0588 (parish) *Tintagol c.*1137 (mid 12th), Robert de *Tyntagel,* de *Tintajoel* 1208, 'the island of *Tyntagel* and Richard's castle' 1233 (*c.*1300), 'church of *Sancta Merteriana* de *Tynthagel*' 1259. Probably 'fort of a constriction', *din* + probably *tagell.* The pronunciation of the *g* as 'dj', already in existence by 1207, counts against *tagell* as second element; but it can be explained as due to Norman influence in this name, of which the main fame was in romances. The 'fort' of the name would refer to the Dark-Age occupation of the headland; and the 'constriction' would be the narrow neck joining the promontory to the mainland. Tintagel Head X0489 (coast) is *Tintagell Head* 1748. Until the 20th century, the name Tintagel referred to the castle, the manor and the church, but not to the village here. That was called Trevena as recently as 1907, formerly *Trewarvene* 1259, *Trevenna c.*1870; 'farm on a hill', *tre* + *war* + *menydh* (with mutation of *m* to *v*).

Torpoint X4355 (Antony) *The Torr, Tor parke* 1617 (fields), *Tar Point* 1736, *Tor-point* 1746, *Torr Point* (hamlet) 1748. An eighteenth-century new town, named from the nearby point. English, 'crag-headland', *torr* + *point.* The variant spelling with *Tar* seems to be a temporary re-interpretation or corruption; the older field-names show that *torr* is original. The same headland seems to be the one known at an earlier date by the name of *Stertpoynt* 1608: English, *steort* 'tail of land' (compare START POINT in Tintagel and elsewhere). Evidently the nearby field called *Torr* caused the replacement of *steort* with *torr* between 1608 and 1736.

Towan Head W7962 (coast, St Columb Minor) *Towan point* 1699, *Towan Head* 1748; named from the nearby settlement called *Tewyn* 1289, *Towyn* 1504, Cornish *tewynn* 'sand-dunes'. The place survived as an independent settlement, *Towan* 1748 (different from *New Key*), but by 1813 the two places had merged: *New Quay alias Towan.* It seems to have been a different place from Towan Blistra, the alternative name of NEWQUAY.

163

Towednack W4838 **(parish)** 'Parish of *Sanctus Tewenno-cus*' 1327, *Tewynnek* 1524, *Twidnack* c.1605. From the dedication of the parish church to St Winwaloe, in the pet-form *To-Winnoc* (containing *to-* 'thy'). See ST WINNOW for details of the saint and his cult. This name shows late Cornish *dn* from *nn*.

Townshend W5932 **(Crowan)** *Townsend* 1867. A 19th-century village, created by the Townshend family (Dukes of Leeds), who had inherited the Godolphin lands in this area: compare LEEDSTOWN.

Traboe W7421 **(St Keverne)** *Trefwurabo* 977 (11th), 1059, *Treurabo* c.1240 (14th), *Trerabo* 1611. 'Farm of Gorabo', *tre* + personal name, with mutation of *g* to *w* and then the loss of that syllable. Pronounced 'Trebba'.

Trebartha X2677 **(North Hill)** *Triberthan* 1086, *Trebartha* 1284, 1302; *tre* + unknown word or name. Compare a lost place called *Polbartha* 1333, perhaps in Advent parish; and the second part of POLBATHICK. There is a Welsh stream-name Barthen, Cardiganshire, also unexplained.

Trebetherick W9378 **(St Minver)** Ralph de *Trebederich* 1284, *Trebedrek* 1302, *Trebethrick* 1657. 'Farm of Pedrek', *tre* + saint's name, with mutation of *p* to *b*. Note that Pedrek has become 'Petherick', just as at LITTLE PETHERICK nearby. The name here is probably connected with the monastery of St Petrock (Pedrek) at PADSTOW, just across the estuary. In the Life of St Petrock it is claimed that the saint, on first arriving in Cornwall, struck a spring of water here in the middle of the dry sand; but no connection of ownership with the monastery is known.

Trebudannon W8961 **(St Columb Major)** *Trebedannan* 1279, *Trepydannen* 1355. Probably 'farm of *Pydannan*', *tre* + personal name (with mutation of *p* to *b*), though no exact equivalent of such a personal name is found elsewhere.

Treburley X3477 **(Lezant)** *Treburley* 1538. Compare William *Borlay* in the parish in 1327. The place-name is probably an example of a late *tre*, formed with the surname of the medieval family, 'Borlay's farm'. The surname itself is likely to come from Devon, from Burley Down in Lewtrenchard, or Burleigh in South Huish.

Tredavoe w4528 (Paul)   William de *Trewordavo* 1298, Treworthavou 1328, *Tredavo alias Trewardavow* 1633. 'Farm of Gorthavow', *tre* + personal name, with mutation of *g* to *w*.

Tredinnick w9270 (St Issey)   Roger de *Treredenek* 1286, *Tredenek* 1406. 'Brackeny farm', *tre* + *reden* + *-ek*.

Tredrizzick w9576 (St Minver) *Tredreyseg* 1262. 'Brambly farm', *tre* + *dreys* + *-ek*.

Treen w3923 (St Levan) *Trethyn* 1284 (1446), *Treen* 1699. 'Farm of a fort', *tre* + *din*, with mutation of *d* to *dh*, and its subsequent loss, turning the name into a monosyllable. The reference is to the nearby promontory-fort called Treryn Dinas, W397222 (*dinas* 'fort'); it is first mentioned as 'castle of *Trethyn*' 1478.

Tregadillett x2983 (Launceston St Thomas)   *Tregadylet* 1076 (15th), *Tregadilet c.*1212 (15th). Probably 'farm of Cadyled', *tre* + personal name (with mutation of *c* to *g*); but there is no evidence for such a name. There is a personal name *Cadwoled*, but it would not fit the early spellings so well.

Tregeare x2486 (Egloskerry)   Richard de *Tregyer*, John de *Trengyer* 1284. 'Farm by the fort', *tre* + (*an*) + *ker*, with mutation of *k* to *g*; note the optional definite article in one of the forms. The fort is the earthwork on Tregeare Down, X249867.

Tregeare Rounds x0380 (fort, St Kew)   *Tregaer Castle* 1876. Dialect 'rounds' in the sense 'hill-fort'; named from the neighbouring farm of Tregeare X033797 (*Tregayr* 1425), 'farm by a fort', *tre* + *ker*, with mutation of *k* to *g*. In antiquarian writings the spurious name 'Dameliock Castle' (*c.*1735 and later) was bestowed upon this fort, owing to a misunderstanding of the text of Geoffrey of Monmouth's *History of the Kings of Britain*, where the name *Dimilihoc* occurs, actually referring to Domellick, W943585 in ST DENNIS parish.

Tregidden w7522 (St Keverne) *Tregudyn c.*1190, 1331; *tre* 'farm' + unknown word or name: *cudynn* 'hair' would fit, but makes no sense; possibly a personal name *Cudynn*. The hamlet now called Tregidden was formerly Tregidden

Mill (first mentioned as 'mills of *Tregudyn*' in 1331), and the original farm of Tregidden is a quarter-mile to the south, at W753225.

Tregole x1998 (Poundstock) *Turgoil* 1086, *Tregoul* 1270, *Tregaul* 1293, *Tregowel* 1306. Obscure. The first word may be *tre* 'farmstead', if the earliest form has *Tur* in error for *Tre*; the second word is completely obscure.

Tregonetha w9563 (St Wenn) *Tregenhetha* 1341, *Treganeytha* 1357. 'Farm of Kenhetho', *tre* + personal name, with mutation of *k* to *g*.

Tregonning Hill w6029 (hill, Breage/Germoe) So found in 1687. The hill is named from the nearby farm of Tregonning (in Breage, W605303). The farm was *Tregonan* in 1341; 'farm of Conan', *tre* + personal name, with mutation of *c* to *g*. There was a Cornish name for the hill, found as 'hille of *Pencair*' c.1540; 'top of a fort', *penn* + *ker*, with reference to the hill-fort on the summit; but that name has not survived.

Tregony w9245 (Cuby) *Trefhrigoni* 1049, *Treligani* (*l* for *r*) 1086, 'borough of *Trigoni*' 1201, *Tregeny* 1214, *Tregny* c.1540. Probably 'farm of Rigni', *tre* + personal name, but the form of such a personal name is uncertain. *Rigni* would be best, for then the vowel between *g* and *n* would be epenthetic and unstressed, 'Tre-*rigony*', becoming 'Tregony'. That would explain both the variation in that vowel in the early forms (*o*, *a* and *e*), and also the unexpected modern stress on the first syllable, a stress which is at least 400 years old, as shown by the form of c.1540. If that vowel were not epenthetic, it would have borne the stress, and the name would then have been stressed 'Tre-*rigony*', giving modern 'Tre*gony*'. However, there is little justification for a personal name of the form *Rigni*, as required.

Tregurrian w8565 (St Mawgan in Pydar) *Tregurrian*, *Tregurrion* 1606. Obscure, for lack of earlier forms: *tre* 'farm' + unknown word or name.

Treknow x0586 (Tintagel) *Tretdeno* 1086, *Trefnou* c.1245, *Trenou* 1337. 'Farm of a valley', *tre* + *tnow*; it is situated at the head of a short side-valley to the north of the main valley running down to the coast. Note the epenthetic *e* in

1086 (later lost again); and the early reduction of the diphthong -*ow* to -*o*, also in 1086.

Trelan w7418 (St Keverne) *Treland*, *Trelant* 1086, *Trelanmur* c.1260, *Trelan* 1288. Probably 'farm at a church-site', *tre* + *lann*; the forms often have *meur* 'great' attached, in contrast with Trelanvean (*byghan* 'small') at W752197. No early church-site is known in the area, but there is an Iron-Age (unenclosed) cemetery half-way between Trelan and Trelanvean, and it might be connected with the name in some way. The final *d/t* in the earliest forms is odd. It might suggest *nans* 'valley', instead of *lann*; but there is no valley at either site, so that will not do. The ideal meaning might have been 'farm in moorland', for both places are situated on the edge of Goonhilly Downs; but there is no Cornish word corresponding to French *lande* 'moorland'.

Treligga x0584 (St Teath) *Treluge*, *Treluga* 1086, *Treluga* 1304, *Trelygy* 1569; *tre* 'farm' + unknown word or name — probably a personal name of the form *Luga*, though there is little justification for such a form.

Trelights w9979 (St Endellion) *Trefflectos* 1302, *Treleghtres* 1425; *tre* 'farm' + unknown word or name. Trelash (in Warbstow, X186903) has the same derivation (*Trefleghtres* 1355). There is a Welsh place-name Llechryd, meaning 'slab-ford' (three instances). A corresponding Cornish word would suit the forms moderately well, though it would be necessary to assume an intrusive *t* between the two words (*legh-rys* becoming *leghtrys*), which would be irregular. But it would not suit the sites of the places, since both are at the heads of streams rather than at fords.

Trelill x0478 (St Kew) *Trelulla* 1262, *Trelille* c.1540. Probably 'farm of Lulla', *tre* + personal name. *Lulla* is an Old English personal name, not a Cornish one.

Trelissick w8339 (Feock) John de *Trelesyk* 1275, Matthew *Trelesyc* 1327. Probably 'farm of Ledik' *tre* + personal name, with change of *d* to *s*. Other examples of Trelissick (in St Erth and Sithney) were formerly *Trewolesyk* (so in 1358, St Erth) or the like, 'farm of Goledik', *tre* + personal name, with mutation of *g* to *w*; but the place in Feock has no such spellings to indicate a similar origin.

Trelowarren w7224 (St Mawgan in Meneage) *Trellewaret*, *Treluueren* 1086, *Trelewarent* 1227, *Treleweren* 1290; *tre* 'farm' + unknown word or name. The early spellings, and the stress, show that the second word cannot be *lowarn* 'fox'; but the name may later have been felt to contain that word. Note that the forms seem to show final *nt* becoming *n*, with loss of *t*, instead of giving *ns* as normally.

Tremail x1686 (Davidstow) *Tremail* 1086, *Tremayl* 1284 (1602), 1327. 'Farm of Mel', *tre* + personal name. Note the lack of the expected mutation (*m* to *v*) here in east Cornwall.

Tremaine x2389 (parish) 'Chapel of *Tremen*' c.1230 (15th), *Tremene* 15th, *Tremaine* 1582. 'Farm of a stone', *tre* + *men*. The early forms show that a tentative derivation previously given, 'farm of monks', *tre* + *menegh*, plural of *managh*, cannot be right.

Tremar x2568 (St Cleer) *Tremargh* 1284, 1305. 'Farm of Margh', *tre* + personal name, is more probable than 'farm of a horse', *tre* + *margh*.

Trematon x3959 (St Stephen by Saltash) *Tref meu tun* mid-11th, *Tremetone* 1086, *Tremeton* 1201, *Trematon* 1337; *tre* + unknown word or name *meu*, with the subsequent addition of English *tún* 'farm, estate'.

Trenance w8567 (St Mawgan in Pydar) *Trenans* 1327. 'Farm in a valley', *tre* + *nans*. The original settlement was at the head of a short (quarter-mile) valley running down to the coast.

Trenarren x0348 (St Austell) *Tyngharan* 1302, *Tingaran* 1307, *Trenyaren* 1556. 'Fort of a crane', *din* (variant *tin*) + *garan*, with later re-interpretation of *Tin* as *Tren*. The fort is the cliff-castle on BLACK HEAD nearby.

Trendrine Hill w4738 (hill, Zennor/Towednack) So found in 1888; named from Trendrine nearby in Zennor parish, W475394. The farm is first found as *Trendreyn* in 1302; 'farm of the thorn-bushes', *tre* + *an* + *dreyn*. The hill has had several different names. It is first found as *Carne an Watch* 1613, 'crag of the look-out place', *carn* + *an* + English *watch*, a hybrid name. Later it is called Carnminnis 1813, probably 'little crag', *carn* + *munys*; and Merra Hill *c.*1870, of uncertain derivation, possibly from a lost place called *Merther* which seems to have existed in Towednack (*merther*, 'place claiming a saint's relics').

Treneglos x2088 **(parish)** 'Church of *Treneglos*' 1269, 'church of St Gregory of *Treneglos*' 1282. 'Farm of the church', *tre + an + eglos.*

Trenewan x1753 **(Lansallos)** *Trenewien* 1207, *Trenewyen* 1424; *tre* 'farm' + unknown word or name, probably a personal name *Nowyen.*

Trerice w8458 **(Newlyn East)** Odo de *Trereys* 1302, Odo de *Treres* 1326, *Trerees* 1359. 'Farm by a ford', *tre + rys.*

Tresco v8914 **(island, Scilly)** *Trescau* 1305, *Trescaw, Iniscaw*, 'the Isle of Elder, by cawse yt bereth stynkkyng elders' *c.*1540. 'Farm of elder-bushes', *tre + scaw.* Later the name was changed to 'island of elders', *ynys + scaw*, but the change did not last. An older name for the island was 'island of *Sanctus Nicholaus*' 1193 (15th), from the cell of Tavistock Abbey here, dedicated to St Nicholas; the cell is first referred to as 'prior and brothers of *Sanctus Nicholaus*' 1176 (13th).

Trescowe w5730 **(Breage)** *Trescau* 1086, *c.*1210. 'Farm of elder-bushes', *tre + scaw.*

Tresillian w8646 **(Merther/St Erme)** *Tresulyan* 1325, *Tresulian* 1336, *Tresilian* 1451. 'Farm of Sulyen', *tre +* personal name.

Tresmeer x2387 **(parish)** *Treguasmer* 1076 (15th), *Trewasmur*, 'chapel of *Treasmur*' 1185 (15th), *Tresmur* 1275 (15th), 1291, *Tresmere* 1284. Probably 'farm of Gwasmeur', *tre +* personal name, though there is not good evidence for such a name. The early forms show that a derivation previously given, 'great moorland', *ros + meur*, cannot be right.

Trethevy Quoit x2568 **(antiquity, St Cleer)** *Trethevystones*, 'called in Latin *Casa gigantis* [the giant's house], a litle howse raysed of mightie stones' *c.*1605, *Trevethy Stone* 1842, *Trethevy Quoit* 1885. English, 'cromlech at Trethevy', with 19th-century antiquarian use of English *quoit* in the sense 'discus, giant's play-thing'. It is named from the nearby farm of Trethevy, which occurs as *Trethewy* 1284, 'farm of Dewi', *tre +* personal name (with mutation of *d* to *dh*). The change of *w* to *v* is unusual. Note the deliberate antiquarian corruption to *Trevethy* (e.g. in 1842), in order to make the name appear to contain *bedh* 'grave', with reference to the Quoit. In 1872 the name was pronounced 'Tredavy'.

Trethewey w3823 (St Levan) *Trethewy* 1320. 'Farm of Dewi', *tre* + personal name, with mutation of *d* to *dh*.

Trethurgy x0355 (St Austell) *Tretheverki* c.1230, *Trethevergy* 1251, *Trethergy* 1360. 'Farm of Devergi', *tre* + personal name, is much more likely than 'farm of an otter', *tre* + *dowrgi*; in either case there is mutation of *d* to *dh*.

Trevalga x0890 (parish) 'Chapel of *Trevalga*' 1238, *Trevalga* 1262; *tre* 'farmstead' + probably a personal name. The first part of such a personal name could be *Mel-* (Old Cornish *Mael-*), with *ae* borrowed here in east Cornwall as *a*, before it became Middle Cornish *e*; and with mutation of *m* to *v*. The name *Melgi* would be a possibility, if the earliest form already showed reduction of -*i* to *a*; a name *Melga* would suit the forms best, but such a personal name cannot be paralleled. There was an older name for the place, *Melledan* 1086, 'church of *Menelidan*' c.1163 (13th), 'church of *Melidan*' 1201, *Meleneledan* 1238; probably 'broad hill', *menydh* + *ledan*, but the forms are corrupt.

Trevanson w9772 (St Breock) *Trevansun* 1259, *Trevanson* 1284. 'Farm of Antun', *tre* (older *trev*) + personal name, with the original final *v* of *trev* preserved before a vowel; note the change of *nt* to *ns*.

Trevarren w9160 (St Columb Major) Odo de *Treverran* 1201, *Treveran* 1244; *tre* 'farm' + unknown word or name, perhaps a personal name *Meren*, for which there is slight evidence. 'Farm of Meren', if so, with mutation of *m* to *v*.

Trevarrick w9843 (Goran) Amandus *Trevarek* 1327, Nicholas de *Trevarek* 1332; *tre* 'farm' + unknown word or name.

Trevellas w7452 (St Agnes) Ralph de *Trevelles* 1306, *Trevelles* 1337, *Trevellas* 1341; *tre* 'farm' + unknown word or name, possibly a personal name *Melyd*, for which there is slight evidence. 'Farm of Melyd', if so, with mutation of *m* to *v*, and later change of *d* to *s*.

170

Treverva W7531 **(Budock)** Richard *Trewruvo* 1327, John *Trefurvo* 1358, *Trevyrvo* 1407; *tre* 'farm' + unknown word or name. If the earliest form were an error for *Trewurvo*, it would be more consistent with the others. Possibly then 'farm of Urvo', *tre* + uncertain personal name, with the final *v* of *trev* preserved before a following vowel. The spellings indicate *Urvo* (with regular reduction of *-o* to *-a* in the modern form); but there is no parallel for such a name.

Trevigro X3369 **(South Hill)** *Trevigora* *c.*1230 (1348), Nicholas *Trefigerow* 1327; *tre* 'farm' + unknown word or name. Note that the vowel between *g* and *r* seems to be epenthetic; and the later *-o(w)* perhaps a hyper-correction. The original form of the second element should have been either *igra*, with preservation of the final *v* of *trev*, or else *bigra* or *migra*, with mutation of *b/m* to *v*.

Treviscoe W9456 **(St Stephen in Brannel)** *Tref otcere* 1049, Robert de *Trevyscar* 1333, *Treviscoe* 1748. 'Farm of Otker', *tre* + personal name, with survival of the original *v* of *trev*, and later change of *t* to *s*. The modern form, ending in *-oe*, must be a hyper-correction of a pronounced form 'Trevisca', with unusual loss of *r*, though such a form is not actually found. Note that no derivation would have been possible without the form of 1049.

Trevone W8975 **(Padstow)** *Treavon* 1302, Ainger de *Treavon*, de *Treafon* 1333, *Trevone* 1427. A difficult name; *Treavon* looks like 'farm of a river' *tre* + *avon*; but that makes no sense here, unless *avon* could be used of the sea, which is unlikely. Moreover, the modern stress, on the last syllable, and the early loss of *a* (already in 1427) are hard to reconcile with a two-syllable word as second element: it should then have been pronounced 'Tre-*avon*', and the stress would not have landed on the final syllable.

Trevose Head W8576 **(coast, St Merryn)** *Trevose Point* 1699, *Trevose Head* 1748. The headland is named from the nearby farm of Trevose. That was *Trenfos* 1302, 'farm by the bank', *tre* + (*an*) + *fos*. Such a 'bank' suggests a promontory-fort on the headland, and that is confirmed by the name Dinas Head for a part of the headland (W8476, *dinas* 'fort'); but no definite remains are known. However, there is a revetment or bank, of uncertain date, beside the road which leads to the farm (W865756). If old enough, it might be the feature which gave rise to the name.

Trewarmett x0686 (Tintagel) James de *Trewerman* 1302, *Trewarman*, *Treworman* 1337, *Trewarmett* 1599; *tre* 'farm' + unknown word or name, possibly a personal name *Gorman*, with mutation of *g* to *w*: 'farm of Gorman', if so. The 16th-century change from *-n* to *-tt* is odd and unexplained.

Trewarthenick w9044 (Cornelly) Stephen de *Trewythynek* 1284. 'Farm of Gwethenek', *tre* + personal name, with mutation of *gw* to *w*. 'Wooded farm' is not a possible meaning, for the adjective from *gwydh* 'trees' was *gwydhek*, not *gwydhennek*.

Trewassa x1486 (Davidstow) Andrew de *Trewasa*, Agatha de *Trawassa* 1284, *Trewassa* 1305. 'Farm of Gwasso', *tre* + personal name, with early reduction of *-o* to *-a*.

Trewavas Head w5926 (coast, Breage) So found in 1813; named from the neighbouring farm of Trewavas. That was *Trewaevos* 1289, 'farm of a winter-home', *tre* + *gwavos*, with mutation of *gw* to *w*.

Trewellard w3733 (St Just in Penwith) 'Mill of *Trewyllard*' 1307, Philip *Trewylard* 1327; *tre* 'farm' + uncertain second word, perhaps a personal name *Gwylarth*, giving 'farm of Gwylarth', with mutation of *gw* to *w*. There is no direct evidence for such a personal name, but it is more likely than an earlier suggestion, that the second word is a compound containing *ardh* 'a height'. In either case, there is a later change of final *-rth* to *-rd*, found elsewhere.

Trewen x2583 (parish) *Trewen* c.1293 (15th). Probably 'white farm', *tre* + *gwenn* (feminine form of *gwynn*), with mutation of *gw* to *w*. The short vowel in the place-name makes 'farm of Gwen', *tre* + personal name, less likely, for that man's name would have had a long vowel.

Trewidland x2559 (Liskeard) Nicholas de *Trewithelon* 1297, *Trewythelan* 1298. Possibly 'farm of Gwydhelan', *tre* + personal name, with mutation of *gw* to *w*. The personal name would be a Cornish equivalent of Welsh *Gwyddelan*, found in place-names. But the stress in the Cornish name is wrong, for the Welsh name is stressed 'Gwy*ddel*an', whereas the Cornish name was evidently stressed 'Tre-*with*elan', with epenthetic *e*, as shown by the modern form. There is a Welsh word *gwyddlan*, meaning 'churchyard, cemetery', and a Cornish equivalent of that would suit the forms of Trewidland well: 'farm by a cemetery', if so. But there is no record of such a feature here.

Trewint x1897 **(Poundstock)** *Trewynt* 1303, *Trewent* 1336. 'Windy farm', *tre* + *gwyns* (older *gwynt*), with mutation of *gw* to *w*.

Trewithian w8737 **(Gerrans)** *Trewythyan* c.1270 (14th), *Trewythian* 1300. 'Farm of Gwethyen or Gwydhyan', *tre* + personal name, with mutation of *gw* to *w*. The exact form of the personal name is uncertain, for there are several to choose from.

Trewoon w9952 **(St Mewan)** *Tregoin* 1086, *Trewoen* 1284, *Trewoone alias Troone* 1680. 'Farm on the downs', *tre* + *goen*, with mutation of *g* to *w*. The modern pronunciation is 'Trooan'; this must be derived from the shortened form 'Troon' (as in 1680, and compare TROON), with subsequent breaking of the long vowel into a diphthong; the written form Trewoon was already archaic in 1680.

Treyarnon w8673 **(St Merryn)** *Trearvan* (*v* for *n*) c.1210, *Treyarnen* c.1240, *Trearnen* c.1245. Probably 'farm of Yarnenn', *tre* + personal name, though the exact form would be uncertain.

Trispen w8450 **(St Erme)** *Tredespan* 1325, *Trethespan* 1382, *Trevisprin* 1462, *Trispan* 1695. Obscure; *tre* 'farm' + unknown word or name *despan*, with mutation of *d* to *dh*. In the 15th century the *dh* was replaced by *v*, which survives in the archaic form Trevispian Vean nearby ('little Trispen', + *byghan*); but the first two syllables were later conflated to give the modern 'Trispen'.

Troon w6638 **(Camborne)** Simon *Trewoen* 1327, *Trewon* 1430, *Troon* 1768. 'Farm on the downs', *tre* + *goen*, with mutation of *g* to *w*, and later conflation of the two syllables into one. Compare TREWOON, which underwent the same process; but in that case the archaic form continued to be written, whereas here the new pronunciation became the established written form also.

Truro w8244 (city) *Triueru* c.1173, *Triwereu* 1201, *Truru* c.1280, *Trufru* 1289. A difficult name. It is clear that the first element is not *tre*, but *try*-, a prefix meaning 'triple' or 'very' (or possibly 'through, across'). It is unclear whether the second part began with *w* or *v*, though the occasional spellings with *f* suggest original *v* (mutated from *b* or *m*, if so). The second part of the name is anyway obscure. It might be a word *berow* 'a boiling', in which case the whole name ought to mean 'a very-boiling'. That would be perfect in form, but would make little sense; perhaps if the meaning could be '(place of) great water-turbulence' it might be a reasonable interpretation. The town is liable to flood in winter, as two fast rivers meet the sea here at the head of a creek. However, as an alternative possibility, one might compare the Gaulish tribe of the *Treveri*, whose name survives in Trier. Their name is thought to mean possibly 'people of the river-crossing' (compare Old Irish *treóir* 'water-crossing'). This meaning would suit Truro very well, since the two river-crossings are the significant feature of its location; but it is much harder to justify linguistically, for there would be no explanation for the final *-(e)u* in the Cornish name, unless possibly one compared the suffix in *Cornowii*, 'horn-people' (see CORNWALL). The explanation 'three rivers', sometimes suggested, is unfortunately not possible, because there is no word *ber* or *ber(e)w* meaning 'river'.

St Tudy x0676 (parish) *Hecglostudic* 1086, *Seintudi* 1201, *Sanctus Tudius* 1281, *Sanctus Tudicus* 1302, *Seynt Udy* 1522. From the dedication of the parish church. St Tudy is also honoured at various places in Brittany, where he was believed to have been a disciple of St Mawes (Maudez). The first form contains *eglos* 'church' + saint's name. Note the early loss of final *c* in this name; a saint *Tudec* is known in Brittany. It is possible that both *Tudi(c)* and *Tudec* are simply pet-forms for St Tugdual, an important Breton saint of the diocese of Quimper.

Twelveheads w7642 (Kea) New mineral house called *the Twelfe Heades* early 17th. English; 'heads' are the hammers in a set of tin-stamps; the place is at a confluence of streams, and there must have been a set of water-driven tin-stamps here — perhaps two sets, with six heads each.

Tywardreath x0854 **(parish)** *Tiwardrai* 1086, 'church of St Andrew of *Tywardrait*' *c*.1150 (13th), *Tiwardraith* 1235, *Trewardreth* 1367. 'House on the strand', *chi* (older *ti*) + *war* + *treth*, with mutation of the *t* of *treth* to *d*. The written forms of this name (denoting a manor, parish and priory) had a strong influence, enough to preserve the ancient form *Ty*, which here never became *chi*; later it was often re-interpreted as *Tre*. Pronounced 'Tower-*dreth*', with short *e*, though 'dreeth' might have been expected.

Upton Cross x2872 **(Linkinhorne)** So found in 1870. A 19th-century village at a cross-roads, near Upton X279724. In 1839 a field at Upton was called *Cross Park*, but the hamlet apparently did not yet exist. Upton itself was *Uppeton* 1474; 'higher farm', English *upp* + *tún*, here in contrast with Netherton 'lower farm', half a mile away.

Vale of Mawgan or Lanherne w8765 **(valley, St Mawgan in Pydar)** *Vale of Lanherne* 1836, *Vale of Mawgan or Lanherne* 1906. Named from two places in the valley, ST MAWGAN in Pydar, and the settlement at St Mawgan called Lanherne, actually the old name for the churchtown of St Mawgan. The latter was formerly *Lanherueu* 1086 (perhaps for *Lanherneu*?), *Lanhern* *c*.1187, *Lanherno* 1257; *lann* 'church-site' + unknown word or name, probably a personal name, perhaps of the form *Hernow* or similar, though there is little justification elsewhere for such a form.

Vellan Head w6614 **(coast, Mullion)** *Velland Point* 1841. Uncertain, for lack of earlier forms. The name could be *melin* 'mill' or *melyn* 'yellow', with English *point* or *head* added later. 'Mill' would be preferable, since the mutation of *m* to *v* could then be explained by a lost definite article (*an velin* 'the mill'). However, no windmill is recorded here. About a mile to the south-east were fields called Windmill Croft in 1840, implying a windmill at approximately W684144, but they are not quite close enough to explain the name.

Veryan w9139 **(parish)** *Sanctus Symphorianus* 1281, *Severian* 1525, *Seyntveryan* 1534, *Verian* 1607. From the dedication of the parish church to St Symphorian. The first syllable of his name was lost as a result of the change of *St Symphorian* to *Severian*, and the subsequent re-interpretation of *Severian* as *Saint-veryan* (compare ST LEVAN); from *St Veryan* the 'St' was again dropped, leaving *Veryan*. St Symphorian was a Gaulish martyr of the 2nd or 3rd century. It is possible that the dedication to St Symphorian represents a re-interpretation of an earlier, unrecorded, Celtic dedication; but the female saint honoured at ST BURYAN is certainly different, for that name never began with an *S*-syllable, and this one never contained *b*. There was another name for the manor and parish, found as *Elerchi* 1086, now Elerkey W913395: probably 'swan-stream, swan-place', *elergh* + -*i*. Veryan Bay W93 (coast) is so found in 1813.

Victoria W9861 **(Roche)** So found in 1888, from the Victoria Inn here. Inns were frequently named after the queen in the 19th century.

Wadebridge W9972 **(St Breock)** *Wade* 1358, 'chapel of *Wade*' 1382, 'town of *Wade*, bridge of *Wadebrygge*' 1478, *Wadebridge c.*1540. English, 'bridge at *Wade*'. The original name was simply English *wæd* 'a ford' (compare Wade in Suffolk); then in the 15th century a bridge was built and English *brycg* was added to the name. William of Worcester in 1478 described the bridge as having sixteen 'peres' (piers). Leland, in *c.*1540, said that there had been 'a fery a 80 yeres syns', which gives a date of *c.*1460 for the building of the bridge; he is also the first to relate how some of the piers were built on 'pakkes of wolle' to prevent them from sinking into the quick-sand.

Wainhouse Corner X1895 **(Jacobstow/St Gennys)** So found in 1748; named from a nearby place (now lost) called *Winhouse* 1417, *Wynehous* 1440. English, *wínhús* 'winehouse, inn'. There is still an inn at the cross-roads. Near here the name *Wendron Corner* appears in 1699, but if that refers to this place, the form must be corrupt.

Warbstow X2090 **(parish)** 'Chapel of *Sancta Werburga*' 1282, *Warberstowe* 1309, 'parish of *Seynte Warburghe*' 1327, 'chapel of *Warbestowe*' 1342, *Warpstow* 1553. English, 'holy place of St Wærburh' (*Werburga* in Latin), saint's name + *stów*. She was an Anglo-Saxon saint, a princess, daughter of the Anglo-Saxon king Wulfhere of Mercia (the Midlands); she became a nun and her relics, at Chester, were an object of pilgrimage in the Middle Ages.

Warleggan x1569 (parish)   *Wrlegan*   *c.*1250,   *Worlegan* *c.*1260, 1291, *Warlegen* 1380. An obscure name. The first part seems to be *gor-* 'over-, very' (preserved in its archaic form *Wor-* in this parish name), but no good suggestion can be made for the second part. There is an early Welsh verb *gorllwg* 'watches over, guards, follows'. If a Cornish equivalent existed, then with the uncertain suffix *-an*, it might give a word of the right form (*gorlegan*), meaning presumably 'watch-place'; but that is very doubtful. If so, it would probably refer to Carburrow Tor, a mile to the north (X155707), the highest point in the area.

Washaway x0369 (Egloshayle)   So found in 1699. English; probably not 'path to a washing-place' (compare Washway in Lincolnshire), for the place is over a mile from a suitable stream. So note instead English *washway*, meaning either 'part of a road crossed by a shallow stream', or 'a concave road, deeper in the middle than at the sides'. The latter meaning may be the more likely one here.

Watergate Bay w8365 (coast, St Mawgan in Pydar)   So found in 1813. 'Watergate' is a common English place-name in Cornwall and elsewhere (two instances in Devon); presumably it means 'sluice-gate', for a mill-stream or the like. In this case there is no place called that which could have given its name to the bay; and it is unknown where such a feature would have been located. Possibly the name has been transferred from another instance elsewhere.

Week St Mary x2397 (parish)   *Wich* 1086, 'church of *Sancta Maria* of *Wich*' *c.*1170, *Seintemarywyk* 1321, *Wyke* 1327. English, *wíc* 'dwelling, village', with the later addition of St Mary, the patron saint of the church, to distinguish the parish from Pancrasweek and Germansweek, both in Devon (S2905 and X4394, 6 and 12 miles away respectively). The pronunciation 'Week' is unexpected in these names; 'Wike' or 'Witch' might have been expected.

Welloe W5825 **(coast, Breage)** *The Welloe* 1748. Obscure, for lack of early forms. As it stands, possibly from Cornish *gwelow* 'sights' (plural of *gwel*), or *(an) gwella* 'the best' (i.e. best fishing-ground?), with hyper-correction of final *a* to *o*; but nothing can be suggested with assurance.

Wendron W6731 **(parish)** 'Church of *Sancta Wendrona*' 1291, *Seynt Wendron* 1384, *Seynt Gwendurne* 1514, *Wendron* 1522, *Gwendron* 1569. From the patron saint of the parish church, but nothing is known about her. The name was probably originally *Wendern*, though not recorded here in that form: compare the Old Cornish personal name *Wendeern*. Note that the initial *W* evidently did become *Gw* in speech, as expected; but the archaic *W* was preserved in the official forms of this parish name (compare WITHIEL, etc.). The older name of the churchtown was *Eglosiga* 1208, 1224, but the name apparently died out about then, and does not occur at a later date; *eglos* 'church' + unknown word or name. It is unlikely to be a personal name, for when *eglos* is followed by a personal name, it is always the patron saint of the church. At a later date *Egloswendron* 1513, 'church of St Wendron', is found.

St Wenn W9664 **(parish)** 'Church of *Sancta Wenna*' 1236, *Seynt Wenna* 1380, *Seint Wenne* 1439. From the patron saint of the parish church. The female St *Wenna* was believed to have been one of the 24 sons and daughters of King Broccan of Breconshire, according to the Cornish version of the legend.

Werrington X3287 **(parish)** *Ulvredintone* 1086, *Wolvrinton* 1171 (13th), *Wulfrinton* 1249, *Worryngton* 1324, *Werington* 1593. English, 'Wulfræd's farm', personal name + *-ing* + *tún*. In Devon, Worlington S7713 has the same origin, but with a different modern development. Werrington itself was in Devon until 1966.

West Curry: see under C.

Western Rocks V8306 **(coast, Scilly)** *The Western Rocks* 1792. English, self-explanatory.

West Pentire: see under P.

South Wheatley X2492 **(North Petherwin)** *South Whitleigh* 1748. The southern part of the place found originally

178

as *Whytele(ye)* 1249, *Whiteleye* 1332. English, 'bright clearing', *hwít* + *léah*. The other divisions of the place are Middle Whiteley X246940 (formerly *Wheatlywist* 1699 and *North Whetly* 1813), and Higher Whiteleigh in Week St Mary, X246944 (*Wyteleye* 1327, *Wheatly-weeke* 1699).

White Island v9217 **(island, Scilly)** *Whites Iland* 1652, *White Island* 1689. English; if the first form is to be trusted, probably from a surname 'White'; otherwise 'white, bright island'.

Whitemoor w9757 **(St Stephen in Brannel/St Dennis)** *Whitemoor* 1748. English, 'white marsh', *hwít* + *mór*. The place is in the heart of the tinning district called *Blackmoor*, and it may have been named in deliberate contrast with that much older name.

Whitesand Bay w3527 **(coast, Sennen/St Just in Penwith)** *Whitson Bay* 1580 (18th), *Whitsande Baye* 1582. English, self-explanatory.

Whitsand Bay x35 **(coast, Anthony/Sheviock/St John)** *Whitesand Bay* 1813. English, as previous entry.

Whitstone x2698 **(parish)** *Witestan* 1086, *Whyteston* 1333, *Whyston* 1525. English, 'white stone', *hwít* + *stán*. Note the local pronunciation shown in the form of 1525.

Widegates x2857 **(Morval)** *Wide-gates* 1673, *Widegate* 1748. English, self-explanatory. When the hamlet was created (probably in the 17th century), the district would have been open downland, and *gate* is often used in the moorland areas of Devon and Cornwall to indicate 'road (presumably gated) leading onto the downs': compare DOWNGATE.

Widemouth Bay s2002 **(Poundstock)** The holiday village is called *Widemouth* in 1969, *Widemouth Bay* 1971. It takes its name from the neighbouring Widemouth (farms) S202012, a name first found as *Witemot* 1086, *Widemutha* 1181, *Wydemouthe* 1337. English, 'wide gap', *wíd* + *mútha*. The bay itself is first found as *Widemouth Bay* in 1813. English *mútha* normally denotes a river-mouth, but there is no stream of note here, merely a sandy bay. It has been suggested that the 'mouth' is the mile-long gap in the cliffs instead. Pronounced '*Wid*muth'.

St Winnow x1157 (parish) *San Winnuc* 1086, *Sanctus Winnocus* 1166, *Sanctus Guennou* c.1300, *Seyntwynnowe* 1434, *St Gwinnowes* 1577. From the dedication of the parish church. This saint is generally equated with one who has a considerable cult in Flanders (north-east France), where his Life was written in the 9th (?) century: there he was believed to have been of the 'land of the Britons' (either Britain or Brittany), and to have come to the monastery of St Bertin (near St Omer, south-east of Calais), where he lived most of his life. However, there is no evidence that this was the saint to whom the Cornish church was dedicated, and it is more likely that *Winnoc* is here a pet-form of the Cornish and Breton St Winwaloe (see GUNWALLOE and TOWEDNACK). It is notable that there is no cult of a St Winnoc in Brittany. The modern form shows a change of *oc* to *-ow*, first shown in the form *Guennou* c.1300. This form, and some later ones, show the expected Cornish *gw*; but the official form with initial *W* has been preserved in this parish name (compare WITHIEL, etc.).

Withiel w9965 (parish) *Widie* 1086, *Widel* 1201, Thomas de *Wythiel* 1274, *Guythiel* 1355. 'Wooded district, forest', *gwydhyel*, the adjective formed from *gwydh* + *-yel*. The district is not now much wooded; but additional evidence for its former nature is seen in the name of one of the two subdivisions of the parish, Withielgoose X003653, found as *Wythiellgoos* 1434, *Wythiell Goyse woode* 1549: *coes* 'wood', and subsequently English 'wood', have been added to the original name. By contrast, the other division, including the churchtown, was called *Wythyeleglos* 1305 (*eglos* 'church'). The initial *W* is archaic; note the expected initial *G* in the form of 1355 (as in WENDRON and ST WINNOW).

Woodford s2113 (Morwenstow) *Wodeford* 1302. English, 'ford in a wood', *wudu* + *ford*.

Wolf Rock w2612 (coast) *The Gulfe* 1564, *De Wolff* 1584, *The gulfe* 1588, *the Gulf or Woolfe* c.1698, 'called *the Wolf*, from the continued and melancholy howling which the waves make in breaking round it' 1817. English, 'the wolf', either for the reason given, or from its dangerous nature. But the variant *Gulf* is curious; if credited, it would suggest instead that the name was Cornish, and that *Wolf* was an English re-interpretation of the mutated form. Compare *the Ulffes*, perhaps a former name of NAVAX POINT; it is possible that both names are corruptions of some Cornish word, possibly *goelva* 'lookout-place'. Or else, if the English derivation is right, *Gulf* could be due to hyper-correct de-mutation of *W*.

Yeolmbridge x3187 **(Werrington)** *Yambrigge* 13th, William *Yhombregge*, de *Yombrigge* 1308, '*Yalme bridge* of stone' *c*.1540. English, possibly 'river-meadow bridge', *éa* + *hamm* + *brycg*, though that is not very convincing. The *l* from the 16th century on is non-original. It may have been added by analogy with Yealmbridge near Plymouth, x5952, which is named from the River Yealm (*Yalme* 1414), of uncertain derivation.

Zelah w8151 **(St Allen)** *Sele* 1311, *Zela* 1613. English, *sele* 'hall'. For the voicing of the initial *s* to *z*, compare Zeal in Devon (6 instances), with the same derivation. The preservation of the early English final syllable here, unlike the Devon examples, may have been due to the Cornish-speaking environment in which this name existed. This name is often given a derivation in Cornish, 'dry-place' (a compound, *sygh* + *le* 'place'). That cannot be right, both because of the great rarity of *le* in place-names, and because the early spellings show no sign of the required *gh* sound.

Zennor w4538 **(parish)** 'Church of *Sanctus Sinar*' *c*.1170, *Sancta Sinara* 1235, *Sancta Senara* 1270, *Senar* 1522, *Zenar* 1582. From the patron saint of the church. All forms, except the very first, are agreed in making her female, but nothing else is known of her, nor is the name found elsewhere. It has been suggested that she was the same as a princess *Azenor* of Breton legend, mother of St BUDOCK. However, Breton *z* is normally the equivalent of Cornish *dh* or *th*; so a Cornish equivalent of the Breton name ought to have been *Athenor*, or the like. But perhaps if the Breton name has *z* for older *s*, an equation between the two names might be sustained. If so, compare ST KEVERNE and ST NEOT for the loss of initial *A*- in saints' names.

Zone Point w8530 **(coast, St Anthony in Roseland)** '*Savenheer* or the long coved point' 1597, *The Zone Point* 1813:

'long cleft', *sawn* + *hir*, later shortened and anglicised to 'Zone'. The cleft is still visible, though it has now mostly fallen in. In *c*.1870 the name was misprinted *The Zoze Point*, with the (capital) *N* on its side. Through the authority of the Ordnance Survey, that form gained considerable currency, and it is still (1985) to be heard locally — an interesting example of feed-back from the written to the spoken tradition.

Index of Elements

1. Cornish

Note on spelling: There is no one agreed way of spelling Cornish. In my previous book, *Cornish Place-Name Elements* (CPNE), I used the spellings of the original Cornish texts wherever possible. That method produces inconsistencies and misleading spellings which are not suitable for the present book. The spelling of Revived Cornish, which uses a single self-consistent system, is currently under drastic revision. Its new system is a great improvement upon the old; but, in my opinion, it removes itself undesirably far from the spellings of the Middle Cornish texts (which are also, very often, those of medieval Cornish place-name spellings, and are therefore particularly apt here). I have therefore compromised, using many of the suggestions of the new system for Revived Cornish, particularly as regards the vowels, while in other respects, especially among the sibilants, respecting the system of genuine Middle Cornish (which in these respects usually coincides with former Revived Cornish). But a few elements have been cited in Old Cornish forms, if it seems unlikely that they were in use in the Middle period.

To aid those who may wish to cross-check between the systems, references to CPNE are given for all those elements which appear in that book, and the spelling of the new system of Revived Cornish ('KG') follows, when it differs from that used here. Words preceded by the symbol † are respelt words, found in the Cornish texts but not actually in those spellings; those preceded by an asterisk * are not found at all in Cornish texts, and have been invented, usually by analogy from Welsh and/or Breton.

Further discussion of the elements, sometimes extensive on the meanings or forms, will be found in CPNE.

Discussion appears here only when there is substantial addition to be made. A name in brackets in the following list indicates the main entry in this book under which the derivation of the preceding name will be found: thus *Anhaye* will be found under the entry for HEAMOOR.

alter 'altar of a church': Altarnun. (CPNE 4)

*ammal 'edge, boundary': probably in Chapel Amble. (CPNE 5)

an 'the': *Anhaye* (see Heamoor), *Carne an Watch* (Trendrine Hill), Castle-an-Dinas, Chyandour, *Enor* (St Mary's), *Maenenescop* (Bishop Rock), ?Navax Point, *Pen an ulays* (Land's End), *Penvounder* (see Shortlanesend), Ponsanooth, Porthnavas, Praze-an-Beeble, Rosenannon, Trendrine, Treneglos, *Trenfos* (Trevose), *Trengyer* (Tregeare). In some other names (Drift, Greeb Point, Gribbin Head and Grumbla) it is never shown in the early spellings of the names, but its one-time existence is demonstrated by a mutation which can only have been caused by it. However, with some of these names (e.g. Greeb, Grumbla), the mutation may have become fixed in the word, whether or not *an* was present, so that the presence of *an* is not essential in those cases. (CPNE 5)

*-an, suffix meaning 'place of' (?). This suffix is of doubtful existence, but it may occur in ?Carnon, ?Fraddon, ?Ludgvan, ?Manaccan, ?Ruthernbridge, ?Warleggan. (CPNE 7)

*ar 'facing, beside': Perranarworthal. (CPNE 8)

*ardh 'a height': ?Carharrack, Lizard, ?Trewellard. (CPNE 9)

avon 'river': ?Trevone. If present in the name, it must here have the meaning 'sea'. The normal word for 'river, stream' in Cornish was *dowr*. (CPNE 13)

bal 'mine, area of tin-working': Baldhu. (CPNE 15)
†bedh 'tomb, grave': Morvah. (CPNE 20)
ben 'foot': Pendavey (see River Allen), Pentewan. (CPNE 20)
*berow 'boiling, water-turbulence': ?Truro.
†berr 'short': Burras. (CPNE 20)
†besow 'birch-trees': Bissoe. (CPNE 18; KG bedjow)
*bod (Old Cornish) 'dwelling'. (i) qualified by a personal

184

name: Ballowal, Bedruthan, Belowda, Bocaddon, Bocon-noc, Bojewyan, ?Bosavern, Boskednan, Bossiney, Boswinger. Note also Boscoppa, where *bod* may be qualified by a surname. (ii) qualified by a descriptive term: Bodieve, Bodmin, ?Bosullow. Botallack and Burlawn may be qualified by either a descriptive term or a personal name. See also *gwavos*. (CPNE 23; KG bos)

bownder 'lane': *Penvounder* (see Shortlanesend). (CPNE 27)

*bre 'hill': Brewinney (Paul), *Bryanick* (St Agnes), Carn Brea, ?Kelly Bray, Mulfra (see Newmill), (+ -*yer* plural) Bryher. (CPNE 30)

bregh 'arm': *Brechiek* (St Martin's). (CPNE 30)

*brenn 'hill': *Goen bren* (Bodmin Moor). (CPNE 31)

bro 'district, region': Penbro (see Breage). (CPNE 32)

†bronn 'breast, hill': Brown Willy, Camborne, *Penherierd* (see Herodsfoot). (CPNE 32)

*brygh 'speckled': ?Kelly Bray. (CPNE 31)

*bud(er) 'dirty': ?Bude.

*buorth 'cow-yard': Bohortha. (CPNE 35)

byghan 'small': *Boschiwolou-bigha* (Bosullow), Ednoe-Vean (Perranuthnoe), Marazion, Nanpean, Penhalvean, *Pentirevean* (Pentire), *Portbyhen* (Looe), Porthpean, *Ruan Vean* (Ruan Minor), Trelanvean (Trelan), Trevispian Vean (Trispen). (CPNE 21)

†camm 'crooked': ?Cambeak, Camborne, ?Camel, Gilly Gabben (see Crim Rocks). (CPNE 36; KG kamm)

carn 'tor, rock, crag': Canworthy, Caradon, Carn Brea, Carne (meaning 'barrow'), *Carne an Watch*, Carnhell, *Carnminnis* (Trendrine Hill), Carnon, *Carn Peran* (see Perranzabuloe), Carn Towan, Carnyorth. (CPNE 38; KG karn)

carow 'stag': Pencarrow Head. (CPNE 40; KG karow)

*carr-bons 'causeway' (literally 'cart-bridge', compound of *carr* + *pons*): Carbis. (CPNE 38; KG karrbons)

†carrek 'rock': Cargreen, *Carrack Looes en Cooes* (St Michael's Mount), The Carracks, Carrick Roads. (CPNE 41; KG karrek)

castell 'fort, village, rock': Castellack, Castle-an-Dinas, Kestle (singular or plural). The meaning of *castell* is very uncertain in place-names, as the word had such a wide variety of senses. Occasionally, as at Kestle, it was used interchangeably in both singular and plural forms. (CPNE 42; KG kastell)

†**caswydh** 'thicket': Cadgwith. (CPNE 43; KG kadjwydh)

†**chi** 'house, cottage': ?Bosullow, Chyandour, Chysauster, Rinsey; older *ti*, Trethevey in St Mabyn (see River Allen), Tywardreath; for compounds containing *chi*, see *crow-ji*, *melin-ji*, and *meyn-ji*. (CPNE 76; KG tji)

†**cleger** 'cliff': ?Ligger Bay. (CPNE 60; KG kleger)

***codi** (?) (Old Cornish), 'to rise': ?Codda. The existence of this word is very doubtful. The form *codi* would be Old Cornish; if it had survived it would have given Middle Cornish *cosi*, but it is not found. Welsh *codi* means 'to rise' (in the normal sense, and also of a stream); but its older form was *cyfodi*. No record of a Cornish equivalent exists; so it is uncertain whether one may hypothesise that a Cornish equivalent, which would have been *kevodi* originally, would have gone through the same shortening to *codi* as did the Welsh word. However, it would provide a satisfactory explanation for the one place-name.

†**coes** 'wood': *Carrack Looes en Cooes* (St Michael's Mount), Cotehele, Pendoggett, Quethiock, *Wythiell Goyse woode* (see Withiel); see also *troen-goes*. (CPNE 66; KG koes)

***coger** (?) 'winding stream' (?): Kuggar. (CPNE 62; KG koger)

***cordh** 'clan, army': ?*Langorthou* (Fowey). (CPNE 64; KG kordh)

corn 'horn', also 'corner'?: Cornwall, Porthcurno. (CPNE 66; KG korn)

***covrek** (?), perhaps a stream-name, of unknown meaning: Coverack.

***cow-nans** 'ravine' (compound, *cow* 'hollow' + *nans*): Kynance. (CPNE 57; KG kownans)

***crag** 'sandstone': Crackington. (CPNE 68; KG krag)

cres 'middle': *Ammalgres* (see Chapel Amble), Colgrease (see Carines). (CPNE 69; KG kres)

***crew** 'weir': ?Crowlas (or *crow*). (CPNE 70; KG krew)

†**crib** 'comb, crest, ridge': Greeb Point, (plural *cribow*) Cribba Head. (CPNE 70; KG krib)

†**cribynn** 'little crest' (*crib* + *-ynn*): ?Gribbin Head, ?Crim Rocks (CPNE 70; KG kribynn)

***cromm-legh** 'quoit, dolmen' (literally 'curved-slab'): Grumbla. (CPNE 72; KG krommlegh)

†**crow** 'hut': Carines, ?Crowlas. (CPNE 73; KG krow)

***crow-ji** 'hut': Crowdy. (CPNE 73; KG krowdji)

†**crug** 'barrow, tumulus': Carclew, Crugmeer, *Egloscrow* (St Issey). (CPNE 73; KG krug)

†**cudynn** 'tress of hair': ?Cudden Point, ?Tregidden. (CPNE 74; KG kudynn)

davas 'sheep': Porthnavas. (CPNE 81)

devr- 'water': see *dowr*. (CPNE 82)

dew 'two': Duloe, Pendoggett. (CPNE 82)

deyl 'leaves': ?Delabole. (CPNE 81)

***din** 'hill-fort' or 'promontory-fort': ?De Lank, Pendeen, Tintagel, Treen, Trenarren. (CPNE 84)

***dinan** 'fort': Cardinham. (CPNE 85)

***dinas** 'fort': Castle-an-Dinas, St Dennis, Dinas Head (see Trevose Head), Pendennis Point, Treryn Dinas (see Treen). (CPNE 85)

***di-serth** 'very-steep (place)': Dizzard. (CPNE 85)

dor 'ground' ('mainland'): *Enor* (St Mary's). (CPNE 86)

dowr 'water, stream': Chyandour, *Dour Conor* (see Connor Downs), ?Gwenter; variant *devr-* (plural) Devoran. (CPNE 87)

dreyn 'thorn-bushes': Trendrine. (CPNE 88)

dreys 'brambles': Tredrizzick. (CPNE 88)

du 'black': Baldhu, Carthew, *Peden due* (Black Head), Poldhu, ?Retew. (CPNE 89)

ebel 'colt': (plural) ?Menabilly. (CPNE 90)

eglos 'church': *Ammaleglos* (Chapel Amble), *Egglosbrec* (Breage), *Eggloscrauuen* (Crowan), *Egglossanres* (Sancreed), *Egglostetha* (St Teath), *Eglish Hallow* (Illogan), *Eglosberrie* (St Buryan), *Egloscontantyne* (see Constantine Bay), *Egloscrow* (St Issey), *Egloscuri* (Cury), *Eglos Cutbert* (Cubert), *Eglosellan* (St Allen), Egloserme (St Erme), Egloshayle, *Egloshayle* (Phillack), *Egloshellens* (St Stephen in Brannel), *Eglosiga* (Wendron), Egloskerry, *Egloslagek* (Ladock), *Eglos Maderne* (Madron), Eglosmerther (Merther), *Eglosmeylyon* (Mullion), *Eglosnyulyn*

187

(Newlyn East), *Eglospenbro* (Breage), *Eglostephen* (St Stephen in Brannel), *Egloswendron* (Wendron), *Hecglosenuder* (St Enoder), *Hecglostudic* (St Tudy), ?Manacles, Treneglos, *Wythyeleglos* (Withiel). (CPNE 91)

-ek, adjectival ending: ?Callestick, ?Carharrack, ?Castellack, Kelynack, Meneage, Penwithick, ?Port Isaac, Predannack, Quethiock, Sheviock, Stenalees, Tredinnick, Tredrizzick, *Brechiek* (St Martin's), ?Levorrick (Mevagissey), Stennagwyn (see Stenalees); see also *havek* and *tal*. (CPNE 90)

*-el, adjectival ending: ?Brannel (St Stephen in Brannel), ?Carnhell; see also *goethel*; in the form *-yel*, Lostwithiel, Withiel. (CPNE 138)

†elergh 'swan(s)': Elerkey (Veryan). (CPNE 93)

*-el(l), river-name ending: ?Camel (CPNE 93)

†-enn, singular ending for names of trees: Rosenannon; see also *gwydh*. (CPNE 93)

*enyal (?), 'wild, desolate': ?*Innyall Chappell* (see Gurnard's Head). (CPNE 93)

escop 'bishop': *Maenenescop* (Bishop Rock). (CPNE 94; KG epskop)

*eyrik (?), possibly a stream-name, 'fierce one': ?Penjerrick.

*faw 'beech-trees': Fowey. (CPNE 96)

fenten 'spring, holy well': Ventonglidder (see St Clether), *Nanfonteyn* (Little Petherick). (CPNE 97)

†fordh 'road, way': ?Gunver Head. (CPNE 99)

fos 'bank, dyke': Trevose, Ruthvoes. (CPNE 99)

†fros 'stream': Fraddon. (CPNE 100)

garan 'crane': Trenarren. (CPNE 101)

garow 'rough': Garras, ?Garrow Tor. (CPNE 102)

*garth 'ridge': see *hir-yarth*. (CPNE 102)

glas 'grey-green': Pentireglaze (see Pentire Point), ?Stenalees. (CPNE 103)

†go- 'little, sub-': Godolphin. (CPNE 105)

*go-dre 'little farm': Godrevy. (CPNE 106)

†goedh 'goose': see *goeth* 'water-course'. (CPNE 111)

†goel 'fair, festival': Golant, Goldsithney. (CPNE 106)

†goel-va 'lookout-place' (compound, *goel* + *ma*): ?Wolf Rock, ?*the Ulffes* (see Navax Point). (CPNE 113)

†**goeles** 'lower': *Fraddon woolas* (Fraddon), Predannack Wollas. (CPNE 106)

†**goen** 'downland, downs': *Goen bren* (Bodmin Moor), Goonbell, *Goon Carnon* (Carnon Downs), Goonhavern, Goonhilly, Trewoon, Troon. (CPNE 108)

†**goeth** 'water-course' or †*goedh* 'goose': Polgooth, Ponsanooth;th see also *goethel*. (CPNE 111)

*****goethel** 'marshy land' (*goeth* + *-el*): Perranarworthal. (CPNE 111)

golow 'light': ?Bosullow. (CPNE 107)

†**gor-** 'over, super-' (possibly in a word *gorleg* 'to watch over'?): ?Warleggan. (CPNE 109)

*****gor-ge** 'broken-down hedge': Georgia. (CPNE 110)

gover 'stream': Langover. (CPNE 112)

gwartha 'upper': *Frodan wartha* (Fraddon), Predannack Wartha. (CPNE 115)

*****gwavos** 'winter-dwelling' (compound, *gwav* 'winter' + *bod*): Trewavas. (CPNE 116)

†**gwel** 'sight': unlikely in ?Trewellard; plural *gwelow*, or *gwella* 'best': ?Welloe. (CPNE 117)

gwennol 'swallow': (plural *gwennili*) Brown Willy. (CPNE 117)

*****gwig** 'village' (?): Gweek. (CPNE 119)

gwis 'sow, female pig': ?Quies. (CPNE 121)

gwlas 'land': *Pen an ulays* (Land's End). (CPNE 123)

gwragh 'hag, old woman': ?Praa Sands. (CPNE 123)

†**gwydh** 'trees': (+ *-yel* adjective) Lostwithiel, Withiel; (+ *-ek* adjective) Penwithick; (+ *-enn* singular) ?Lawhitton (CPNE 121)

*****gwydh-lann** 'cemetery': ?Trewidland.

†**gwynn** 'white, fair': ?Gunver Head, ?Kenwyn, North and South Petherwin, Portquin, Stennagwyn (see Stenalees), Trewen (or personal name). (CPNE 120)

gwyns 'wind': Trewint. (CPNE 121)

hag 'and': Mevagissey. (CPNE 124)

hal 'marsh, moor': Hallantacka (Newbridge), Hallworthy, *Halldrunkard* (see Hallworthy); (plural) ?*Eglish Hallow*, (Illogan); see also *penn hal*. (CPNE 125)

*****havar** 'summer-ploughed land': ?Goonhavern. (CPNE 127)

*havek 'summer-land': ?Navax Point. (CPNE 124)

hel 'hall': ?Carnhell. (CPNE 128)

†helghi 'hunting, to hunt': ?Goonhilly (or *hyli*). (CPNE 128)

*hen-lann 'ancient church-site' (*hen* 'ancient' + *lann*): Helland, Kehelland. (CPNE 130)

*hen-lys 'old court' (*hen* 'ancient' + *lys*): Helston, Helstone, Helsbury (see Michaelstow). (CPNE 130)

*heyl 'estuary': Cotehele, Egloshayle, Hayle, Helford, *Egloshayle* (Phillack); (+ *-ynn* diminutive), *Porraylan* (see Holywell). (CPNE 127)

hir 'long': *Savenheer* (Zone Point). (CPNE 132)

*hir-yarth 'long-ridge' (compound, *hir* + *garth*): Herodsfoot. (CPNE 133; KG hirardh)

†hyli 'brine' (meaning 'brackish water'?): ?Goonhilly (or *helghi*), ?*Porthiley* (Mevagissey). (CPNE 131)

*-i, name-forming suffix (especially in river-names): Elerkey (Veryan), Fowey, Inney, Tiddy. (CPNE 135)

*igolenn 'whetstone': Nancegollen. (CPNE 136)

†-ik, diminutive ending: Penpillick. (CPNE 135)

*kehoedh (?) 'proclamation': ?Porthcothan.

†kellester 'pebbles': ?Callestick. (CPNE 47)

kelli 'grove, small wood': Kehelland, Kelly Bray, Gilly Gabben (see Crim Rocks). (CPNE 47)

kellys 'lost, hidden': Porkellis. (CPNE 48)

†kelynn 'holly': Kelynack. (CPNE 46)

†keow 'home-field' (?) (literally 'hedges'?): Gugh. (CPNE 57)

*ker 'fort, a round': Cardinham, ?Carharrack, Carthew, Tregeare (2 instances), *Pencair* (Tregonning Hill); variant *kery* (?), ?Caerhays (see St Michael); *kerys* 'fortified', (hypothetical past participle passive of a hypothetical verb *keri*, 'to fortify'), ?Kerris, ?Polkerris. (CPNE 50)

*kevyll (?) 'horse': ?Penkevil (see St Michael). (CPNE 57)

keyn 'back, ridge': ?Kenwyn, ?Kilmar Tor (or *kil*). (CPNE 45)

†kil 'nook, corner': ?Kilmar Tor (or *keyn*), ?*The Kilguthe* (Cape Cornwall). (CPNE 58)

*kylgh 'circle': Kilkhampton. (CPNE 59)

*lann 'church-site': Lamorran, Landulph, Laneast, Lan-

hydrock, Lanivet, Lanlivery, Lanreath, Lansallos, Launcells, Launceston, ?Lawhitton, Lelant, Lewannick, Lezant, Linkinhorne, Ruan Lanihorne, Vale of Lanherne, Lantinning (St Anthony in Meneage), *Landrayth* (St Blazey), *Langustenstyn* (Constantine), Langurra (Crantock), *Lankyp* (Duloe), *Lanuthno* (St Erth), Lanuah (St Ewe), La Feock (Feock), *Langorthou* (Fowey), *Lamayne* (St George's Island), *Lannaled* (St Germans), *Langoron* (Gorran), Lanisley (Gulval), *Lamwenep* (Gwennap), *Lanuste*, Lafrowda (St Just in Penwith), Lanzeague (St Just in Roseland), *Lanhevran* (St Keverne), Lanow (St Kew), *Lavabe* (Mabe), Landithy (Madron), *La Vousa* (St Mawes), Levorrick (Mevagissey), *Lanvyhayll* (St Michael Caerhays), Landegea (Old Kea), *Laffenake* (Padstow), *Lanberan* (Perranzabuloe), *Lamprobus* (Probus), Talland, ?Trelan; see also *gwydh-lann* and *hen-lann*. The meaning formerly given for *lann*, 'enclosed Dark-Age cemetery', may be too narrow: the cemetery was seen as the most important field-monument of Dark-Age Christianity, for it leaves the most obvious archaeological remains; but that ignores that the primary feature must have been a place of worship. So it seems best to translate *lann* as 'church-site'; see the Introduction, section on Saints, for more detail about its implications. (CPNE 142)
†**lannergh** 'clearing': Landrake, Lanner, Muchlarnick. (CPNE 142)
ledan 'broad': ?*Meleneledan* (Trevalga). (CPNE 145)
***lefant** (Old Cornish) 'toad': Polyphant. (CPNE 146; KG lefans)
***legh** 'flat-stone, slab': Penlee Point, Rilla Mill; see also *cromm-legh*, *legh-rys* (?). (CPNE 146)
***legh-rys** (?) 'slab-ford, ford with flat stones' (compound, *legh + rys*): ?Trelights.
leven 'smooth': Porthleven. (CPNE 148)
†**loes** 'grey': *Carrack Looes en Cooes* (St Michael's Mount). (CPNE 153)
***log** 'chapel': Luxulyan. (CPNE 151)
***logh** 'pool, inlet': Duloe, The Loe, Looe, Portloe. (CPNE 152)
***lonk** 'ravine': ?De Lank. (CPNE 153)
lost 'tail': Lostwithiel. (CPNE 153)

lowen 'happy': ?Burlawn. But a personal name, *Lowen*, is more likely. (CPNE 154)

lu 'army, fleet of boats': Newlyn. (CPNE 155)

lusow 'ashes': ?Ludgvan. (CPNE 155; KG ludjow)

†**lynn** 'pool': Newlyn. (CPNE 149)

***lyr** 'liquid, water' (plural *lyryon*): ?Lerryn.

***lys** 'court': ?Crowlas (or *rys*), Lesnewth, Liskeard, Lizard, ?Stenalees; see also *hen-lys*. (CPNE 150)

lyw 'colour': ?Carclew. (CPNE 151)

***ma** 'place, plain, cleared district': Menheniot; see also *goel-va*. (CPNE 155)

†**managh** 'monk': Meneage, ?Manaccan, *Lamayne* (St George's Island); see also *meneghi*. (CPNE 156)

margh 'horse': Kilmar Tor; in Tremar a personal name *Margh* is more likely. (CPNE 157)

marghas 'market': Marazion, Market Jew (Marazion). (CPNE 157)

melin 'mill': Porth Mellin (Mullion Cove), Portmellon, Vellan Head? *Melenowith* (New Mills). (CPNE 160)

***melin-ji** 'mill-house' (compound, *melin* + *chi*): Bolingey. (CPNE 161; KG melindji)

men 'stone': *Maenenescop* (Bishop Rock), ?Manacles, ?Menabilly, Tremaine; see also *meyn-ji*. (CPNE 161)

***meneghi** 'church-land': Bodmin. The precise meaning of *meneghi* is uncertain. It is a derivative of *managh*, 'monk'; in Breton the meaning 'sanctuary' is sometimes given, but that appears to be an error, and it certainly does not suit the Cornish names that show it. Most likely it means 'church-land, land owned by the church', though that too fails to suit all the Cornish place-names which contain it. (CPNE 163)

†**menydh** 'hill': ?*Meleneledan* (Trevalga), Trevena (see Tintagel). (CPNE 163)

***merther** 'saint's grave': Merther, Merthyr (see Morvah), Merther (see Sithney), *Merther* (see Trendrine Hill). (CPNE 164)

meur 'great, big': Crugmeer, Porthmeor, *Bossowolomeour* (Bosullow), *Ammalmur* (Chapel Amble), Polmear Island (see Charlestown), Delamere (see Delabole), *Ponsmur* (Grampound), *Kerismoer* (Kerris), Penhalveor (see

Penhalvean), Uthnoe Veor (Perranuthnoe), *Trelanmur* (Trelan). (CPNE 166)

*meyn-ji 'stone-house' (compound, *meyn*, plural of *men*, + *chi*): Mountjoy. (CPNE 159; KG meyndji)

*moel 'bare': Mulfra (see Newmill). (CPNE 167)

mor 'sea': Morvah, ?Morval; (+ -*ek* adjective) ?Levorrick (Mevagissey). (CPNE 168)

munys 'little': *Carnminnis* (Trendrine Hill). (CPNE 170)

nans 'valley': Golant, Lamorna, ?Langover, ?Lawhitton, Nancegollan, Nancent (St Breock), Nancledra, *Nanfonteyn* (Little Petherick), Nanpean, Nanstallon, Trenance; see also *cow-nans, penn nans*. (CPNE 170)

neved (Old Cornish) 'sacred place, pagan sacred grove': Lanivet. (CPNE 172; KG neves)

†nowydh 'new': Lesnewth, Penoweth (Mylor Bridge), *Melenowith* (New Mills). (CPNE 172)

onn 'ash-trees': (+ -*enn* singular) Rosenannon; (plural *enn*), Inney. (CPNE 174)

orth 'near, towards': Carines. (CPNE 239)

pell 'far': Goonbell, Penpell (see Penpillick). (CPNE 177)

†penn 'head, top, end': Pendogget, Penpillick, Penwithick, Penbro (see Breage), *Penkynans* (see Kynance), *Pen an ulays* (Land's End), *Penvounder* (Shortlanesend), *Pencair* (Tregonning Hill); in sense 'headland', St Michael Penkevil, Pencarrow Head, Pendeen, Pendennis Point, Penlee Point, Penzance, *Peden due* (Black Head). (CPNE 177)

penn-ardh 'headland' (*penn* + *ardh*?): Nare Head, Nare Point, Penare, *Pennarthe* (Gribbin Head). (CPNE 180)

penn hal 'head of a marsh': Penhale Point, Penhalvean. (CPNE 181)

penn nans 'head of a valley': Penjerrick. (CPNE 182)

penn poll 'head of a creek': Penpol, Penpoll. (CPNE 182)

penn ros 'end of a moorland': Penrose. (CPNE 183)

penn rynn 'headland' (literally 'end of a point', *penn* + *rynn*): Penryn. (CPNE 182)

penn tir 'headland': Pentire, West Pentire, Pentire Point, Pentire (see Park Head). (CPNE 183)

pennwedh 'end-district' (?): Penwith.

pibell 'pipe, conduit': Praze-an-Beeble. (CPNE 184)

pig 'point': ?Cambeak. (CPNE 185)

plen 'arena, open space': *Pleyn-goylsithny* (Goldsithney). (CPNE 186)

plu 'parish': Pelynt, *Plu vuthek* (Budock). (CPNE 187)

†**poll** 'pool, cove': Polbathick, Poldhu, Polkerris, Polzeath, Praa Sands (or *porth*); see also *penn poll*; (meaning 'pit') Delabole, Polgooth, Polyphant. (CPNE 187)

pons 'bridge': Polmassick, Ponsanooth, *Ponsmur* (Grampound), Penoweth (Mylor Bridge), *Pons-releubes* (Relubbus); see also *carr-bons*. (CPNE 190)

porth 'cove, harbour': Par, Polperro, Polruan, Porkellis (inland, meaning 'gate, pass' perhaps), Portgaverne, Porthallow, Porthcothan, Porthcurno, Porthleven, Porthmeor, Porthnavas, Portholland, Porthoustock, Porthpean, Porth Reservoir, Porthtowan, Port Isaac, Portloe, Portmellon, Portquin, Portreath, Portscatho, Portwrinkle, Praa Sands (or *poll*), *Por Cadgwith* (Cadgwith), Barrepta Cove (see Carbis Bay), Polmear Island (see Charlestown), *Porthcovrec* (see Coverack), *Porth East* (Gorran Haven), *Porraylan* (see Holywell), *Porthia* (St Ives), *Portbyhen* (Looe), *Porthmawgan* (Mawgan Porth), *Porthiley* (Mevagissey), *Porthennis* (Mousehole), Porth Mellin (Mullion Cove), *Porthe Gone Hollye* (Sennen Cove). (CPNE 190)

pras 'meadow, a green': St Erth Praze, Praze-an-Beeble. (CPNE 193)

Predenn 'Britain': Predannack.

†**pryvenn** 'reptile' (*pryv* 'serpent' + *-enn*): *Inispriven* (Mullion Island). (CPNE 194)

reden 'bracken': Tredinnick. (CPNE 196)

†**reun** 'seal': Cargreen, *an garrak ruen* (see Carrick Roads). (CPNE 203)

roeth 'juice, liquid' (?): Ruthernbridge.

ros 'moorland': Garras, ?Garrow Tor, Rose, Rosenannon; see also *penn ros*; in Roseland and Rosemullion, *ros* has the sense 'promontory'. (CPNE 199)

†**rudh** 'red': Redruth, Ruthvoes. (CPNE 204)

rynn 'point of land': Rinsey; see also *penn rynn*. (CPNE 199)

†**rys** 'ford' (Old Cornish *rid*): Burras, Crowlas (or *lys*), Redruth, Rejerrah, Relubbus, Retew, Rilla Mill, Roseworthy, Seworgan, Trerice. (CPNE 197)

sans 'holy': Penzance; meaning 'a saint', in the older form *sant*, plural *synt* or *se(y)nt*, ?Nancent (St Breock), *Lanhoghou seynt* (St Kew). (CPNE 204)

sawn 'cleft, gully': Zone Point. (CPNE 205)

†**scath** 'boat, large rowing-boat': plural *scathow*, Portscatho. (CPNE 205; KG skath)

scaw 'elder-trees': Tresco, Trescowe. (CPNE 205; KG skaw)

seth 'arrow' or 'pot': ?Seaton. (CPNE 209)

sevi 'strawberries': Sheviock. (CPNE 209)

skidi (?) (Old Cornish) 'to clear land of roots, to assart': ?Talskiddy. (KG skidji)

†**sten** 'tin': Stenalees, Stennagwyn. (CPNE 212)

†**stok** 'tree-stump': (+ *-yer* plural), Sticker. (CPNE 212; KG stokk)

stras 'broad valley': Stratton. (CPNE 212)

stumm 'bend': *Stymkodda* (Codda). (CPNE 213)

†**sygh** 'dry': ?Polzeath. (CPNE 207)

***tagell** 'constriction, narrow neck': Tintagel. (CPNE 214)

tal 'brow': Talland, Talskiddy; (+ *-ek* adjective), Botallack (or personal name *Talek*). (CPNE 214)

tew 'fat, thick': ?Retew (or *du*).

tewynn (?) 'bright' (river-name): Pentewan.

†**tewynn** 'sand-dunes': Carn Towan, Porthtowan, Towan Head, Towan Blistra (Newquay). (CPNE 222)

tnow 'valley': Treknow. (CPNE 218)

to- (Old Cornish) 'thy' (in pet-forms of saints' names): Towednack, Landegea (Old Kea). (CPNE 218; KG te-)

tre 'farmstead, estate, hamlet': Drift; see also *go-dre*. Qualified by a descriptive term: Tredinnick, Tredrizzick, Treen, Tregeare (2), ?Tregidden, Treknow, Trelan, ?Trelights, Tremaine, Trenance, Trendrine, Treneglos, Trerice, Tresco, Trescowe, ?Trevone, Trevose, Trewavas, ?Trewellard, Trewen, Trewint, Trewoon, Troon, Trevena (see Tintagel). Qualified by a personal name (Celtic unless otherwise specified): Traboe, Trebetherick (saint), Trebudannon, Treburley (surname), Tredavoe, Tregadillet, ?Tregaverne (see Portgaverne), Tregonetha, Tregonning, Tregony, ?Treligga, Trelill (Old English), Tremail, Tremar, Tresillian, ?Tresmeer, Trethevy, Trethewey, Trethurgy, Trevanson, Trevisker, ?Trewarmett, Trewarthenick, Trewassa, ?Trewellard, Trewidland, Trewithian, Treyarnon.

Qualified by an unknown word or name: Trebartha, Tregole, Tregurrian, Trelissick, Trelowarren, Trematon, Trenewan, Trevalga, Trevarren, Trevarrick, Trevellas, Treverva, Trevigro, Trispen, Trewrickle (see Portwrinkle). It has been suggested that the meaning formerly given for *tre*, 'farm, estate', is too narrow, and that the vaguer meaning 'hamlet' should be added; that seems very likely to be right. (CPNE 223)

†**treth** 'beach, strand': Portreath, Tywardreath, *Landrayth* (St Blazey), *Pirran in Treth* (Perranzabuloe). (CPNE 223)

troen-goes 'wood on a nose of land' (literally 'nose-wood', compound, *troen* 'nose' + *coes*): *Halldrunkard* (see Hallworthy). (CPNE 235)

†**try-** 'triple, very': Truro. (CPNE 233)

us 'chaff': ?Port Isaac. (CPNE 237)

war 'upon': Trethevey in St Mabyn (see River Allen), Trevena (see Tintagel), Tywardreath. (CPNE 238)

*-**yel**, adjectival ending: see *-el*.

-**yer**, plural ending: Bryher, Sticker. (CPNE 139)

yn 'in the': *Carrack Looes en Cooes* (St Michael's Mount).

†**-ynn**, diminutive ending: ?Carnon, ?Fraddon, ?Rutherbridge, ?Seaton; see also *cribynn, heyl*.

†**ynys** 'island': Carines, *Porthennis* (Mousehole), *Inispriven* (Mullion Island), *Iniscaw* (Tresco). (CPNE 93)

†**yorgh** 'roebuck': Carnyorth. (CPNE 140)

yow 'Thursday': Market Jew (Marazion). (CPNE 140)

*yuv 'lord': Bodieve. (CPNE 140)

2. English

It is a convention in English place-name studies normally to cite elements in Old English forms. In Cornwall that is often an anachronism, since many of the names must have been given well after the Old English period; but, for purposes of comparison with other counties, I have kept to that convention where it is convenient to do so. Old and Middle English words are marked with (OE) and (ME); Old English words are cited in West Saxon forms if there is a choice. The Old English letters 'eth' and 'thorn' have been transliterated as *th*, as in the rest of the dictionary. Modern English words are unmarked, and no meaning is given for them unless it is unexpected. Occasionally both an Old English word and its modern descendant are given separately, when they have differing usages or meanings (e.g. *dún* and *down*, *héafod* and *head*).

ác (OE) 'oak-tree': Braddock (or *hóc*)
æsc (OE) 'ash-tree': Saltash

bæc (OE) 'back, ridge': Siblyback
bath: Bathpool
bay: Bude Bay, Carbis Bay, Cawsand Bay, Watergate Bay, Widemouth Bay
beacon: Fire Beacon Point
beak: Cambeak
bearu (OE) 'grove, small wood': Harrowbarrow
beorg (OE) 'hill, tumulus': Bilberry, Clubworthy, Flexbury, Hensbarrow Downs
bishop: Bishop Rock
blæc (OE) 'black': Black Head (2), Blackwater, *Blaketore* and *Black Rock* (see Rock)
brád (OE) 'broad, wide': Braddock, Broad Sound
bróc (OE) 'brook, stream': Millbrook
brycg (OE) 'bridge': Bridgerule, Mylor Bridge, Newbridge, Ruthernbridge, Wadebridge, Yeolmbridge
bula (OE) 'bull': Bullapit (see Polapit Tamar)
burh (OE) 'fort, borough': *Cardinan lebiri* (Cardinham), *Croftholburgh* (Crafthole), Helsbury (see Michaelstow)

calu (OE) 'bare hill': Callington
camb (OE) 'comb, crest': Cambeak
cape: Cape Cornwall
castel (OE) 'castle': Boscastle
chace 'hunting-ground': Chacewater
chapel: Chapel Point
cíeping (OE) 'market': *Langchepyng* (Summercourt)
cirice (OE) 'church': Marhamchurch
clob (dialect) 'mud': ?Clubworthy
cól (OE) 'cool': Colliford
copped 'pollarded': Coppathorne
cot (OE) 'cottage': Bennacott, Brazacott, Eastacott, Grimscott, Luckett
court 'court-yard': Summercourt

cow: ?Cawsand
croft (OE) 'enclosed land': Crafthole
crow: ?Crow Sound
cyta (OE) 'kite, buzzard': Kit Hill

down 'downland, rough grazing': Carnon Downs, Connor Downs, Downgate, Hensbarrow Downs, Longdowns
dún (OE) 'hill, downland': Caradon, Golberdon, Red Down, *Dounhed* (Launceston)

éa (OE) 'river': Ottery, ?Yeolmbridge
eald (OE) 'old': Oldwit (see Lawhitton), *Oldestowe* (Padstow)
éast (OE) 'east': Eastcott, East Taphouse
eddy 'water-turbulence': Eddystone Rocks
end: Land's End, Shortlanesend

feire (ME) 'fair, market': *La Lunge feire* (Summercourt)
fire: Fire Beacon Point
fleax (OE) 'flax': Flexbury
ford: Colliford, Helford, Hessenford, ?Rumford, Tideford, Woodford
fót (OE) 'foot': Herodsfoot
fox: Foxhole

gate: Downgate, Lockengate, Marshgate, Widegates; see water-gate
gós (OE) 'goose': Gooseham
green 'village green': Coad's Green, Carnhell Green
gull 'sea-gull': Gulland Rock
gurnard 'gurnard fish': Gurnard's Head

hæfen (OE) 'harbour': Bude Haven, Crackington Haven, Gorran Haven
hæg (OE) 'enclosure': Haye, Heamoor
hægtesse (OE) 'witch': Hessenford
hætt (OE) 'hat': Hatt
hálig (OE) 'holy': Holywell
hamm (OE) 'river-meadow': Gooseham, Otterham, ?Yeolmbridge
hár (OE) 'grey', possibly 'on a boundary': Harrowbarrow
head 'headland': Black Head (2), Gribbin Head, Gurnard's Head, Gwennap Head, Nare Head, Park Head, Pencarrow Head, Rame Head, Rosemullion Head, Towan Head,

Trevose Head
héafod (OE) 'head': *Dounhed* (Launceston)
henn (OE) 'hen': Henwood
highway: Highway, St Kew Highway
hind (OE) 'hind, female deer': Hensbarrow Downs, ?North Hill
hóc (OE) 'hook (of land)': Braddock (or *ác*)
hogg 'pig': *Hogswall* (Dobwalls)
hóh (OE) 'heel, spur of land': Hugh Town
hol (OE) 'hole': Foxhole, Mousehole
hwít (OE) 'white': South Wheatley, Whitemoor, Whitesand Bay, Whitsand Bay, Whitstone, ?White Island
hyll (OE) 'hill': ?Crafthole, Kit Hill, Tregonning Hill, Trendrine Hill

-ing (OE), meaningless connective particle: Werrington
læc (OE) 'marsh': Latchley
lacu (OE) 'stream': *Stingede-lace* (Codda), Gunnislake
land (OE) 'land': Blisland, Gulland Rock, Land's End, Roseland, Stoke Climsland. In a good number of names of manors in Devon and Cornwall, *land* and *tún* were used interchangeably, to denote respectively the lands of the manor and its centre. Thus one finds, for instance, pairs such as *Bliston* and *Blislonde*, Launceston and *Launceland*, Callington and *Calilond*; and, in Devon, *Hertitona* and Hartland, Walkhampton and *Walcumlond*. It seems to be mere chance which of the pairs has survived to become the modern name, though forms with *tún* have done so more often.
lane: Shortlanesend, *Malla downe lane end* (Bray Shop)
lang (OE) 'long': Longdowns, Longships, *Langchepyng* (Summercourt)
léah (OE) 'wood' or 'clearing in a wood': Latchley, ?Ley, ?North Hill, South Wheatley
locking: Lockengate
logan (dialect) 'rocking, movable': Logan Rock
lutel (ME) 'little': Little Larnick (see Muchlarnick)

mægden (OE) 'maiden': Maidenwell
mersc (OE) 'marsh': Marshgate
mór (OE) 'moor, marsh': Bodmin Moor, *Foy Moor* (Bodmin Moor), Heamoor, Henmoore (see Hensbarrow Downs),

Redmoor, Whitemoor

mucel (ME) 'great': Muchlarnick

mús (OE) 'mouse': Mousehole

mútha (OE) 'mouth, river-mouth, gap': *Crakemude* (Crackington Haven), *Hægelmutha* (see Egloshayle), Falmouth, Widemouth Bay

myln (OE) 'mill': Millbrook, Newmill, New Mills, Rilla Mill

mynster (OE) 'endowed church': *Menstre* (Manaccan)

næss (OE) 'headland': ?Sharpnose Point (2) (or *nós*). Compare Old Norse *nes*.

níwe (OE) 'new': Newbridge, New Grimsby, Newmill, New Mills, Newquay, Newtown in St Martin

nós (OE) 'nose, headland': ?Sharpnose Point (2) (or *næss*)

oter (OE) 'otter': Otterham, Ottery

park 'deer-park': Park Head

píl (OE) 'stake, post': Pillaton

place: Playing Place, Sandplace

pohha (OE) 'pouch, bag' (of uncertain meaning in place-names): ?Poughill

point 'headland, promontory': Chapel Point, Dodman Point, Fire Beacon Point, Pendennis Point, Penhale Point, Penlee Point, Pentire Point, Sharpnose Point (2), Start Point, Torpoint

pól (OE) 'pool': Bathpool, ?Polapit Tamar

porth (dialect) 'cove': *Holy Well Porth* (Holywell Bay), Mawgan Porth, Perranporth; compare *porth* as a Cornish element.

pund (OE) 'animal-pound': Poundstock

pytt (OE) 'pit': Polapit Tamar

quay: Newquay

quoit 'discus, giant's plaything': Trethevy Quoit

réad (OE) 'red': Redmoor

riht (OE) 'straight': ?Red Down

road 'roadstead for ships': Carrick Roads, The Road; 'railway station': Bodmin Road, St Columb Road, Grampound Road

roke (ME) 'rock': Logan Rock, Rock, Wolf Rock

round (dialect) 'fort, curved enclosure': Tregeare Rounds

rúh (OE) 'rough': Rough Tor

rúm (OE) 'wide': ?Rumford

rynel (OE) 'water-channel': Runnel Stone

sand (OE) 'beach, sand': Cawsand, Kingsand, Sandplace, Whitesand Bay, Whitsand Bay

scearp (OE) 'sharp': Sharpnose Point (2)

scoria (ME) 'mining-waste': Scorrier

sealt (OE) 'salt': Saltash

sele (OE) 'hall': Zelah

seofon (OE) 'seven': Seven Stones

ship: Longships

shop 'workshop, smithy': Bray Shop, Shop (2)

short: ?Shortlanesend (or surname)

smith: *Smitheck* (Falmouth), Mawnan Smith

sound 'strait, sailable channel': Broad Sound, Crow Sound, St Mary's Sound, Smith Sound

stán (OE) 'stone': Eddystone Rocks, Runnel Stone, Seven Stones, The Stone, Whitstone

steort (OE) 'tail, point of land': *Penwihtsteort* (Land's End), Start Point, *Stertpoynt* (Torpoint)

stoc (OE) 'settlement': Calstock, Poundstock, Stoke Climsland, *Neotestoce* (St Neot)

stów (OE) 'church-site': Davidstow, Jacobstow, *Martistowe* (St Martin by Looe), Michaelstow, Morwenstow, *Nietestou* (St Neot), Padstow, *Oldestowe* (Padstow), Warbstow

street: High Street

stybb (OE) 'tree-stump': Stibb

summer: Summercourt

tap-house 'ale-house, inn': East Taphouse

thorn 'thorn-tree': Coppathorne

torr (OE) 'rocky outcrop, crag': Garrow Tor, Kilmar Tor, *Blaketore* (see Rock), Rough Tor, Torpoint

town 'village, farmstead': Canonstown, Charlestown, Halsetown, Higher Town, Hugh Town, Leedstown, Newtown in St Martin

tún (OE) 'farmstead, settlement': Albaston, Antony, Boyton, Callington, Crackington, Helston, Helstone, Kilkhampton, Launceston, Lawhitton, Pillaton, Stratton, North Tamerton, Trematon, Upton, Werrington, *Bliston* (Blisland), Connerton (see Connor Downs), Fawton (see River Fowey), *Landerhtun* (Landrake), Rillaton (see Rilla

Mill), Climsom (see Stoke Climsland). See *land* for the interchange between that word and *tún* in Cornish place-names.

twifeald (OE) 'double': Twelvewood (see Doublebois)

upp (OE) 'higher': Upton

wæd (OE) 'ford': Wadebridge

washway 'road with a water-channel': Washaway

wall: Dobwalls, *Hogswall* (Dobwalls)

watch 'look-out place': Pendeen Watch (see Pendeen), *Carne an Watch* (Trendrine Hill)

water 'stream, settlement on a stream': Blackwater, Budock Water, Canworthy Water, Chacewater

water-gate 'sluice-gate': ?Watergate Bay

wíc (OE) 'settlement': *Smitheck* (Falmouth), Week St Mary

wíd (OE) 'wide': Widegates, Widemouth Bay

wiella (OE) 'well, spring': Holywell, Maidenwell, Markwell, ?Poughill

wín-hús (OE) 'wine-house, inn': Wainhouse Corner

worthig (OE) 'enclosure, farm': Canworthy, Chilsworthy,

wudu (OE) 'wood': Twelvewood (see Doublebois), Henwood, Woodford

wulf (OE) 'wolf': ?Wolf Rock

3. Old Norse

ey 'island': New Grimsby

hagi 'pasture, enclosure for grazing': ?Agnes

nes 'headland': ?Agnes. Compare Old English *næss*

4. French (cited in Modern French forms)

beau 'beautiful': Barripper, Berepper

bois 'wood': Doublebois

brisants 'breakers, reef': The Brisons

double 'double': Doublebois

grand 'great': Grampound

mal 'bad': Malpas

marais 'marsh': ?Moresk

pas 'step': Malpas

pont 'bridge': Grampound

repair 'a retreat': Barripper, Berepper

roche 'rock': Roche

Index of Personal Names

The spelling of personal names in Cornish is an even greater problem than the spelling of ordinary words. As mentioned in the Introduction, very few Cornish personal names remained in use after the eleventh century. When they are recorded at all, it is therefore in Old Cornish forms. The elements have been cited in spellings approximating to their Middle Cornish forms; but to do that with Cornish personal names would be historically unjustifiable; and in east Cornwall it would anyway be a pointless exercise, for the names are mostly fossilised in their Old Cornish forms in that part of the county.

Many of the personal names found in Cornish place-names are not recorded at all in Cornish, but must be invented by analogy from Welsh and Breton. Moreover, such names as are recorded in Old Cornish are found either in Anglo-Saxon spellings (not always the most accurate for showing their true forms), or in native Old Cornish spellings (in the List of saints), which are even more misleading to the untrained eye.

The solution attempted here is to use the same spelling-system as in the Index of Elements, but to use it to give the names in their Old Cornish forms, rather than their Middle Cornish ones. (I have made one exception to this principle, and have allowed the Middle Cornish ending *-ek* into the forms, when strictly speaking it should be *-euk*, spelt *oc* in Old Cornish, giving *Pedreuk*, *Caranteuk*, and so on. The ending *-euk* became *-ek* in the late eleventh century, so that the forms given below represent an actual stage of development in about 1100.) The problem about this method is that, in some cases, the exact form of a personal name is uncertain; so the forms should mostly be taken as tentative. In the list which follows, the symbol †
indicates a name which has been re-spelt from Old Corn-

ish or by direct extrapolation from Welsh and/or Breton; the asterisk * is reserved for names which are not recorded in any of the three languages, but which have been invented, by re-combining elements used in the personal names in those languages. In a few cases (stated), there is no evidence at all for the name, but it seems a likely one.

An attempt is made to give the conjectured meanings where possible; but for many personal names (which have been even less studied than place-names, and are even trickier) that is not possible. Note that most of these names are compounds, not phrases; and have the according stress and mutation. Others are from a single element, with the addition of a suffix such as *-an*, *-ynn* or *-ek*.

The forms of saints' names are even more tentative. Often the sole evidence of a name is the Cornish dedication, which may not be recorded until the thirteenth century, and then in a form written by English diocesan officials. Where no equivalent is given here, the form is based solely upon those of the place-name in question, or upon references to the saint as patron saint of that place. A saint's name is not cited in the following list if it appears under approximately its expected place in the main body of the dictionary. (Thus St Ewa, St Gerent and St Teon, for instance, are omitted, since the references would be simply to the place-names St Ewe, Gerrans and Tean.)

1. Cornish

†**Aghevran** (saint): St Keverne. Old Cornish *Achobran*.

Anta (?) (saint): Lelant.

†**Antun**: Trevanson. From Latin *Antonius*, equivalent to early Welsh *Antun* (later *Annun*). Note the later Cornish *ns* from *nt*. When there is another *n* following *nt*, as here, this standard change often fails to appear (e.g. *fenten* 'a spring', not *fensen*); but note *briansen* 'throat', where the change does appear, as in Trevanson.

†**Avarn**: Bosavern. No exact equivalent, but compare early Welsh *Awarnach* (where *w* = *v*, Modern Welsh 'Afarnach').

Beryen (saint): St Buryan. Old Cornish *Berion* (List).

†**Bran**: Brane. Compare Old Breton and Old Welsh *Bran*.

Branwalader (saint): St Breward.

Bryvyth (saint): (see Lanlivery).

*Cadwen: Bocaddon. Many names start with *Cad-* ('battle') in Welsh, Cornish and Breton; for the ending *-wen*, compare Old Cornish *Onwen*, and *Gwen* below.

*Cadyled: Tregadillett. For *Cad-*, see previous entry; there is no parallel for the ending *-yled*, but Old Breton *Catuuolet* provides a slightly similar name (which would have given Old Cornish *Cadwoled*).

†Carantek (saint): Crantock. Early Welsh *Carantoc(-us)*, Modern Welsh *Carannog*; 'lovable one'. Compare *Correk*.

Cleder (saint): St Clether.

†Clodri: Nancledra. Equivalent to early Welsh *Clotri* (literally 'fame-king').

Coan (saint): (see Merther).

†Conan: Tregonning. Equivalent to Old Welsh and Old Breton *Conan*, Modern Welsh *Cynan*; from *con-* 'hound'.

†Conek (or Kenek): Boconnoc. Equivalent to Old Welsh *Cinauc* (*con-* 'hound').

 Corentin (saint): Cury (compare *Keri*?).

*Correk: Langurra (Crantock). *Correk* may be a pet-form of the saint's name *Carantek*.

Costentin (saint): Constantine, Constantine Bay.

Crida (saint): Creed. Old Cornish *Crite*.

*Cudynn: Tregidden? No parallel has been found.

†Devergi: Trethurgy. 'Otter', literally 'water-hound', *devr-/dowr* + *ki*; equivalent to Welsh *dyfrgi*, 'otter', Old Irish personal name *Dobarchú*. Note that the historical forms of the place-name seem to show a change from *devr-* to *dowr*.

Dewi: Trethevy, Trethewey. Welsh *Dewi*, Middle Cornish *Dewy*, 'David'.

Dilic (saint): Landulph.

†Doghow (saint): Lanow (see St Kew). Welsh *Dochau*.

Entenin (saint): Lantinning (St Anthony-in-Meneage). Old Cornish *Entenin* (List).

Ergh (saint): St Erth. Irish *Erc*.

Euny (saint): *Unyredreth* (Redruth), (and see Lelant).

*Eustek (?): Porthoustock. No equivalent found, but compare Old Breton names beginning with *Eu-* (possibly meaning 'wish, desire').

†**Feleg** (saint): Phillack. Old Cornish *Felec* (List).

†**Fili** (saint): Philleigh. Old Cornish *Filii* (List).

†**Gavran**: Portgaverne? Equivalent to Old Welsh *Gabran* (from *gafr*, 'goat'). Or *Gavran* could be a stream-name.

†**Goedhgen**: Seworgan. Equivalent to early Welsh *Guoidcen* (literally 'wild-skin'?).

Goedhyan (saint): Gwithian. Old Cornish *Guidian* (List).

†**Goledik**: Trelissick in St Erth and Sithney (see Trelissick in Feock). Compare Old Breton *Uuoletec*, but that has *-ec*, whereas the Cornish names seem to have *-ik*. Probably contains *go-* 'sub-', so not the same as Welsh *gwledig* 'leader', as formerly thought.

†**Gorabo**: Traboe. Equivalent to Old Welsh *Guorabui, Guorapui*. Note that the final diphthong of the Cornish personal name had already become simple *-o* before the date of the earliest place-name form, *Tref-wurabo* 977 (11th): compare the similar development seen in *Kenhetho*.

†**Gorgi**: Hallworthy. Old Cornish *Wurci*, Welsh *Gwrgi* ('super-hound', *gor-* + *ki*).

†**Gorhi**: Roseworthy. Equivalent to early Welsh *Gurhi* (*gor-* 'super-').

***Gorman**: Trewarmett. Compare Old Breton names in *Uuor-* 'super-' and *-man* (possibly 'good'). This name should normally have become *Gorvan*. For the preservation of *m*, one could either compare Welsh *Garmon* (which may, however, be a literary form), or else compare other instances in east Cornwall (where Trewarmett is) where *m* survives when it should have been mutated to *v* (e.g. Tremail, Tremaine, Tremar).

†**Gorthavow**: Tredavoe. Equivalent to Old Welsh *Gurtavau, Gurdauau* (*gor-* 'super-'?).

†**Gorvoy** (?): Rejerrah? Perhaps equivalent to early Welsh *Guorvoe*, with early loss of *v* (*Gorvoy* becoming *Goroy*). For the subsequent reduction of *-oy* to *-o* (giving *Goro*), compare remarks under *Kenhetho*.

***Gwasmeur**: Tresmeer. No equivalent is known; the name would mean 'great lad', from *gwas* 'lad' and *meur* 'great' (a phrase, not a compound). Compare early Welsh and Breton names starting with *Gwas-*, and Old Breton names ending with *-mor*.

†**Gwasso**: Trewassa. Old Cornish Wasso, Waso; *gwas* 'lad, devotee'.

Gwelvel (saint): Gulval.

†**Gwen**: Trewen? (but *gwynn* is more likely in the place-name). Compare early Welsh *Gwen* (man's name), meaning either 'smile, good-will' or 'prayer, wish'.

Gwendeyrn (saint): Wendron; from *gwynn* 'white, fair', or compare *Gwen*, and *teyrn* 'lord'.

†**Gwenek**: Lewannick. Compare the Breton saint's name *Guenoc, Guenec*, and Llanwenog in Cardiganshire.

†**Gwengor**: Boswinger. Old Cornish *Wengor*; *gwynn* 'white, fair' or *gwen* 'smile, etc.', and perhaps *cor(dh)* 'family, tribe'.

†**Gwethen**: Lawhitton? Equivalent to Old Breton *Gueten* (with *t* for *th*), possibly from *gueith* 'battle'.

†**Gwethenek**: Trewarthenick; (saint) *Laffenake* (Padstow). Old Cornish *Geuedenoc* (List), Old Breton *Uuethenoc*, etc.

†**Gwethyen** or †Gwydhyen: Trewithian. *Gwethyen* would be equivalent to Old Breton *Uuethien*, Old Welsh *Gueithgen* (possibly from *gueith* 'battle'), and *Gwydhyen* to Old Welsh *Guidgen*, Middle Welsh *Gwydyen*.

†**Gwydhelan**: Trewidland? Equivalent to Welsh *Gwyddelan*, seen in Dolwyddelan (Caernarvonshire) and Llanwyddelan (Montgomeryshire); a Cumbric equivalent of the Welsh name has been suggested in Tarn Wadling (Cumberland). But in both the Cornish and the Cumbric names, the stress is wrong for an exact equivalent to be present, and Trewidland may contain a common noun, *gwydh-lann*, instead.

***Gwylarth**: Trewellard? No parallel is known, but compare Old Welsh *Guil-biu*, and Old Breton names starting with *Arth-* 'bear'.

Gwynnwalo, To-wynnek, Gwynnek (saint): Gunwalloe, Towednack, St Winnow. Old Breton *Uuinuualoe*.

Helent (?) (saint): *Egloshellens* (St Stephen in Brannel).

***Hernow** (?): Lanherne? No parallel is known, but compare Old Breton names starting with *Hoiarn-* 'iron', and early Welsh *Haearn-llen*.

Hydrek (saint): Lanhydrock.

*Hynyed or †Hunyad: Menheniot. *Hunyad* would be the equivalent of Old Welsh *Huniat*, but no equivalent for the preferred form *Hynyed* has been found.

Idi (saint): St Issey, Mevagissey. Old Cornish *Iti* (List), Middle Cornish *Yse*.

†**Ke** (To-ge) (saint): Kea, Old Kea. Middle Welsh *Kei*.

†**Kebi** (saint): *Lankyp* (Duloe). Middle Welsh *Kybi*.

†**Kenek**: *see* Conek; *con-/ken-* 'hound'.

†**Kenhetho**: Tregonetha. Equivalent to Old Welsh *Kan-haethoe*. The second part of that personal name appears, with its diphthong already reduced to simple *-o*, in the Old Cornish personal name *Mor-haytho*; and compare *Gorabo*, above, for a similar early simplification of a diphthong.

†**Kenhoarn**: Linkinhorn. Equivalent to early Welsh *Kyn-hayarn*, *Cunhearn*, Old Breton *Conhoiarn*; literally 'hound-iron'.

*Kennon: Boskednan. No exact equivalent: the *e*, double *n* and probably the *-on* in this name all make it different from *Conan* (above).

Keri (saint): Egloskerry (compare Corentin?)

†**Kerwyd**: Liskeard. Equivalent to early Welsh *Kerwyt*, *Kerwid*.

†**Kerys**: Polkerris? Welsh *Cerist* (?).

†**Keyn** (saint): St Keyne; compare Kenwyn. Welsh Cain, Ceinwen.

†**Kyni**: Bossiney. Equivalent to early Welsh *Cini*.

*Ledik: Trelissick? For *Led-* compare Old Breton *Let-monoc*.

*Livri: Lanlivery. No parallel is known, but compare Welsh *Llifris*, and the Breton place-name Lanlivry.

*Loude: Belowda. Compare other names starting with *Lou-* (Old Cornish *Lou-march*, *Lou-cum*, Old Breton *Lou-morin*), possibly 'light, bright'; no exact equivalent for *-de* has been found.

*Louhal: Ballowal. Compare Old Cornish *Lou-* (as in previous entry); and early Breton names ending in *-hael* 'generous', also Old Cornish *Hal-uiu*.

*Lowen: Burlawn (or the adjective *lowen*, 'happy'). Compare Old Cornish *Lowenan*, Old Breton *Louuenan* (both with suffix -*an*); also Old Cornish *Wur-lowen* and other Old Breton names in -*louuen*.

*Luga (?): Treligga? No parallel for such a name is known; it might possibly come from Latin *Lucas*, 'Luke'. The preservation of the second syllable would be irregular, but one could compare other biblical names which failed to lose their final syllables.

Mab (saint): Mabe

Mabon (saint): St Mabyn

†Madek: Polmassick. Equivalent to early Welsh *Matauc*, *Matoc*, Old Breton *Matoc*, *Madoc* (from *mad* 'good').

Managhan (?) (saint): Manaccan

†Margh: Tremar. Old Cornish *Marh*, Old Welsh *March* (from Latin *Marcus*).

Mawseth (?) (saint): St Mawes

†Mel: Tremail. Equivalent to early Welsh *Mael* ('prince').

†Melgi or ***Melga**: Trevalga? *Melgi* would be equivalent to Old Breton *Melchi*, 'prince-hound' (compare Welsh *Maelgwn*); *Melga* would be without a known equivalent.

†Melyd (?): Trevellas? Equivalent to the Welsh saint's name *Melyd*; but there is some doubt as to whether that is a native name or not.

†Meren: Trevarren? Equivalent to Old Breton *Meren*, found only in the place-name *Lan-meren* and, compounded, in the personal name *Ed-meren*.

Meva (saint): Mevagissey. Old Cornish *Memai* (List).

Mewynn (saint): St Mewan. Old Cornish *Megunn* (List).

Milyan: Rosemullion. Old Cornish *Milian*; compare early Welsh *Milgen*. Probably connected with *mil*, 'wild animal'.

†Morek: (Mevagissey); or *morek* 'of the sea', adjective of *mor*. *Morek* would be equivalent to Old Breton *Moroc* (possibly from *mor* 'sea'?).

Moren (saint): Lamorran

Morwenna (saint): Morwenstow

†Nennyd (saint): Pelynt

Nonn (saint): Altarnun

*Nowyen: Trenewan. No equivalent is known. Compare early Welsh *Nouy*, *Nowy*. Compare also an early Welsh St *Nuuien*, but the form of his name is doubtful.

Otker: Treviscoe. Old Cornish *Otcer*, with later change of *d/t* to *s*.

Padern (saint): North, South Petherwin. Welsh *Padarn*.

Pedrek (saint, 'Petrock'): Padstow, Little Petherick, Trebetherick. From *Peder* (from Latin *Petrus*) + -*ek*.

*Pera or ***Pyra**: Polperro? Compare early Welsh *Peryf* or *Pyr*; also Old Cornish *Perem*, which may have *m* for *v*, 'Perev'; the *v* could have been lost early, giving *Pere* and hence *Pera*.

*Pydannan: Trebudannon. No equivalent has been found.

†Reydhogh: Lanreath. Compare early Welsh *Rydoch*, though the forms of the Cornish place-name show a diphthong, *ey*, whereas the Welsh personal name has the single vowel *y*.

*Rigni: Tregony? Compare Old Breton names starting with *Ri*- 'king'; no parallel has been found for the ending -*gni*. Old Breton and Old Welsh *Riceneu* would have had an equivalent *Rigenow* in Cornish, but that does not suit the forms of the place-name so well.

*Rihoarn: Ruan Lanihorne. No equivalent is known, but compare Welsh and Breton names beginning with *Ri*- ('king'), and many Old Breton ones ending with -*hoiarn* ('iron'): compare Kenhoarn.

*Rudhynn: Bedruthan. From *rudh* 'red' with a suffix; compare Old Breton *Rudheder*.

†Ruveun: Polruan; (saint) Ruan Lanihorne, Ruan Minor. From Latin *Romanus* (personal name); Old Cornish *Rumon* (List), Old Welsh *Rumaun*, Modern Welsh *Rhufon*.

*Salwys or ***Selwys**: Lansallos. No equivalent has been found.

†Sant: Lezant, *Eglossant* (Sancreed), Nancent? (St Breock). Early Welsh *Sant*.

†Selevan (saint): St Levan. Old Cornish *Salamun* (List).

Senar (saint): Zennor

†Sulyen: Luxulyan, Tresillian. Equivalent to early Welsh *Sulien*, *Sulyen*.

Sydhni (saint): Goldsithney, Sithney

*Syek: Lanzeague (St Just in Roseland). Compare the Breton saint *Seoc*, though it is not an exact equivalent.

†**Talan**: ?Nanstallon. Equivalent to Old Breton and early Welsh *Talan* (from *tal* 'brow').

†**Talek**: Botallack (or see *tal*). From *tal* 'brow'.

To-ge (saint): *see* Ke.

To-wynnek (saint): *see* Gwynnwalo.

*****Urvo**: Treverva? There would be no exact equivalent for *Urvo*; but compare early Welsh *Urvei*.

Uvel (saint): St Eval.

*****Uyon** (?): Bojewyan. No equivalent known.

Ya (saint): St Ives.

*****Yarnenn**: Treyarnon. No exact equivalent known (*Yarnan* is possible instead); compare Old Cornish and Old Breton names starting with *Iarn-* (probably the same as *hoiarn* 'iron').

†**Yust** (saint): *Porth East* (Gorran Haven), St Just (in Penwith), St Just in Roseland. Old Cornish *Iust*: (List).

Old English (and Old Norse, 'ON')
Ælmarch: Markwell

Æl-??: Albaston

Anta: Antony

Billa: Bilberry

Boia: Boyton

Bynna: Bennacott

Ceol: Chilsworthy

Grim: Grimscott

(ON) Grímr: Grimsby

Gunna: Gunnislake

Leofa: Luckett

Lulla: Trelill

Marwen or Merwenn :(saint): Marhamchurch

Pohha: Poughill?

Wærburh :(saint): Warbstow

Wulfræd: Werrington

Middle English and surnames
Borlay: Treburley

Boterel (Botreaux): Boscastle

Bray: Bray Shop

Brosya: Brazacott

Burrell or Birrell (?): Berryl's Point
Charles (Christian name): Charlestown
Coad: Coad's Green
Coppa: Boscoppa
Daryte: Darite
Dobbe: Dobwalls
Dudman: Dodman Point
Edgcumbe: Mount Edgcumbe
Fridia: Freathy?
Gwennap: Gwennap head
Halse: Halsetown
Hawke: Mount Hawke
King: Kingsand?
Leeds (dukes of): Leedstown (see also TOWNSHEND)
Parkyn: Shop (in St Merryn)
Rayne or Rame (?): Rame? (in Wendron)
Ruald: Bridgerule
Shorte: Shortlanesend?
Sibyly: Siblyback
Silvester: Chysauster
Smith: Smith Sound
Townshend: Townshend (compare Leeds)
White: White Island (or *hwít*)

Further Reading

Cornish place-names

Any of the writings of Charles Henderson, most notably his *Essays in Cornish History* (Oxford, 1935), *Old Cornish Bridges and Streams* (Exeter, 1928), and *A History of the Parish of Constantine in Cornwall* (Truro, 1937)

O. J. Padel, *Cornish Place-Name Elements* (English Place-Name Society, Nottingham, 1985)

P. A. S. Pool, *The Place-Names of West Penwith*, 2nd edition (Penzance, 1985)

Oerjan Svensson, *Saxon Place-Names in East Cornwall*, Lund Studies in English, 77 (Lund, 1987)

Personal names

Bodmin Manumissions: the most accessible text for readers in Cornwall is that printed by George Oliver, *Monasticon Dioecesis Exoniensis* (Exeter, 1846), pp.431-36. The best edition is by Max Foerster, 'Die Freilassungsurkunden des Bodmin-Evangeliars', in *A Grammatical Miscellany Offered to Otto Jespersen*, edited by N. Bogholm and others (London and Copenhagen, 1930), pp. 77-99 (in German)

The Saints' List: B. Lynette Olson and O. J. Padel, 'A Tenth-Century List of Cornish Parochial Saints', *Cambridge Medieval Celtic Studies*, 12 (Winter, 1986), pp. 33-71.

Early Welsh personal names are taken mostly from J. Gwenogvryn Evans and J. Rhys, *The Text of the Book of Llan Dâv* (Oxford, 1893), and from P. C. Bartrum, *Early Welsh Genealogical Tracts* (Cardiff, 1966); and early Breton ones from J. Loth, *Chrestomathie bretonne* (Paris, 1890).

Cornish language and dialect

M. A. Courtney and T. Q. Couch, *Glossary of Words in Use in Cornwall* (London, 1880)

Ken George, *The Pronunciation and Spelling of Revived Cornish* (Cornish Language Board, 1986) (The best account of the sounds of Cornish)

R. Morton Nance, *A New Cornish-English Dictionary* (Federation of Old Cornwall Societies, 1938)

English place-names

Margaret Gelling, *Signposts to the Past* (London, 1978) and *Place-Names in the Landscape* (London, 1984) (The best general works on Engish place-names)

J. E. B. Gover and others, *The Place-Names of Devon*, 2 volumes (English Place-Name Society, Cambridge, 1931-32)

Welsh and Breton place-names

There are unfortunately very few general works on Welsh and Breton place-names. The following are mostly difficult to obtain, but they are the most useful:

Rhestr o Enwau Lleoedd: A Gazetteer of Welsh Place-Names, edited by Elwyn Davies, 3rd edition (Cardiff, 1967)

Melville Richards, *Welsh Administrative and Territorial Units* (Cardiff, 1969)

W. B. S. Smith, *De la toponymie bretonne: Dictionnaire étymologique*, Language Monograph no. 20; supplement to *Language*, 16 (1940)

Bernard Tanguy, *Les noms de lieux bretons*: I. *Toponymie descriptive* (Studi no. 3: Rennes, 1975)

R. J. Thomas, *Enwau Afonydd a Nentydd Cymru* (Cardiff, 1938) ('The names of Welsh rivers and streams'; in Welsh)

Ifor Williams, *Enwau Lleoedd*, 3rd edition, (Liverpool, 1969) ('Place-names'; in Welsh)